HUMAN SERVICES IN CONTEMPORARY AMERICA

PAUL SCHMOLLING, JR., is a clinical psychologist trained at the N.Y.U. Graduate School of Arts and Science. His clinical experience includes ten years as a psychologist at a child guidance center, and he has also worked as a ward psychologist at New York City's Bellevue Hospital. Currently he teaches at Kingsborough Community College, where he is associated with the Community Mental Health Program. Paul is an active researcher and has published a number of articles on cognitive processes in schizophrenia. He has a special interest in stress and is studying the long-range psychological impact of confinement to Nazi concentration camps. He is also interested in the effects of family destabilization on the mental and physical health of college students.

MERRILL YOUKELES is a certified social worker who received his M.S.W. from the University of Pennsylvania. More recently, he completed doctoral studies on aging at Columbia University, with the aid of a grant from the Administration on Aging. Merrill has over 30 years of experience as a practitioner, consultant, and educator. His work in agencies, clinics, and community organizations has given him a broad and realistic view of the human services field. He is presently director of the Human Service Program at Kingsborough Community College of the City University of New York. A staunch advocate of prevention programs, Merrill is an active member of the New York City Coalition for Prevention in Mental Health.

WILLIAM R. BURGER received his doctorate in social psychology, but his academic background also encompasses the fields of educational psychology and philosophy of education. While attending graduate school at Harvard University, he was awarded a research assistantship for his work in the area of community decision making. Bill is a faculty member in the Community Mental Health Program of Kingsborough Community College of the City University of New York. He has served as a consultant to a variety of human services programs in New York and Massachusetts, has lectured at various colleges and universities, and has written a number of guest editorial articles for various newspapers.

HUMAN SERVICES IN CONTEMPORARY AMERICA

Paul Schmolling, Jr.

Merrill Youkeles

William R. Burger

Kingsborough Community College

Brooks/Cole Publishing Company
Monterey, California

Brooks/Cole Publishing Company
A Division of Wadsworth, Inc.

Printed in the United States of America

10 9 8 7 6 5 4 3 2 1

Library of Congress Cataloging in Publication Data

Schmolling, Paul.
  Human services in contemporary America.

  Bibliography: p.
  Includes index.
    1. Social service—United States—Addresses, essays,
lectures.   2. Social service—Vocational guidance—
United States—Addresses, essays, lectures.   3. United
States—Social policy—Addresses, essays, lectures.
I. Youkeles, Merrill.   II. Burger, William, 1949–
III. Title.
HV91.S294   1985   361'.973   84-23079
ISBN 0-534-04692-4

Sponsoring Editor: *Claire Verduin*
Editorial Assistant: *Pat Carnahan*
Marketing Representative: *Gerry Levine*
Production Editor: *Fiorella Ljunggren*
Manuscript Editor: *Lorraine Anderson*
Permissions Editor: *Carline Haga*
Interior Design: *Juan Vargas*
Cover Design: *Vernon T. Boes*
Cover Illustration: *Gene Takeshita*
Photo Researcher and Editor: *Judy K. Blamer*
Typesetting: *Instant Type, Monterey, California*
Printing and Binding: *R. R. Donnelley and Sons Company, Crawfordsville, Indiana*

Photo credits: p. xviii, Steve Hansen, Stock Boston, Inc.; p. 4, Marcia Roltner,
Brooks/Cole Publishing; p. 13, Paul S. Conklin, Monkmeyer Press Photo Service;
p. 21, Joan Liftin, Archive Pictures, Inc.; p. 36, Owen Franken, Stock Boston, Inc.;
p. 47, San Francisco Child Abuse Council, Inc.; p. 52, Peter Menzel, Stock Boston,
Inc.; pp. 80, 104, and 126, The Bettmann Archive; p. 132, The Harvard University
News Office; p. 146, Christopher Morrow, Stock Boston, Inc.; p. 170, Mimi Forsyth,
Monkmeyer Press Photo Service; p. 176, Joel Gordon, DPI; p. 185, Charles
Harbutt, Archive Pictures, Inc.; p. 195, Ellis Herwig, Stock Boston, Inc.; p. 202, Joel
Gordon, DPI; p. 216, Freda Leinwand, Monkmeyer Press Photo Service; p. 224, J.
C. Pigozzi, Archive Pictures, Inc.; p. 233, U.S. Dept. of Health and Human Services;
p. 246, Joel Gordon, DPI; p. 256, Owen Franken, Stock Boston, Inc.
Table 1-1, p. 31, the "Social Readjustment Rating Scale," by T. H. Holmes and R.
H. Rahe, from the *Journal of Psychosomatic Research*, 1967, *11*, pp. 213-218.
Copyright 1978 by Pergamon Press, Inc. Reprinted by permission.

*To my wife, Patricia, and my son, Paul Thomas,
who make up a very special support system.*

P.S.

*To Marcia, Lisa, Adam, and Golde,
who make it all worthwhile.*

M.Y.

*To my wife, Mary, and my daughter, Kim,
who help me maintain a balanced perspective
and keep my priorities in order.*

W.R.B.

FOREWORD

In the best of all possible worlds, good intentions would invariably compel their desired positive results. But the reality of contemporary American society produces a road to social improvement fraught with detours, hazards, and delays that good intentions alone cannot successfully overcome. Since human services are formulated, devised, and implemented within a social milieu in which human needs are but one of many policy considerations, the value of *Human Services in Contemporary America* lies in the realism it fosters in its readers. As a sociologist, I welcome the authors' approach because it departs from the often simplistic cause-and-effect characterizations and "how to help" syndrome of many standard introductory human services texts. Optimism and idealism are not enough. They are, at best, necessary but insufficient prerequisites to progress. That recognition, coupled with the careful explanation of its implications, is perhaps the greatest strength of the book you are about to read.

Social scientists are sometimes criticized (and often rightfully so) by human services professionals for the distance they seek to maintain from the issues they research. It is as if the dispassionate, objective nature of the research process demanded an aloof neutrality of spirit on the part of the researcher. Similarly, human services professionals are sometimes criticized (and, again, often rightfully so) by social scientists for plunging headfirst into action programs without benefit of careful, reasoned analysis. This tension between researcher and activist, between analysis and action can engender an unproductive stalemate in which the real losers are those among us who are genuinely in need of assistance. Perhaps the best way to avoid such an impasse is to promote meaningful dialogue instead of indulge the tendency of each group to bemoan among themselves the misguided efforts of "those other folks," whether "those other folks" are academics with their heads in the clouds or human services workers with their hearts in their hands. But how do we bridge this gap I've noted and transcend the limitations of too narrow academic training? How do we go beyond a trained incapacity to respect the validity of another's point of view?

Although I am not so naively optimistic to believe that there is a single, easy solution to this dilemma, I do see reasons for at least a cautious optimism. *Human Services in Contemporary America* is a rare text in that it genuinely seeks to cross traditional disciplinary boundaries. The interrelatedness of personal troubles and public issues and the interplay of analysis and action are prominent themes of the book. Such themes do, in my view, encourage that meaningful dialogue across disciplinary lines that I mentioned earlier. An exemplary introductory-level text in any field provides more than a cursory survey of accumulated knowledge in a subject matter. It is an invitation to adopt a new perspective, to enhance your vision in that you might see in a new light things you merely looked at before but didn't truly see.

As do most good books, *Human Services in Contemporary America* raises far more questions than it answers. But having read it, you will likely ask more perceptive questions, be less satisfied with simplistic, pat answers, and be ready to tackle new intellectual challenges, armed not simply with more information but with a broader, more critical perspective on the real issues before us. For both students and teachers, this might well be more than they've bargained for. Certainly it is more than we've come to expect in an introductory text. But perhaps we should learn to accept nothing less. For, if beginning students in human services fields continue to find in their texts a "cookbook" approach detailing simple solutions to complex social problems, they will be impotent to effect change in a political world they scarcely comprehend. And, similarly, if beginning students in the social sciences continue to find in their texts theories and abstractions divorced from a consideration of their practical application, they too will be unable to play an active role in the improvement of our society. *Human Services in Contemporary America*, in striking a balance between realism and idealism, pessimism and optimism, theory and application, and analysis and action, sheds welcome light on some of our most pressing social issues.

Stephen L. Markson
University of Hartford

> In future societies, the most valuable people might be, not those
> with the greatest ability to produce material goods, but rather
> those who have the gift to spread good will and happiness through
> empathy and understanding. Such a gift may be innate in part but
> could certainly be enhanced by experience and education [René
> Dubos, *Celebrations of Life.* New York: McGraw-Hill, 1981, p. 229].

We wrote this text in the hope of enhancing the student's capacity to
facilitate the lives of others. We believe, along with Dubos, that this
capacity can, to a large extent, be taught and learned. The ability to
help others in a professional context requires a base of knowledge
along with a range of helping skills. We intend this text to help the
beginning student take the first steps toward acquiring the needed
knowledge and skills.

This book provides a general introduction to the field of human
services and is designed for introductory college courses in human
services, mental health technology, social work, community mental
health, and other human services programs. We expect that most
students who read this text are headed toward careers that involve
direct contact with people. However, the book would also be useful
to those considering administrative work in the human services.

Students in the human services typically begin their training
with hopes of helping other people lead more fulfilling lives. Unfortunately these hopes are sometimes dampened by the realities of the
outside world. The humanistic society of the future described by
Dubos is not yet here. Although humanistic values do play an important role in present-day America, they must compete with other
motives such as profit, power, and self-aggrandizement. In order to
be effective, the human services worker must be able to face the
harsh realities of our complex, imperfect society. Of course, the
worker can keep the ideal society in mind and work toward it in a
realistic way.

In the pages that follow, we have sought a balance between
idealism and realism. We certainly do not intend to dampen the

idealistic feelings of students. However, our collective experience as teachers of human services students has shown us that the students who become discouraged are often those who expect too much of clients, helping agencies, and themselves. This disillusionment can be avoided if the student develops a realistic idea of what to expect.

Aside from these aims, we offer a great deal of valuable information about human services, a field whose scope and complexity have greatly increased in recent decades. The material is presented in a provocative manner, raising issues not usually addressed in introductory texts. The impact of political, economic, and social pressures on human services is explored.

The text begins with an account of the goals, functions, and organization of human services seen in the context of contemporary social problems, followed by a description of target populations— the groups of people who receive help from human services. A history of attempts to help persons in need provides a background against which current efforts can be viewed. There is also coverage of the major theories that govern helping efforts, as well as a review of the techniques and methods of helping. The student is also provided with some practical information about career options in the human services field.

The final chapters are certainly unusual in an introductory text. We feel it is important for students to know something about how social policies are developed and about how human services workers might influence policies. These policies, which determine who receives what kind of help, have a great impact on worker and client alike. It is undeniable that today's student is the policymaker of tomorrow.

In the chapter on prevention, we demonstrate a strong bias in favor of programs aimed at preventing problems and dysfunctions from developing in the first place. Frankly, we try to persuade students, instructors, and human services agencies that prevention programs should play a major role in the future of human services.

The text concludes with a sampling of current controversies affecting human services. We offer this selection with the intent of fostering a realistic understanding of conflicts and issues that confront human services workers.

The introductory course in human services is perhaps the most important a student will take. It is here that the student's attitudes and philosophy are developed. We believe that a humanistic perspective, combined with a realistic awareness of societal problems, provides the best foundation for creative and effective helping.

Acknowledgments

We wish to express our gratitude to the many individuals who provided input, advice, and support during the preparation of this text. In particular, we appreciate the contributions of Dean Sam Goldstein of the Wurzweiler School of Social Work, Dr. Arthur Schwartz, Director of Consultation and Education of the Sound View Throggs Neck Community Mental Health Center, Dr. Scott Mykel, Director of Consultation and Education of the Queens Hospital Community Mental Health Center, and Ellen Gorman, President of N.Y.C. Coalition for Prevention in Mental Health.

Our special thanks go to Ethel Rosenberg, our secretary, who typed more pages of manuscript than she would like to remember. We are deeply grateful for her seemingly endless supply of warmth, patience, and good will.

To Claire Verduin and her staff at Brooks/Cole, we express our appreciation for their expert help and support. Special thanks to Fiorella Ljunggren, who shepherded the book through the production process, and to Lorraine Anderson, who did the final editing of the manuscript.

Finally, we wish to thank the reviewers of the manuscript for their helpful comments and suggestions. They are Betty Brown-Chappell of the University of Chicago, Soraya Coley of California State University at Fullerton, Dennis Cogan of Georgia State University, Gloria Davenport of Santa Ana College, David Foat of the University of Minnesota, Irene Glasser of Eastern Connecticut State College, Jeanette E. Kimbrough of St. Louis Community College, Margaret P. Korb of Santa Fe Community College, Jean Macht of Montgomery County Community College, Mary Lou O'Phelan of Lakewood Community College, Lonnie Watts of Westark Community College, and Catharine S. Zimmerman of Camden County College.

Paul Schmolling, Jr.
Merrill Youkeles
William R. Burger

CONTENTS

HUMAN SERVICES IN
CONTEMPORARY AMERICA

HUMAN SERVICES IN THE UNITED STATES TODAY

INTRODUCTION

Over the years, human services in the United States have evolved
into a network of programs and agencies that provide an array of
services to millions of Americans. The one feature shared by all of
these services is that they are designed to meet human needs. Since
services are invariably linked to needs, it is important to understand
the full range of human needs. Thus this chapter begins with a
consideration of human needs, and the kinds of services that seek to
meet them. Some service agencies are devoted mainly to helping
people meet basic survival needs such as food and shelter, while
some are concerned with helping clients achieve more satisfying
relationships or attain other kinds of personal fulfillment. Primary
social supports, such as family and friends, also play a role in
meeting human needs, and we examine that role in this first
chapter.

There is controversy about just what needs should be met by
agencies supported by public funds. There is, in fact, a great deal of
controversy about questions involving the scope and quality of
human services. In this chapter we provide an overview of the
human services that raises some of these questions. Critics argue
that human services are wasteful and inefficient, while supporters
are convinced that more should be done to meet people's needs.
Some social planners want to cut funds for services, while others
demand increased funding. Since these conflicts are fought out
primarily in the political arena, it is vital to grasp the liberal and
conservative positions that underlie the countless debates about
specific programs. We outline these positions in this chapter.

The chapter also includes a survey of some contemporary
problems that may affect the ability of Americans to meet their own
needs. For example, a person involved in a natural disaster such as a
hurricane or earthquake is very likely to need help from human
services on an emergency basis. Social problems such as discrimination, poverty, and unemployment may also reduce a person's ability
to be self-supporting. Some victims of these problems need help
only temporarily, while others receive help for an extended
period.

So this chapter introduces some of the topics basic to a study of
contemporary human services. At first glance, they may appear to be
simple topics, but closer examination shows them to be very complex—so much so that the brief preliminary information given in this
introductory chapter is elaborated throughout the book.

HUMAN NEEDS: FOCUS OF HUMAN SERVICES

A number of schemes have been proposed for conceptualizing human needs. The one suggested by Maslow (1968) is useful for present purposes. He conceived of needs as existing in a kind of pyramid or hierarchy, as shown in Figure 1-1.

At the base of the pyramid are the basic *physiological needs* such as hunger, thirst, and the need for oxygen. These needs are matters of life and death. It is only when survival needs are satisfied that the individual focuses on *safety needs*, which involve the need for a stable, predictable, and secure environment. Clearly, this includes decent housing in a safe neighborhood.

Once partial satisfaction of safety needs has been attained, the need for *love and belongingness* begins to emerge, expressed as a desire for affectionate relations with others. This includes accep-

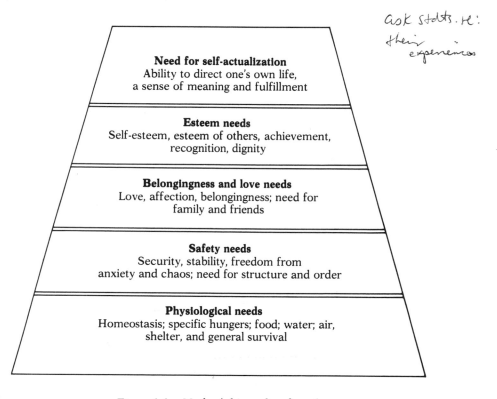

Figure 1-1. Maslow's hierarchy of needs.

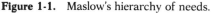

Distinguished American psychologist Abraham Maslow.

tance by one's family, lover, or some larger group. Once the three lower needs have been partly satisfied, *esteem needs* come to the fore: these include the need to be respected as a competent or even a superior person. Most of us desire the recognition and appreciation of others.

The highest need, for *self-actualization*, has to do with fulfilling one's innate tendencies and potentials. This need involves expressing one's inner nature and talents. For one person, the path to self-actualization might be artistic creativity; for another, it might be studying Eastern religions. This highest level of motivation generally becomes prominent in later life. Young adults are generally preoccupied with making a living and winning the love and approval of others. Maslow (1970) estimated that the average American has satisfied about 85% of physiological needs, and that the percentage of needs satisfied declines at each step up the hierarchy. At the top step, only 10% have attained satisfaction of self-actualization needs.

How does the hierarchy of needs relate to human services? Social planners agree that society must provide for those who are unable to meet basic survival needs. The needs for food, some sort of shelter, and emergency medical care are considered essential.

Some human services devote themselves to safety needs. The criminal justice system, which includes law enforcement and corrections, is designed to meet safety needs. Citizens want to live in secure communities and go about their daily activities without fear of being threatened, robbed, or assaulted. To this end, the public spends millions for police, courts, and corrections. In Chapter Two, we discuss some reasons for the partial failure of the criminal justice system to create a safe environment.

One of the most consistent findings of social research is that the risk of suicide or mental illness is greatest when the individual cannot find a place in the social order (Freeman, Jones, & Zucker, 1979). Some human services help people to feel that they belong and are valued members of a group. It is expected that such membership may help keep a person out of an institution and, therefore, serve an important preventive purpose. For example, some agencies set up senior clubs for elderly persons who would otherwise be living a lonely, isolated life. Another example is the establishment of psychiatric residences for former mental patients who have no family.

Some human services agencies are primarily concerned with meeting the higher needs for esteem and self-actualization. Others help indirectly by meeting basic needs, thus allowing the individual to pursue higher needs on his or her own initiative. Education, particularly at the higher levels, is attuned to helping students attain fulfillment and satisfaction through pursuit of a career. In general, human services workers encourage people to function at their highest possible level. More tangible kinds of help are provided in the form of scholarships and grants that are offered by a number of governmental and private agencies.

THE ROLE OF PRIMARY SOCIAL SUPPORTS IN MEETING NEEDS

Most people seek gratification of needs through a network of social relationships. For example, needs for nurturance and intimacy can be met by family, friends, and peer groups. Religious and social groups help meet needs for belongingness, esteem, and spiritual enrichment. A job satisfies crucial economic needs and also provides a setting for social interaction with coworkers. Additional support may also come from informal social contacts. For example, bartenders and hairdressers are well known for listening sympathetically to the problems of their customers. This network of relationships, which makes up the primary social support system, is the traditional source of need satisfaction in our culture. One important feature of this support system is that there is usually some sense of mutual obligation underlying the transactions. In other words, a person is expected to give something, to meet certain needs of others, in exchange for what is received. Sometimes, it is enough to simply let others know that one is ready to help if the need arises.

The importance of this primary network to a person's well-being can hardly be overestimated. A study of the Chinese-American community in Washington, D.C. showed that psychiatric symptoms were more commonly reported among unmarried people, those with low-paying jobs, and those with weak social supports (Lin, Simeone, Ensel, & Kuo, 1979). Another study showed that social supports can help people to counteract the effects of a difficult or challenging situation (Sarason, 1980). Lack of a support system can also increase the chances of serious illness, including coronary artery disease (Lynch, 1977). These are just a few of the many studies that have shown that the availability of a social support system can help a person to maintain good health in both emotional and physical areas.

Many people in this country are sadly lacking in primary social supports. They may have no friends, no family, no job, and, therefore, no way to meet important needs. In some cases, a person may have family and friends who would be willing to help but who lack the means to do so. As detailed in Chapter Three, certain human services came into being to meet the needs of persons who have nowhere to turn for help. Over the years, human services have expanded greatly, and now go far beyond helping the poor, sick, and disabled. Gradually, they have taken over some of the functions of primary social supports. For example, the task of caring for poor elderly persons, once assumed by the family, is increasingly being accepted by governmental human services agencies.

AN OVERVIEW OF HUMAN SERVICES

"What are human services, anyway?" is one of the questions most frequently asked by students. We would like to be able to provide an "official" or generally accepted definition, but there is no such thing. Hasenfeld (1983) suggested that human services are organizations designed to "protect or enhance the personal well-being of individuals" (p. 1). This is a rather broad definition that includes almost any kind of helping service. Azarnoff & Seliger (1982) discussed the definition presented in the Allied Services Act of 1974: "Human services are those which enable the consumers of service to achieve, support, or maintain the highest level of economic self-sufficiency and independence" (p. 1). This definition is narrower than the first since it places strong emphasis on economic services.

It is clear that experts do not agree on the range or type of helping activities that should be included in human services. We propose the following somewhat arbitrary definition. Human services are organized activities that help people in the areas of health care, mental health including care for retarded persons, disability and physical handicap, social welfare, child care, criminal justice, housing, recreation, and education. Another type of service that might be included is income maintenance, a term that refers to programs like unemployment insurance and social security that provide income to people who are unemployed or retired.

It should be noted that human services do not include the help given by family, friends, or other primary supports. The help is provided by some type of formal organization, be it a clinic, hospital, nursing home, agency, bureau, or other service institution.

Obviously, human services cover a lot of ground. During recent decades, human services have increased greatly in size and scope in the United States. This increase is reflected by the fact that the total cost of social welfare programs was about $500 billion in 1977 compared to only $35 billion in 1950 (U.S. Bureau of the Census, 1980). During that period, there were comparable increases in expenditures for human services by federal, state, and local governments. About half the huge federal budget is now earmarked for social programs of one kind or another. About 12% of all employed persons in this country work in human services, either providing direct services or administering them (Hasenfeld, 1983). By any standard, human services is one of the largest industries in the United States.

Human Services Workers

The personnel at human services agencies can be divided into four general categories: (1) those who provide direct service to consumers of the service, (2) supervisory personnel, (3) administrators who determine the policies of the agency, and (4) support personnel who do clerical, maintenance, and security work. In addition, some settings, such as hospitals and nursing homes, require kitchen, housekeeping, and other support workers. In smaller agencies, workers sometimes have to do work in several of these categories.

The term *human services worker* usually refers to those who are involved in direct contact with clients, and to their supervisors. A great many job titles, positions, and professions are included under this general heading. These range from positions that require relatively little formal training, such as mental hospital aide and teacher assistant, to those that require extensive formal training and education. Clinical and counseling psychologists, psychiatrists, social workers, and nurses are included in the latter category. Chapter Six goes into detail about a wide range of career options in the field.

There is considerable variation in the extent to which different professionals identify themselves as human services workers. Social workers, for example, have generally been more accepting of the term than psychologists or psychiatrists. The term *human services worker* is more than a way of identifying workers in a particular field; it carries with it a certain attitude or philosophy about the field. The underlying idea is that the separate disciplines should emphasize what they have in common—serving people's needs—rather than their differences.

Some activists would like to phase out specialty training in favor of generalist training in human services. However, there is considerable resistance to this idea from professionals who wish to preserve separate identities as psychologists, social workers, psychiatrists, and so on. We apologize if all this sounds confusing; it *is* confusing, because the field of human services is undergoing rapid change. It is not possible to know for certain how human services workers of the future will be trained or what their job titles will be.

Kinds of Help Provided

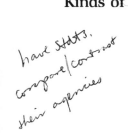

Human services provide help in a variety of direct and indirect ways. Perhaps the most basic kind of direct aid consists of *tangible items* such as food, clothing, shelter, tools, and other useful articles. Victims of natural disasters and homeless poor persons may be in dire need of this kind of help. The Salvation Army and the Red Cross are well known for providing hot meals and shelter to homeless people.

In most situations, *cash transfers* can be considered a form of direct aid because the money can readily be exchanged for needed goods and services. Social security, welfare, and unemployment insurance are among the most important benefits of this kind because millions depend on them for economic survival. These cash benefits can be used in any way the recipient sees fit. This freedom worries some politicians who fear that the money will be used for nonessential or even destructive items. This explains why some benefits are offered with strings attached—in other words, the benefits can be used only for some specified purpose. Food stamps, for example, are given to eligible poor persons but can be used only to buy food. Another example is a housing subsidy paid directly to the landlord for a welfare recipient's rent.

In addition to these direct forms of aid, there are indirect ways of promoting the client's health, well-being, and self-reliance. These indirect ways include services that are meant to increase clients' capacities to gain satisfaction of needs by their own efforts. The next few paragraphs give brief preliminary definitions of some of the major kinds of indirect intervention. All will be discussed in more detail in later chapters.

Primary prevention refers to services designed to prevent people from developing an illness or psychological problem. These services are usually offered to healthy or relatively well-functioning individuals, and often have an educational or informative component. A school program designed to inform teenagers of the hazards of alcohol abuse is an example of primary prevention.

Counseling helps people to consider their choices and options in life. Counseling may focus on career choice, budgeting, legal matters, or marital problems. Career counseling, for example, may help a client to select a suitable occupation, while marital counseling may focus on a decision about continuing a marriage. Some forms of counseling become involved in helping a client deal with personal problems, and, therefore, overlap with the following service.

Psychotherapy has the general goal of changing a client's behavior or emotional responses so as to improve psychological well-being. Typical goals of therapy are to reduce anxiety, to improve social relationships, and to control undesirable behavior patterns. There is an implication that the client suffers from some degree of psychological impairment.

Crisis intervention is a special form of help designed to meet the needs of a person faced with an unusually difficult life situation. The word *crisis* implies that the person's usual coping mechanisms may not be enough to handle the situation. There is a risk of severe emotional upset or even disorganization. Situations that might trigger a crisis include loss of a loved one, or being the victim of rape, assault, serious accident, or large-scale disaster. The helper provides support and suggests effective ways of coping with the crisis. The goal is not to change the person's personality but to restore the client to the precrisis level of functioning. Crisis intervention may be done in the context of face-to-face meetings or by means of a hotline. The latter is a telephone service that allows the caller to get in touch with a counselor at any time of night or day. The most familiar hotlines are designed to help suicidal persons. Hotline services are also available to rape victims and to persons actively struggling with alcoholism or other chemical dependency.

Rehabilitation is designed to help handicapped and disabled persons achieve the highest possible level of productive functioning. Some experts make a distinction between habilitative and rehabilitative programs: the former aim to help those who have never been productive, while the latter focus on restoring skills to those who were once capable. In either case, the emphasis tends to be on practical skills such as those involved in self-care and earning a living. The type of disability may be physical, emotional, or developmental.

Social support may be offered in various forms to those who can benefit from a strengthening of social ties. An example is a club for senior citizens that enables them to get together with peers once or twice a week. Other familiar examples are the athletic and social programs for teens provided by many Ys and community centers. In addition, many self-help programs such as Alcoholics Anonymous emphasize social support in their therapeutic approach.

Community organizing represents another indirect form of support for those in need. The general idea is that the human services worker works with community leaders to provide some program needed by an unserved population in the community. For example, the worker may help the community set up a training school for retarded persons.

Many human services agencies provide a mix of direct and indirect benefits to clients. Both mental hospitals and prisons, for example, provide direct aid in the form of food and shelter, and may also provide indirect aid in the form of counseling, therapy, or rehabilitation. The employment services of some states link direct cash benefits to job and career counseling. At the other end of the scale are smaller programs that offer only one or a limited range of services to clients.

Sponsors of Human Services

Human services organizations may be sponsored—that is, organized and funded—by private citizens, by religious and other groups, and by government.

Private agencies may be operated on either a profit-making or nonprofit basis. Nursing homes, rehabilitation hospitals, and agencies providing home nursing care are often private profit-making corporations that are run in basically the same way as other businesses. This means that management is under pressure by owners to keep costs down and to show a profit at the end of the year.

Many other private agencies are organized on a not-for-profit basis. Youth employment and child care agencies are sometimes nonprofit. The Red Cross and the March of Dimes are examples of large nationwide private human services agencies operated on a nonprofit basis. Typically, such agencies are controlled by a board of directors that lays down general policies and selects the administrative officers who are responsible for day-to-day operation of the agency. These agencies raise money by appealing to the general public for donations. An important advantage of nonprofit status is that it exempts the agency from certain taxes, which, in effect, allows more of the income to be used for helping consumers of the service.

Religious and other groups also sponsor nonprofit helping agencies. The Federation of Jewish Philanthropies, Catholic Charities, and the Lutheran Brotherhood are supported by major organized religions. In addition, unions, fraternal organizations, and ethnic groups sponsor countless helping agencies all across the country. The necessary funds are raised by appealing to parishioners and members for donations. Increasingly, both private and religious agencies are making use of professional fund-raisers who are paid on the basis of a percentage of the income they raise.

Without minimizing the importance of private and religious human services agencies, it is certain that governments (local, state, and federal) have become the major providers of direct and indirect aid to those in need. The scope and purpose of huge federal programs like social security will be discussed in the next chapter. State governments play a major role in education, administer employment insurance, and manage most of the nation's mental hospitals. Local governments are responsible for actual administration of welfare programs, and also provide many other kinds of help such as programs for seniors and teens.

Studying Human Services Firsthand

One of the best ways to learn about human services is to identify and study the different agencies and facilities within your geographical area. This kind of study lends itself readily to a team approach since students can divide the work and share information with one another. The information can come from many sources, including literature available at agencies, on-site visits, and meetings with staff members.

Your class might list all of the human services agencies, programs, and facilities in your area, and provide answers to the following questions:

have stats.
Compare their experiences

- What are the *stated* goals of the agency?
- What needs does the agency attempt to meet? What population is served? Roughly how many people does the organization serve? Hundreds? Thousands?
- What does the service cost the consumers? What are the eligibility criteria?
- Where does the money come from? If several sources are involved, list them in order of contribution.
- How many and what kinds of human services workers are employed by the human services agency?

Students may also share their subjective impressions of the agencies they visited. Did they feel welcome? Did the service seem to be well organized? How were clients treated by staff?

SOURCES OF NEED SATISFACTION

Figure 1-2 is a flowchart that illustrates the relationship between needs, primary sources of help, and human services. A person in need often seeks help from primary sources such as family and friends before going to a human services agency. For example, a person with financial difficulties may seek help from the family before applying for welfare. Similarly, a person with emotional problems may seek advice from a priest, minister, or rabbi before going to a psychiatric clinic. It is often more comfortable to appeal to familiar persons rather than to an impersonal agency for help. The bureaucratic procedures of some agencies make people hesitate to go to them: some agencies make clients wait for hours, require that complicated forms be filled out, and process the claims in a cold, perfunctory manner.

In some circumstances, however, a person may prefer to go to a human services agency rather than to primary sources. For example, an individual may want to conceal an unwanted pregnancy from family and friends. Others may feel too embarrassed about certain behaviors to even discuss them with friends or family. Child abusers, gamblers, and drug addicts may well fall into this category. In these cases, the human services agency offers the opportunity to deal with the problem in a confidential manner. And to those lacking in primary social supports, the human services often represent the last defense against personal disaster.

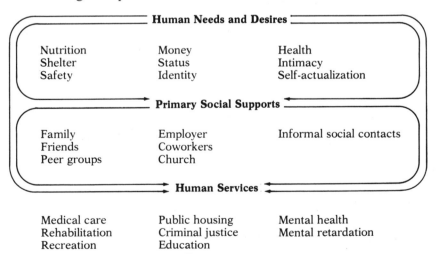

Figure 1-2. The Relationship between Needs, Primary Social Supports, and Human Services.

FALLING THROUGH THE SAFETY NET

An unknown number of persons need help from human services but don't get it. These are the persons who fall through the safety net provided by basic services. Some needy persons are not eligible for help based on the criteria of the agency in question. For example, a worker may not be eligible for unemployment benefits if he or she did not work for a specified number of months during the previous year. Other needy persons may simply be unaware of existing programs. For example, some illegal immigrants do not know about programs designed to help them. Still other needy persons may be fully aware of programs but too proud to accept the help available.

What happens to these people who are not helped by either primary social supports or by human services? The number is by no means insignificant. It is estimated that there are over 30,000 homeless "street people" in New York City alone. There are many additional thousands in towns and cities across America. Some depend on handouts from passers-by, and may supplement their diet with meals provided by private charities such as the Salvation Army. Some are long-term alcoholics whose life span is reduced by the rigors of life in the streets. During severe weather, some of them try to secure admission to jails or mental hospitals on some questionable basis. From time to time, there is a debate about what to do with these people—usually with one agency trying to shift the responsibil-

[handwritten margin notes: concept of outreach / Self determination]

A "bag lady," one of thousands of homeless people living in the streets of our cities.

ity to others. By and large, however, these people are relegated to a limbo of unmet needs.

Up to this point, we have emphasized the role of human services in attempting to meet needs. However, human needs are only one consideration in the design and delivery of services. Let's examine some other potent factors that influence human services in this country.

POLITICAL CONTROVERSY AND HUMAN SERVICES

The magnitude, scope, and purpose of human services are shaped only in part by the needs of people. Other considerations are the resources available for helping and the attitudes of various groups toward human services. Unfortunately, there is no consensus of opinion about the issue of who should receive what kind of help. The ultraconservative views is that government support for human services should be cut to the barest minimum. Liberals see the need for increases in all human services. In our society, there is constant conflict between those who would cut and those who would increase expenditures for human services. This has resulted in an ebb and flow of governmental support for human services. One unfortunate consequence is that human services have not been allowed to develop in an orderly, rational manner. Services are initiated under one administration only to be limited or eliminated by the next administration. The political forces underlying these conflicts are generally labeled liberal and conservative. Of course, people are not consistent within these frameworks. A particular individual may take a liberal position about one kind of service but a conservative position on another. Let's look more closely at these positions.

A Conservative Point of View

Conservatives wish to preserve traditional American values, including a strict adherence to the Constitution and respect for the rights and property of others. They profess a deep respect for the values of the American pioneer with a strong emphasis on hard work, perseverance, and self-reliance. Jealous of their personal liberty, conservatives tend to distrust big government, and wish to limit its role to the barest essentials. This resentment against interference extends into the economic sphere. Generally, conservatives favor a free market, and maintain that free enterprise and the pursuit of private profit have made the United States the richest nation on earth.

Conservatives perceive liberals as sentimentalists who spend billions of dollars of the taxpayers' money on ill-devised and ineffective social programs. For example, Barry Goldwater (1978), a leading conservative spokesman, attacked the liberal political movements for offering federal financing as the answer for every problem that ever confronted the American people. Federal spending for housing, health, education, civil rights, equal employment opportunities, urban renewal, and revamping farms had totaled billions of dollars in recent decades. Yet, Goldwater argued, all this government expenditure had solved no domestic problems and in some cases had made things worse. Goldwater expressed the conviction that the individual is often ignored in all of this liberal organizational activity. Conservatives place great value on the concept of Americans as rugged individualists who believe in pulling themselves up by the bootstraps.

Conservatives no longer oppose social programs in an automatic, reflexive fashion. They recognize that there are some circumstances when people, through no fault of their own, require help from government. Few, if any, conservatives now favor elimination of the social security program, although some would favor a reorganization along the lines of a voluntary insurance program. Conservatives also accept the need for some form of welfare benefits for those who are unable to meet immediate needs. However, they would like to see incentives built into the system that would induce individuals to become self-supporting. They are horrified by the specter of long-term welfare dependency extending from one generation to the next. Conservatives also generally favor unemployment insurance, partly in recognition of the fact that workers are often caught up in economic problems far beyond their individual control. It must also be recognized that all of these programs are beneficial to the economy because they help individuals maintain purchasing power.

Conservatives are likely to oppose programs that go beyond meeting basic survival needs. They express concern that help from the government tends to weaken the initiative of the recipient, creating an attitude of passive dependency. They also believe that the federal government has assumed excessive control over our lives through its massive programs and that power and control should be returned to the individual states.

A Liberal Perspective

Liberals see themselves as champions of the disadvantaged. They are convinced that conservative rhetoric about liberty and self-reliance doesn't mean very much to a person who is hungry, broke, and unemployed. Arthur Schlesinger (1962), the noted historian and liberal spokesman, suggested that American conservatism began on a lofty idealistic plane but degenerated into a concern about immediate class interest—that is, it became increasingly concerned with the profits of the business community. The control of government by big business, Schlesinger continued, drove the country to the brink of revolution. In fact, the Great Depression of the 1930s followed about 50 years during which business interests were predominant in American political life (Ebenstein, Pritchett, Turner, & Mann, 1970). The Depression was an economic disaster during which nearly one out of every three workers was unemployed; there was no money to borrow, and no real opportunity to begin any kind of new enterprise. The frontier with its opportunities had vanished. Millions were helpless victims of a complex industrial society beyond their control or comprehension.

The New Deal of the Franklin Delano Roosevelt administration initiated a period of liberal dominance of our country's political life. The basic premise of the New Deal was that government must help people to do what they cannot do by their individual effort. The principles of F. D. R. and the New Deal were soon translated into ambitious governmental programs. Slum clearance and public health programs were put into effect along with insurance programs for aged, disabled, and unemployed persons. Assistance programs for families with dependent children and for blind persons were created in the mid-1930s along with an array of other kinds of help for those in need. There was a basic shift of political power from big business to big government. The liberal tradition was carried on by the administrations of Harry Truman, John F. Kennedy, and Lyndon Johnson. All perceived that government must take a leading and responsible role in working for the health, safety, and welfare of the people.

During periods of liberal ascendancy, conservatives have been alarmed by the vast increase in the size of government, by the increased taxation needed to support wide-ranging social programs, and by the tendency of liberals to spend more money than they raise. The financial near-collapse of New York City during the late 1970s was seen by conservatives as the inevitable result of liberal mismanagement. Political momentum began to swing in a conservative direction.

CASE STUDY: Ward James

> In his book *Hard Times*, Studs Terkel (1970) reported interviews with many people who had lived through the Great Depression of the 1930s. Ward James told Terkel that up until

1935 he had a good job with a publishing house and was feeling rather secure. Then he was fired with no reasons given. In the following excerpts, he tells about his subsequent experiences.

> I kept going from one publishing house to another. I never got past the telephone operator. It was just wasted time. One of the worst things was occupying your time, sensibly.... The days was long. There was nothing to do evenings. I was going around in circles. It was terrifying. So I just vegetated.
>
> With some people I knew, there was a coldness, shunning: I'd rather not see you just now. Maybe I'll lose my job next week. On the other hand, I made some very close friends, who were merely acquaintances before. If I needed $5.00 for room rent or something, it was available.*

After discovering that he was not eligible for unemployment insurance, which had just been put into effect, James applied for welfare benefits.

> I finally went on relief. It's an experience I don't want anybody to go through. It comes as close to crucifixation as.... You sit in an auditorium and are given a number. The interview was utterly ridiculous and mortifying. In the middle of mine, a more dramatic guy than I dived from the second floor stairway, head first, to demonstrate he was gonna get on relief even if he had to go to the hospital to do it.
>
> I came away feeling I didn't have any business living any more. I was imposing on somebody..."[pp. 421–423].

James eventually began to receive $9 a month in welfare payments. Even though he was later successful in landing some good jobs, he suffered the constant dread that he could lose his job at any time.

The ordeal of Ward James gives some idea of the insecurity many felt during the Great Depression. The chronically unemployed in present-day America are going through an economic depression that is all the more frustrating because of the affluence all around them.

*From *Hard Times: An Oral History of the Great Depression*, by Studs Turkel. Copyright © 1970 by Studs Terkel. This and all other quotations from the same source are reprinted by permission of Pantheon Books, a Division of Random House, Inc.

The Reagan Brand of Conservatism

Ronald Reagan was carried into office by the nation's swing toward conservatism. Once in office, he put into effect a conservative economic program designed to reduce the inflation that over the years had sharply eroded the purchasing power of the dollar. Considerable success in controlling inflation was achieved but only at the expense of causing the high unemployment and economic recession of the early 1980s.

During the 1980 elections, Reagan criticized the previous administration for lagging behind Russia and the communist bloc nations in overall military strength. Once in office, President Reagan acted promptly to increase spending for national defense. To the dismay of some conservatives, the Reagan Administration began spending more money than it received, eventually creating the largest budget deficit in United States history. Conservative notions of fiscal responsibility, which stress a balanced budget, were ignored. The spending for weapons systems and the growing deficit intensified pressure to cut spending for social programs. There were reductions in school lunch programs, more stringent criteria for aid to disabled persons, cuts in medical insurance benefits, and so on.

In line with conservative policies, the Reagan Administration increased the freedom of each state to deal with social programs in its own way. This was done by giving federal money to the states in the form of block grants that allowed each state considerable leeway in deciding how to spend the money (Bloom, 1984). The states were provided with block grants for health services, including specific funds for mental health and for alcohol and drug abuse programs. Since these grants were accompanied by an overall reduction in federal spending for social programs, state leaders were faced with a painful dilemma: either they had to raise money by increasing state taxes or they had to cut services. These developments clearly illustrate the bottom line impact that political philosophies can have on human services, and are discussed further in Chapter Nine.

The Ebb and Flow of Support for Human Services

One factor that determines the degree of public support for human services is the state of the economy. In good times, tax revenues increase and more money is made available for human services. During economic downturns, funding for services is likely to be reduced.

Changes in the public's attitude toward government also affect funding for services. In recent years, the public's confidence in government seems to have reached a low point. Some people feel that the less money you sent to government, the less it will have to waste. Taxpayers periodically rebel against the relentless pressure for increased tax revenues. A case in point was the victory in 1978 of California's Proposition 13, a referendum that restricted the taxing of property. A similar proposition has been introduced in Massachusetts and several other states.

Supporters of human services argue that it is futile to attempt to save money by cutting funds for human services programs. For example, if we pay less for child care services now, we will have to spend more later for supporting people in mental hospitals and correctional facilities. If we cut back on funds for probation, we reduce our chances of rehabilitating offenders. Overcrowding in our prisons coupled with a lack of therapeutic programs is responsible for the high rate of recidivism. Is there really any long-run saving to be derived from "dumping" ex-mental patients into communities that are unable or unwilling to provide supportive services for them? By shortchanging human services agencies, we prevent them from reducing the number of dependent and dysfunctional persons.

Human services programs need sufficient funding to fulfill their missions, and an orderly predictable flow of funds from one year to the next. In fact, government seems to provide for human services on a hand-to-mouth basis with the threat or actuality of significant cutbacks always possible. These variations in funding are usually related to political and economic factors that have little to do with the needs of the agency or its clients. It is difficult to do an effective job, maintain employee morale, and keep the confidence of the clients under such unstable conditions. This is why human services workers are increasingly seeing the need to organize effective lobbying groups. They recognize that well-organized groups such as the gun lobby, the tobacco lobby, and other special interest groups are often successful in securing legislation favorable to themselves. On a practical level, the political system works through the application of this kind of direct pressure. Unrepresented groups, no matter how worthy their cause, are likely to be overlooked.

THE IMPACT OF CONTEMPORARY PROBLEMS ON NEEDS

Human services do not operate in a vacuum; they are shaped by social, environmental, political, and economic conditions that prevail in a given time and place. The purpose of this final section is to pinpoint some contemporary problems that affect the ability of Americans to meet their own needs.

In recent years, Americans have started to ameliorate long-standing social problems such as poverty and racism. At the same time, there have been decreases in population in both farming areas and in the centers of our large cities. Many people have left the Northern, industrial states for the Sunbelt—that is, the tier of Southern states ranging from California to Florida. This is also a time of rapid social and technological change. While all of these changes may bring opportunities for some, they create problems for others. In order to be fully effective, human services need to be based on an up-to-date grasp of the obstacles confronting people. Services need to be constantly modified to keep pace with changing needs.

Natural Disasters

Because natural disasters have occurred since antiquity, it is necessary to explain why this topic is included in a discussion of contemporary problems. The reason is that the rate of casualties from natural disasters is increasing sharply and will continue to go up in the foreseeable future. A disaster is a social phenomenon that occurs when the awesome forces of nature come into contact with people. On a worldwide basis, nearly a quarter of a million people die in natural disasters each year (Frazier, 1979). Earthquake, flood, hurricane, tornado, and volcanic eruption are among the natural hazards with the greatest potential for destruction.

In this country, several trends are acting to increase disaster tolls. One is the vulnerability brought about by increasing dependence on interlinked computer systems and surface electrical power lines. The New York City power blackout of 1977 was triggered by a lightning strike on electronic switching equipment. Another trend that increases the potential for disaster in this country is the shift in population. More and more people are moving into floodplains, seismic risk zones, and coastal areas exposed to hurricane winds, storms, and erosion. There is also an increased risk due to the spread of population to California where landslides and earthquakes are serious hazards. More than half the population now live in places highly susceptible to natural disasters (Frazier, 1979).

In the event of a disaster, people usually first seek help from family, friends, and neighbors. However, if the disaster is severe, local service agencies are called upon to help the sick and homeless. The police, fire department, church organizations, social welfare groups, and medical services may all play important roles, depending on the nature of the disaster. Restoring communication, effecting evacuations, rescuing survivors, and providing temporary shel-

A young girl contemplates the devastation of her hometown by flood waters.

ter and emergency first aid are just some of the important jobs that may need to be done. It is obvious that well-trained, well-organized service workers function more effectively than untrained ones. People tend to turn to large disaster relief organizations such as the Red Cross or Civil Defense only as a last resort (Quarantelli & Dynes, 1972, 1979). Many of these observations apply just as well to man-made disasters such as mine cave-ins or collapse of buildings and other structures. (See the following case study on the Hyatt Regency disaster.)

CASE STUDY: Kansas City Responds to a Disaster

During July 1981, the nation was stunned by the report of a major disaster in Kansas City. Two aerial walkways that spanned the lobby of the Hyatt Regency Hotel suddenly collapsed. The walkways fell to the dance floor below, killing 113 people and injuring many others. It was estimated that 5000 persons, including rescue workers and family and friends of the victims, were at risk of developing negative reactions to the crisis (Bloom, 1984).

The seven community mental health centers that served Kansas City had no plan or guidelines for dealing with the crisis. However, a communitywide response was developed within 72 hours of the tragedy by a team effort of the community mental health centers, the local mental health association, the Red Cross, and the local office of the federal Department of Health and Human Services. Gist and Stolz (1982) described the three components of their joint effort: (1) the creation of support groups at each of the mental health centers; (2) the development of a training program for mental health professionals and ordinary citizens in supportive counseling; and (3) the preparation of a mental health information campaign that was distributed by the mass media.

More than 10% of the at-risk population contacted a mental health center for assistance. According to Gist and Stolz (1982), the support provided by the mental health community helped to reduce the longer-term negative consequences of the tragedy.

This case study illustrates a high degree of cooperation between private and governmental human services organizations. They helped mobilize and coordinate the helping efforts of private citizens, the media, and service agencies.

The victims of disasters are a small percentage of those who receive aid from human services. Most people who receive help are victims of social conditions such as poverty, discrimination, and technological change. These are examined in the following sections.

Poverty

Poverty was the norm among the successive waves of immigrants to this country during the previous century. Most immigrants regarded it as a temporary state that could be overcome by hard work and a bit of luck. During the 1800s this optimism was justified by the dynamic growth of the nation and by the ample space for expansion westward. There were abundant opportunites for the enterprising individual, and it was expected that the second generation would surpass the immigrant parents in financial achievement.

In modern times, however, poverty tends to persist from one generation to the next. As Harrington (1968) pointed out, poverty may become a self-fulfilling prophecy, a kind of vicious cycle that robs the individual of the means to escape. The poverty cycle is due to the fact that the disadvantages of poverty hinder the next generation's chances to succeed. The high prevalence of broken homes and single-parent families sometimes results in insufficient supervision and encouragement of children. Poor language skills and a lack of early environmental stimulation may make it difficult for children to take full advantage of educational resources. It becomes difficult for children to develop the skills and attitudes necessary to break out of the poverty cycle.

Of all social problems, poverty is the one that has received the largest share of attention from social planners. Poverty is a critical problem because so many other problems are linked to it; juvenile delinquency, criminality, drug abuse, and mental illness are disproportionately represented in poor communities. Serious health problems and high rates of infant mortality are also found in poor neighborhoods. Affluent persons are often appalled by the conditions existing in poverty areas, and sometimes blame the victims for choosing to live so badly. The poor, on the other hand, think of themselves as having few options, and as trapped by the culture of poverty.

Poverty is a particular problem in the inner cities. Many of the big cities of this country contain decaying neighborhoods occupied mainly by poor households, and devastated by arson, vandalism, high crime rates, and abandoned housing. Since World War II, thousands of relatively affluent households, especially those with school-age children, have moved to the suburbs (Bradbury, Downs, & Small, 1982). The result is that the cities are tending to concentrate poor residents who have a great need for services and a limited ability to pay for them. In some big cities, one out of five residents is living on public assistance. There is controversy about what to do about this immense problem. Some social planners have thrown up their hands and suggested that it is futile to pour any more money into inner cities. They fear that increased services would only attract more poor people to the cities. Others have proposed that city governments should do everything possible to encourage middle-class people to return to the big cities. This would provide additional tax revenues, which could be used to benefit the poverty population. By and large, however, the inner cities still constitute an enormous reservoir of unmet needs.

Prejudice and Discrimination

The problems of poverty, racism, and prejudice are so deeply intertwined in this country that it is difficult to talk about one without referring to the others. Prejudice is based on preconceived attitudes and feelings about certain races, religions, or ethnic groups. These attitudes reflect negative stereotypes that are often nothing more than simpleminded overgeneralizations about certain groups. Typically, these attitudes are not based on real experience with the group in question but are learned from prejudiced individuals. Prejudicial attitudes not only attack the self-esteem of victims but are often the basis for discrimination in employment, housing, and education. Patterns of discrimination aim to keep certain minorities at the bottom of the economic ladder and in a specific neighborhood or ghetto. Although this country has made progress in reducing discrimination in recent decades, the lingering effects of mistrust are still with us.

Discrimination against Blacks, Hispanics, and women is discussed in the following sections. These groups are highlighted because of their large numbers, and because of their great importance to human services. There are, of course, many other groups that have been victims of discrimination, and you are invited to study these independently. Probably no other group has been treated with such consistent savagery as the American Indian. Brown's (1971) *Bury My Heart at Wounded Knee* provides a moving account of this shameful episode in American history. At times, Oriental Americans, including Japanese-Americans, have been victimized by the White majority. See the Additional Reading section at the end of the chapter for recommended books on this and related topics.

Discrimination against Blacks. For a number of historical reasons, Blacks for many years were denied access to the political and social life of this country. They were segregated in regard to where they lived and went to school. They were relegated to low-level jobs that often provided little more than a marginal income. Family life was disrupted by many factors including the greater availability of jobs for Black females than for Black males. While successive waves of European immigrants were being assimilated into mainstream America, Blacks were held back by their obvious racial features. Even when Blacks achieved wealth and fame, they were not readily accepted by affluent White communities. Discrimination tended to force Blacks into a circular pattern in which limited education barred them from higher education and career opportunities.

Black people made slow but definite progress toward equality during the century following emancipation. This was followed by a period of accelerated progress beginning in the mid-1960s. The political initiatives of the 1960s and 1970s, to be described in Chapter Three, were successful in achieving a higher level of opportunity for Blacks. These positive trends continue to the present day. Blacks are gaining in political power; their income is on the rise and more are now seeking higher education then ever before; a small but significant Black middle-class has been established. It is also clear that much remains to be done. Many Blacks are still deeply rooted in poverty and deprivation. Per capita unemployment is significantly higher among Blacks than Whites, and Black teenagers have high rates of unemployment. By 1982 the rate among young Blacks reached 48%, compared to 20% for White teenagers and 9.5% for all Americans (Crewdson, 1983).

As a result of discrimination, Blacks are overrepresented among those who need help from human services. There is, for example, strong evidence of an association between race and poor health (Julian, 1980). On the average, the life expectancy for White males is about five years longer than for Blacks, with a less pronounced difference in the same direction for Black and White females (U.S. Bureau of the Census, 1983). The infant mortality rate for Blacks is almost twice that of Whites. Partly because of limited access to preventive medical care services, including immunization, Blacks suffer from a higher incidence of disease than do Whites. The stress associated with being poor and Black may also account for the fact that there is a disproportionate percentage of Blacks in mental hospitals (Seham, 1973). Blacks are also overrepresented among those who receive welfare payments, food stamps, and public housing. Enough has been said to show a direct relationship between racial discrimination and increased needs for supportive services.

Discrimination against Hispanics. Spanish-speaking Americans have also been victims of a pervasive pattern of discrimination that limits their opportunities for advancement. Virtually every indicator of well-being reflects the results of this discrimination: their unemployment rates tend to be high; their health is not as good on the average as that of Whites; and their educational achievement scores tend to be low, partly because of the language barrier (Freeman et al., 1979). — growing. will be # 1 by turn of century

Although Hispanics are a smaller group than Blacks, it is difficult to determine their precise number in this country. Included in their ranks are a large but unknown number of illegal aliens. Migrant workers are another group not usually included in census surveys. In any case, Hispanics cannot be considered a homogeneous group. Some can trace their ancestry back to the origins of this country and are well established in their communities. Many others are recent immigrants who came here looking for work. Those who came from Mexico tend to be concentrated in the Southwest, while Puerto Ricans tend to live along the East Coast. Many Cubans have settled in the greater Miami area. Other Spanish-speaking persons have come here from Central and South America. The tendency of these various subgroups to retain their separate identities has frustrated efforts to join together to advance political and economic objectives.

One group in urgent need of help are the migrant workers who follow the harvest from south to north along the Pacific Coast. The plight of these workers, who are mostly of Mexican origin, has been publicized in books, movies, and magazine articles. However, they have not benefited greatly from this media attention. They work for low pay and are often provided with filthy, substandard housing. The state laws regarding living conditions are sometimes ignored because of official indifference and corruption (Garza, 1973). Not only are they exploited by the growers but by recruiters who take a percentage of their wages. Perhaps the best hope of improving their living conditions comes from the increasing strength of agricultural unions.

Illegal aliens are another group in need of assistance. Although undocumented workers, as they prefer to be called, come from India, the Caribbean, Asia, and poor countries all over the globe, the great majority are Spanish-speaking, with Mexicans making up the largest single subgroup. How many foreigners are here without permission? The answer, according to Crewdson (1983), is that no one really knows. Illegal workers usually take great pains to maintain a low profile. They risk being deported if they come to the attention of the authorities.

The arrest statistics of the Immigration and Naturalization Service (INS) do give some idea of the order of magnitude of illegal immigration. In 1961 only 80,000 illegals were apprehended and sent home; the number reached 325,000 in 1970 and soared to nearly a million in 1980 (Crewdson, 1983). The great majority of those arrested are Mexicans who are picked up at or near the border. The vast increase in the number apprehended gives some idea of the large number of people who want to enter the United States.

Undocumented workers work in agriculture, the garment industry, factories, hotels, restaurants, gas stations, and many other settings. For the most part, they get the jobs that are dirty, demeaning, boring, and that offer little hope of advancement and pay badly to boot (Crewdson, 1983). They typically lack union representation, and do not usually receive sick leave, insurance benefits, or other fringe benefits. Their illegal status makes them easy prey for unscrupulous employers. To make matters worse, many American citizens resent their presence in this country and blame the illegals for taking away scarce jobs.

These workers are also periodically accused of taking advantage of social services, such as welfare and unemployment compensation, to which they are not legally entitled. The evidence reviewed by Crewdson (1983) suggests that they use social services far less than American citizens. They tend to shy away from contact with authorities, and sometimes even avoid services that are legally available to them. For example, they are sometimes reluctant to seek medical treatment except in emergency circumstances. This poses a serious public health problem in Southern California and other areas of high concentration because illegals suffer higher rates of infectious disease than do American citizens. Obviously, these workers are not examined for communicable diseases before entering the country.

These people are clearly in need of medical care and other human services that they do not receive because of their illegal status. A good deal of controversy is stirred up by the question of just what their legal status should be. Legislation introduced in Congress in 1984 would extend amnesty to those illegals who have lived in this country for a certain number of years. The same proposed bill would penalize employers for knowingly hiring those not entitled to amnesty, this on the theory that illegals would not come here if they could not work. Some American citizens are strongly opposed to amnesty of any kind for illegals. Others accept their *de facto* presence in this country and would grant them legal status. It is certain that these workers will not fully avail themselves of human services until the threat of deportation is taken away.

Discrimination against Women.   It is ironic that women, who make up the majority of the U.S. population, are also the largest "minority" group. They are considered a minority group in the sense that they have been victimized by prejudice in much the same way as members of certain racial or ethnic groups. *Sexism,* discrimination against a person on the basis of sex, has its roots in prehistory. In early societies, the physical strength of males determined their dominant position as hunters, warriors, and leaders. Females were relegated to food preparation, child care, and other domestic chores. Modern sex stereotypes, oversimple ideas about the differences between the sexes, still reflect this early division of labor. Men are seen as "naturally" more aggressive, venturesome, and dominating. Women are supposed to be relatively more expressive, "intuitive" (irrational), nurturing, and submissive. While these qualities may have some inherited basis, they are largely produced by differential patterns of upbringing for boys and girls.

Of immediate relevance is the impact of sexism on the economic status of women. One important factor is that women have been discouraged from entering certain jobs or career fields. For example, mechanical work, physical sciences, administration, engineering, and police work have traditionally been considered male provinces. In line with prevailing sex stereotypes, women have been thought to be too tender and emotional for some of these occupations. Females have been regarded as more suited to clerical and secretarial jobs as well as certain nurturing professions such as nursing and social work.

Sexism has other important consequences for the economic lives of women. One is that women tend to be paid less than men even when performing the same job. Furthermore, promotional opportunities for women are fewer than those for men. Aside from sexism, certain realistic factors also tend to limit the advancement of women; these include pregnancies and child-rearing responsibilities. Some young women choose to interrupt their paid careers by becoming full-time mothers and homemakers. This possibility makes employers think twice about promoting young women to more responsible positions.

By 1980, the majority of American women were enrolled in the labor force (Ryan, 1983), and they made up about 40% of the total labor force. The average working woman earned only about 59% of the male average income, a difference that was related to the high concentration of females in low-paying office, clerical, and sales jobs (Ryan, 1983). However, there have been some recent signs that women are making progress in their struggle to attain economic parity with men. Despite the resistance of some conservatives who wish to preserve traditional sex roles, women are breaking into male-dominated professions. For example, the proportion of female lawyers rose from 4% in 1972 to 13% in 1980, and about one in five medical students are now females (Ryan, 1983).

Despite these clear signs of progress, women are still at a disadvantage compared to men. The average woman now works at a salaried job, but comes home to a second job that consists of her traditional duties of caring for a home and children. Most men are not yet ready to share these traditional "female" duties on a fifty-fifty basis. The fact that women are seriously challenging the traditional roles has sometimes generated serious conflict between the sexes and may be responsible for some disruption of family life.

One important consequence of the relative disadvantage of women is that they are more likely to need help from human services than men. About 75% of those who receive benefits from welfare and social programs are women. Details are provided in the next chapter.

Social Change

Americans are gradually changing their attitudes toward the poor and minority groups. Actually, this change is only one aspect of what amounts to a revolution in customs and attitudes that has taken place in the last few decades. One major trend has been a liberalization of attitudes toward sexual behavior. Homosexuals are pressing for social acceptance of their sexual preference. Sex is more openly discussed than ever before, and premarital sexual relations are accepted by many teenagers. At the same time, women are challenging traditional roles, and there is much public discussion of alternative lifestyles. The rapid pace of social change, particularly during the late 1960s and early 70s, stimulated a conservative reaction that aimed to preserve traditional social roles and customs. For example, members of the so-called Moral Majority championed a return to values based on fundamentalist religious beliefs. Without taking sides in these controversies, we can note that the rapid pace of these developments has created a sense of insecurity in many individuals. The contemporary American is faced with a bewildering range of options in regard to sexual behavior, role, and lifestyle.

The soaring divorce rate of the late 1960s and 1970s was associated with changing attitudes toward authority, religion, and traditional family structure. There was a significant increase in single-parent homes as well as an increase in reconstituted families—that is, families with children from previous marriages. One response to this destabilization of family life was the rapid development of family therapy. Institutions sprang up all over the country to train therapists to deal with family problems. Human services professionals demonstrated an ability to anticipate the need for a certain kind of service. At this point, it is difficult to predict future needs around family problems. For example, the extent to which current children of divorce will need help is simply not known. Previous generations do not provide a basis for judgment because the attitude toward divorce was more negative than it is now.

Technological Advance

The impact of technological change on people and their needs is sometimes powerful indeed. For example, the mechanical cotton picker, which appeared in the early 1940s, drastically reduced the number of hours needed to gather a bale of cotton, thereby eliminating the need for millions of workers. This and other advances in farm technology caused a huge shift in population from rural to urban areas. Between 1940 and 1960 no less than 3½ million Blacks moved from the rural South and journeyed north (Ryan, 1983). This migration contributed to the concentration of poor people in the inner cities that has already been described.

The replacement of human labor by machines is very much an ongoing process. Automated, programmed machines are replacing assembly line workers in the automobile and other industries. "Robot" machines are doing welding and assembling jobs once done by human beings. Of course, someone has to design, build, sell, and deliver the new machines, and office workers are needed to process the accompanying paper work. It is not certain if automation will reduce or increase the total work force in the long run. However, it seems clear that automation will tend to reduce job opportunities for poorly educated, unskilled workers. Recent innovations in communication technology including data processing also tend to increase demand for skilled as opposed to unskilled workers.

It is not only the unskilled worker who faces dislocation due to technological advances. Some highly skilled technicians and engineers find that their technical skills are becoming obsolete as they get older. Recent graduates with more advanced training in new technologies are often preferred for positions. Some older workers need counseling to help them consider opportunities in other fields where workers are presently needed.

Psychological Stress

The large-scale problems just described have their final impact on individuals. In our complex, rapidly changing culture, it is probable that an individual will sometimes be frustrated in trying to meet the needs described at the beginning of this chapter. All kinds of obstacles including prejudice, poverty, and other factors just reviewed can stand in the way of fulfilling needs. Typically, disadvantaged persons are preoccupied with basic survival needs, while the more affluent are concerned with higher needs relating to self-esteem and fulfillment of creative urges. To some extent, everyone experiences the pressure of these needs, and this is one important source of psychological stress.

Stress is sometimes defined as the strain imposed on an individual by threatening life events. However, it has been found that some desirable events, such as a job promotion, may also impose a strain on the individual. Bloom (1984) covered both possibilities by defining stressful life events as "those external events that make adaptive demands on a person" (p. 244). These events may be successfully handled or, in some instances, may lead to illness or psychological breakdown.

A team of researchers studied life events that occurred shortly before the onset of serious illness (Holmes & Rahe, 1967; Rahe & Arthur, 1978; Rahe, 1979). They developed a list of 43 life events and scaled them in terms of how much stress they evoke. The list is reprinted here as Table 1-1. It is not particularly surprising that death of a spouse ranks as the most stressful kind of event. It is surprising that joyful life events such as marriage or marital reconciliation proved to be more stressful than financial catastrophes such as bankruptcy or mortgage foreclosure. All of the events listed in Table 1-1 have one feature in common: they require a person to adjust to change in life situation.

Some people are better able to tolerate stress than others. It has already been pointed out that stress tolerance is partly dependent on

Table 1-1
Social Readjustment Rating Scale

Life Event	Mean Value
Death of spouse	100
Divorce	73
Marital separation	65
Jail term	63
Death of close family member	63
Personal injury or illness	53
Marriage	50
Fired at work	47
Marital reconciliation	45
Retirement	45
Change in health of family member	44
Pregnancy	40
Sex difficulties	39
Gain of a new family member	39
Business adjustment	39
Change in financial state	38
Death of a close friend	37
Change to a different line of work	36
Change in number of arguments with spouse	35
Mortgage or loan for major purchase (home, etc.)	31
Foreclosure of mortgage or loan	30
Change in responsibilities at work	29
Son or daughter leaving home	29
Trouble with in-laws	29
Outstanding personal achievement	28
Wife begins or stops work	26
Begin or end school	26
Change in living conditions	25
Revision of personal habits	24
Trouble with boss	23
Change in work hours or conditions	20
Change in residence	20
Change in school	20
Change in recreation	19
Change in church activities	19
Change in social activities	18
Mortgage or loan for lesser purchase (car, TV, etc.)	17
Change in sleeping habits	16
Change in number of family get-togethers	15
Change in eating habits	15
Vacation	13
Christmas	12
Minor violations of the law	11

the amount of emotional support one receives from other people. This is why divorce or death of a loved one is particularly stressful; it leaves the victim to face the situation without familiar supports.

Certain personality traits also play a role in how a person handles stress. Kobasa (1979), for example, studied how a person can remain healthy in the face of great stress. She reported that those who do so have a clear sense of their values, goals, and capabilities; a strong tendency toward active involvement with the environment; and a belief in their capacity to control and transform life experiences.

Developmental Crises

Psychological stress is intensified at certain phases of a person's development or maturation. This kind of stress is the unavoidable consequence of moving from one phase of development to the next. The stages of development include the prenatal period, infancy, childhood, puberty, adolescence, young adulthood, middle age, old age, and death. During each transition from one stage to the next, a person is subjected to novel challenges and tasks that tend to increase anxiety. The changes might involve new responsibilities, bodily alterations, and new ways of relating to others. For example, the individual entering young adulthood has reached physical maturity and is expected to make serious plans for a career and to begin serious sexual relationships. The major thrust of a person's activities is toward the achievement of independent, self-supporting status. With support and nurturance from others, most are able to successfully master the demands of the new phase.

However, developmental stresses can be overwhelming to some individuals, particularly those whose needs for support and nurturance are not being met. There is a wide variation in how people react to developmental transitions. What is a crisis for one may be an interesting challenge for another. A crisis occurs when an individual feels overwhelmed by the demands of the next phase of development. If a person is completely unable to master the requirements of the next developmental stage, further growth is prevented. The consequences of this failure may range from temporary emotional disturbance to serious disorganization of personality.

During recent decades there has been a marked change in attitudes of human services workers toward persons in crisis. It is now accepted that people may become anxious or upset during transitions in development, and that such reactions are not necessarily a sign of serious mental illness. Hoff (1978) pointed out that modern crisis theory has established a new approach to people with such problems. It is no longer assumed that they are completely irrational or that they cannot help themselves. Furthermore, it is becoming more accepted that it does not require a highly trained psychotherapist to help people get through a crisis. Counselors, police officers, nurses, lay persons with training in crisis intervention, and family members can be very helpful in getting someone through a difficult development phase.

Interaction among Problems

For purposes of description, contemporary problems have been treated here as separate and distinct from one another. In real life, there is a dynamic interplay among these factors. Close examination shows that certain individuals or groups may have to struggle against the cumulative impact of many stressful factors. For example, a technological change that puts a poor Southern agricultural worker out of work immediately places the family under stress. The need for money may force the older children to quit school and seek work, which reduces their chances of escaping the poverty cycle. If the family relocates to a Northern ghetto in search of work, they may be disappointed to find many others like themselves also out of work. The hopelessness of the situation may promote attempts to temporarily escape by means of drugs or alcohol. High levels of violence, crime, and gang activity may also threaten family cohesion. Medical care may be poor or completely inadequate in the community. These negative influences tend to accumulate to the point that cause and effect act in a circular fashion. For example, the mental breakdown and hospitalization of a mother may be traced to poverty and other factors; in turn, her breakdown becomes a major obstacle to the adjustment of her children, who may be shunted from one person or institution to another. The cycle goes on.

ADDITIONAL READING

Brown, D. (1971). *Bury my heart at Wounded Knee: An Indian history of the American West.* New York: Holt, Rinehart & Winston.

Button, J. W. (1978). *Black violence.* Princeton, NJ: Princeton University Press.

Crewdson, J. (1983). *The tarnished door: The new immigrants and the transformation of America.* New York: Times Books.

Gilder, G. (1981). *Wealth and poverty.* New York: Basic Books.

Kreisberg, L. (1979). *Social inequality.* Englewood Cliffs, NJ: Prentice-Hall.

Moore, J. W. (1977). *Mexican-Americans.* Englewood Cliffs, NJ: Prentice-Hall.

Oates, S. B. (1982). *Let the trumpet sound: The life of Martin Luther King, Jr.* New York: Harper & Row.

Petersen, W. (1971). *Japanese Americans: Oppression and success.* New York: Random House.

Pettigrew, T. F. (1975). *Racial discrimination in the United States.* New York: Harper & Row.

Ryan, M. P. (1983). *Womanhood in America: From colonial times to the present.* New York: Franklin Watts.

Sowell, T. (1981). *Ethnic America.* New York: Basic Books.

Steinberg, S. (1981). *The ethnic myth: Race, ethnicity, and class in America.* New York: Atheneum.

Toffler, A. (1980). *The third wave.* New York: Morrow.

Tsongas, P. (1981). *The road from here: Liberalism and the realities in the 1980s.* New York: Knopf.

West, G. (1981). *The national welfare rights movement: The social protest of poor women.* New York: Praeger.

REFERENCES

Azarnoff, R. S., & Seliger, J. S. (1982). *Delivering human services.* Englewood Cliffs, NJ: Prentice-Hall.

Bloom, B. L. (1984). *Community mental health: A general introduction* (2nd ed.). Monterey, CA: Brooks/Cole.

Bradbury, K. L., Downs, A., & Small, K. A. (1982). *Urban decline and the future of American cities.* Washington, DC: The Brookings Institution.

Brown, D. (1971). *Bury my heart at Wounded Knee: An Indian history of the American West.* New York: Holt, Rinehart & Winston.

Crewdson, J. (1983). *The tarnished door: The new immigrants and the transformation of America.* New York: Times Books.

Ebenstein, W., Pritchett, C. H., Turner, H. A., & Mann, D. (1970). *American democracy in world perspective* (2nd ed.). New York: Harper & Row.

Frazier, K. (1979). *The violent face of nature: Severe phenomena and natural disasters.* New York: Morrow.

Freeman, H. E., Jones, W. C., & Zucker, L. G. (1979). *Social problems: A policy perspective* (3rd ed.). Chicago: Rand McNally College Publishing.

Garza, H. A. (1973, Spring). Administration of justice: Chicanos in Monterey County. *Aztlan, 1,* 137–146.

Gist, R., & Stolz, S. B. (1982). Mental health promotion and the media: Community response to the Kansas City hotel disaster. *American Psychologist, 37,* 1136–1139.

Goldwater, B. (1978). *The conscience of a majority.* Englewood Cliffs, NJ: Prentice-Hall.

Harrington, M. (1968). In L. A. Fenman & J. L. Kornbluh (Eds.), *Poverty in America* (Preface). Ann Arbor: University of Michigan Press.

Hasenfeld, Y. (1983). *Human service organizations.* Englewood Cliffs, NJ: Prentice-Hall.

Hoff, L. A. (1978). *People in crisis: Understanding and helping.* Menlo Park, CA: Addison-Wesley.

Holmes, T. H., & Rahe, R. H. (1967). The social readjustment rating scale. *Journal of Psychosomatic Research, 11,* 213–218.

Julian, J. (1980). *Social problems* (3rd ed.). Englewood Cliffs, NJ: Prentice-Hall.

Kobasa, S. C. (1979). Personality and resistance to illness. *American Journal of Community Psychology, 7,* 413–423.

Lin, N., Simeone, R. S., Ensel, W. M., & Kuo, W. (1979). Social support, stressful life events, and illness: A model and an empirical test. *Journal of Health and Social Behavior, 20,* 108–119.

Lynch, J. J. (1977). *The broken heart.* New York: Basic Books.

Maslow, A. H. (1968). *Toward a psychology of being* (2nd ed.). New York: Van Nostrand Reinhold.

Maslow, A. H. (1970). *Motivation and personality* (2nd ed.). New York: Harper & Row.

Quarantelli, E. L., & Dynes, R. R. (1972, February). When disaster strikes (It isn't much like what you've heard and read about). *Psychology Today*, pp. 66–70.

Quarantelli, E. L., & Dynes, R. R. (1979). Response to social crisis and disaster. *Annual Review of Sociology, 3*, 23–49.

Rahe, R. H. (1979). Life change events and mental illness: An overview. *Journal of Human Stress, 5*, 2–10.

Rahe, R. H., & Arthur, R. J. (1978). Life change and illness studies: Past history and future directions. *Human Stress, 4*, 3–15.

Ryan, M. P. (1983). *Womankind in America: From colonial times to the present.* New York: Franklin Watts.

Sarason, I. G. (1980). Life stress, self-preoccupation and social supports. In I. G. Sarason & C. D. Spielberger (Eds.), *Stress and anxiety* (Vol. 7). Washington, DC: Halstead.

Schlesinger, A. (1962). *The vital center.* Boston: Houghton-Mifflin.

Seham, M. (1973). *Blacks and American medical care.* Minneapolis: University of Minnesota Press.

Terkel, S. (1970). *Hard times: An oral history of the Great Depression.* New York: Pantheon.

U.S. Bureau of the Census. (1980). *Statistical abstract of the United States* (101st ed.). Washington, DC: U. S. Government Printing Office.

U.S. Bureau of the Census. (1983). *Statistical abstract of the United States* (104th ed.). Washington, DC: U.S. Government Printing Office.

TARGET POPULATIONS

INTRODUCTION

Target populations can be defined as groups of people selected for help by human services. The poor, the elderly, mental patients, abused children, and teenage runaways are examples of groups that have been targeted by specific programs and agencies. There is nothing permanent about target populations. Depending on public opinion, availability of funding, and political climate, some groups may be relatively favored at a particular time. Populations that have always existed may suddenly be chosen for benefits. For example, victims of crime have only recently been targeted for benefits in a systematic way. The critical question of who determines which groups will receive aid is discussed in Chapter Seven.

Since there are literally hundreds of target groups of varying sizes, we can't cover all of them here. We limit our discussion to some of the larger groups that are being helped in an organized way. For each group, we give a rough estimate of the number of people included, along with a brief account of some of the programs and services provided. In regard to kinds of help provided, we place emphasis on large-scale federal programs, since these have become the vital bedrock of support for millions of Americans. You are encouraged to investigate on your own some of the smaller target populations as well as some of the local and private helping agencies.

AMERICA'S POOR

The United States is one of the wealthiest nations in the world: its gross national product (the value of all goods and services) is higher than that of any other country. In one recent year, median family income was $23,430, which means half of all families earned more than this amount and the other half earned less. About 20% of American families earned more than $35,000 (U.S. Bureau of the Census, 1981). Despite the high level of affluence in this country, the wealth is distributed in a strikingly uneven manner. The wealthiest 1% of the population own 10% of the real estate in private hands and more than 50% of corporate stock. At the other end of the scale, the poorest 20% of American have only 5% of the national income (Julian & Kornblum, 1983). There is a continuing national debate about these poor Americans. How many are living in poverty? Is there truth to the reports that thousands of Americans are actually going hungry?

Measuring Poverty

Exactly how many Americans are living in poverty? There is no definite answer to this question because the number depends on the standard used to define poverty. Perhaps the most useful measure of poverty is the threshold, or poverty line, provided by the Social Security Administration. This is the income needed to provide the typical family of four with an adequate diet, assuming that one third of family income is spent for food. Due to increases in the cost of living, the poverty line increased from around $3000 for an urban family in the 1960s to $10,178 in 1983. The percentage of Americans living in poverty was 17.3% in 1965—that is, at the start of President Johnson's War on Poverty. It declined to about 11% in the mid-1970s but increased again during the Reagan Administration. The national poverty rate reached 15.2% in 1983, which meant that over 35 million Americans were living in poverty (Pear, 1984). Critics charged that many Americans were indeed going hungry. Administration spokespeople pointed out that the poverty rate is overstated because the poverty threshold does not acknowledge noncash benefits such as food stamps, public housing subsidies, and health insurance payments. There is a continuing debate about the degree of hardship faced by the nation's poor people.

Who Are the Poor?

Obviously, poor people are those with a relative lack of money, resources, and possessions. Beyond this shared characteristic, America's poor may have little else in common. One important subgroup of poor people consists of those who have suffered a temporary setback that has reduced their ability to be self-supporting. These groups include workers who have been laid off, women who have been deserted by a spouse, and persons needed at home in a family crisis. Most of these persons would be considered *able-bodied poor* since they are potentially employable.

A quite different subgroup of poor, sometimes called the *deserving poor*, is made up of persons who are not able to be self-supporting. Included are the aged poor, young children of poor families, some discharged mental patients, and persons who are permanently disabled.

According to Brieland, Costin, & Atherton (1980), this diversity among subgroups of poor has been an obstacle in developing satisfactory programs to help the poor; programs that suit one group may be inadequate for another. To encourage able-bodied poor to enter the job market, an aid program should pay only low benefits. However, low benefits would be an undeserved penalty to a person who could not work in any case.

We pointed out in Chapter One that a disproportionate number of poor can be found among minority groups. Nearly 36% of Blacks were living in poverty in 1982 compared to about 28% of Hispanic Americans and 12% of Whites (Pear, 1984). Women are also over-represented in the ranks of the poor. In fact, three out of every four Americans living in poverty are women; they are the major recipients of social security benefits, food stamps, and many other human service programs. Some of these are older women who have outlived their husbands. Others are women with dependent children who have been abandoned by their husbands. It seems quite obvious that the patterns of discrimination discussed in Chapter One have a powerful impact in determining membership in America's poor.

Welfare and AFDC

At present, the most important single weapon in the war on poverty is public welfare. It is difficult to provide a clear picture of welfare since it is not one but many programs. Local, state, and federal governments are all involved in a complex, interlocking fashion. The basic responsibility rests with local (county or city) governments, which determine who is eligible for welfare and what benefits will be given. There is great variation in benefits paid by the various states, even when differences in cost of living are taken into account. Southeastern states, for example, tend to pay much less than California or some Northern industrial states.

Aid to Families with Dependent Children (AFDC) is the program most people mean when they refer to welfare. Before this program was enacted, there were few acceptable options available to the parent with no means of supporting young children. One alternative was to turn the children over to an orphanage; another was to seek work outside the home, leaving the children unsupervised. Neither alternative was satisfactory to the family or to the community. Considerations such as these led to the birth of the AFDC program in 1935. This program provides benefits to the mother and child. Although there is also some provision for husbands with limited income, over 80% of those receiving aid are members of female-headed households.

The federal government pays 50 to 80% of AFDC benefits, while state and local governments administer the program. The federal government also pays half the administrative costs, but there is variation in the proportion paid by state and local governments.

Some states take on the entire nonfederal portion, while other states require local communities to pay some portion of the nonfederal share. The lack of uniformity has contributed to the creation of a monstrous bureaucratic maze with agencies having different regulations and eligibility requirements.

AFDC has probably generated more political controversy than any other social program. Part of the difficulty centers around the great increase in the size of the program. The number of recipients increased from around 3 million in 1960 to nearly 11 million in the mid-1970s. As the costs of the program soared, critics began to express alarm about the "welfare explosion."

What caused the surge in welfare rolls? Part of the answer is that the civil rights movement of the 1960s and 1970s encouraged poor people to think of welfare as a right rather than a privilege. Previously, many poor people who were eligible had not applied. Some actually did not know about their entitlements; others were too ashamed to apply. Increasingly, poor people rejected the idea that they were to blame for their destitution. At the same time, the liberal political climate caused welfare agencies to be more receptive toward applicants than they had been. Civil rights attorneys were successful in reducing the harassment to which applicants were subjected in many communities. For example, the practice of grilling female applicants about their sexual activities was declared illegal in some states as were the "midnight raids" by welfare officials to check for male cohabitants. All of these changes encouraged poor people to apply for benefits in larger numbers than ever before.

Aside from growing costs of the program, criticisms about other aspects of AFDC were raised by conservative and some liberal commentators. Perhaps the most serious is that AFDC works against keeping the family together. The assumption underlying this criticism is that the program influences some fathers to leave home. These are usually men without technical skills whose income is low, and who may not be able to work on a steady basis. They are often the last hired, the first fired. In contrast, the welfare income is regular and also provides other benefits which the father could not provide. For example, welfare status usually assures eligibility for health insurance—an important consideration in these days of rising health costs. The net effect is that the poor father may help the family by leaving it. If he elects to stay with the family, he cannot earn more than a limited amount without jeopardizing the welfare benefits.

Some commentators blame welfare for the increase in the proportion of female-headed families in recent years, a trend that is most pronounced among Blacks. Since 1960, the number of Black families headed by women has more than tripled; in 1984, half of all

Black families with children were headed by women, and more than 60% of these families lived in poverty (Joe & Yu, 1984). However, welfare policies could not possibly account for all of this huge increase because the welfare rolls have remained about the same since the mid-1970s. The above-cited authors pointed out that the increase in Black female-headed families has been accompanied by a decline in the percentage of Black men who are actively participating in the work force. Perhaps human services should place more emphasis on helping Black men to enter the labor force. This would seem to be a prerequisite for enabling more of them to play active roles as husbands and fathers.

Bethel (1980), a conservative commentator, suggested that welfare not only fails to cure poverty but perpetuates it. He cited the results of welfare experiments in Seattle and Denver to support the view that welfare programs may have negative effects on the recipients. Several thousand people were given a guaranteed income for a period of years. It was found that work productivity dropped off sharply and that the rate of family breakup increased. It may be that husbands tend to leave the family when welfare payments undermine their role as providers. In any case, Bethel suggested, the pattern of family breakup tends to perpetuate the cycle of poverty.

The evidence reviewed by Patterson (1981) suggests that only about 5% of AFDC families were broken up because of AFDC, although it may well be true that the availability of benefits induces some mothers to think twice about remarrying. Patterson and others believe that the main reason for family breakdown among the poor is not welfare but poverty itself. The father often becomes demoralized by his inability to provide a decent, steady income. The chronic frustration about never having quite enough money may lead to excessive drinking, marital discord, even to child abuse. As difficulties multiply, the chances of holding the family together become less and less.

A related criticism is that AFDC encourages poor women to have lots of children. This is one of the myths surrounding welfare. The fact is that welfare families have an average of 2.2 children—a figure not much higher than the national average. In any case, there is no financial gain from additional children since the expenses are greater than the additional benefits.

A final criticism of AFDC is that it weakens self-reliance. Before 1967, recipients were given little incentive to work because any earnings had to be subtracted from welfare checks. In order to increase the incentive to work, Congress, at the request of the Nixon Administration, enacted the Work Incentive Program (WIN). The basic goal of the plan was to break the cycle of poverty by requiring AFDC recipients age 16 and over to accept work training or a job.

Unemployed fathers and young adults were to be selected first. In addition, funding for day care centers would allow welfare mothers to seek training. The plan allowed recipients to keep the first $30 per month they earned plus one-third of amounts above it (U.S. Department of Labor, 1970).

One reason for the partial failure of this "workfare" program, as it was called, was that many who were trained became discouraged by the low pay of jobs available to them (Patterson, 1981). In other cases, welfare mothers did not want to leave their children with strangers. Some states required the mother to leave the children with other welfare mothers who were not trained day care workers. Perhaps the most important drawback was simply that welfare mothers were really needed at home.

Other Programs for the Poor

The federal government provides a number of other programs for persons with limited income. In 1982, 7.2 million families received food stamps, 5.6 million received free or reduced-price school lunches, 3.2 million received housing subsidies, and 8.1 million received Medicaid benefits (Pear, 1984). We'll take a closer look at some of these programs here.

Some low-income families are eligible for food stamps, which can only be used for the purpose of buying food in an authorized food market. They cannot be used for buying liquor, beer, cigarettes, soap, paper products, or other nonfood items. The stamps cannot be redeemed for cash. At present, the majority of recipients earn less than $6000 a year.

Poor persons may also be eligible for various kinds of help with housing. Some communities provide low-cost housing, often called "projects," for poor people. In some cases, welfare provides a rent subsidy for those unable to pay the full amount of their rent. Homeless persons are put up in low-cost hotels until a permanent place is found. Regardless of the form of housing, poor people tend to be placed together in ghetto-like environments where crime, addiction, and substandard conditions are common.

The federal government provides benefits to those of limited income through Medicaid, which is a system of health insurance. It provides for an array of inpatient and outpatient medical services. Although it has helped poor people gain access to improved medical care, the program is riddled with abuses, especially in poor areas. Some unscrupulous persons set up "Medicaid mills" in poor neighborhoods where the patient is routinely run through a lengthy series of tests and procedures, many of which are unnecessary. Another limitation of the Medicaid system is that many doctors simply refuse to accept Medicaid patients because the level of reimbursement is too low.

Not all programs for the poor are concerned with basic survival needs. For example, many city and state governments provide low-cost or free college educations for low-income persons. Many of these colleges have an open enrollment policy, and make some provision for the underprepared student in the form of remediation courses.

Most of the above programs are means-tested, which means that a recipient's total financial support must fall below a certain level before he or she is eligible. Although these and other programs have improved the quality of life for many poor persons, life for the poor is far from easy. There continues to be a strong undercurrent of hostility toward the poor in this country. The "freeloading chiselers" on welfare are condemned not only in the street but from the political platform. Many hardworking Americans, convinced that welfare recipients are lazy and/or immoral people, bitterly resent paying tax money to support them. The poor themselves sometimes have incorporated these negative attitudes into their thinking. They feel ashamed of not being independent and self-reliant, important values to Americans. These attitudes may be shared by the politicians who establish budgets and eligiblity requirements as well as by the workers who administer the programs. It is not surprising that welfare recipients often band together into informal groups where they may find not only understanding and support, but more practical kinds of help.

This section can best be closed by recalling Will Rogers' remark: "It's no crime to be poor but it might as well be."

CHILDREN IN NEED

Children are endangered not only by poverty but by illness, rejection, lack of understanding, the inability of parents to socialize them properly, and many other factors. Human service workers realize that children are a high-risk group for developing all sorts of physical and emotional problems. Children often haven't fully developed the skills and defenses needed to deal with the stresses of life. Although some remarkable children do well in spite of grave hardships, most require some minimal care, love, and guidance. If these are not adequately supplied, the risk of developing a serious disorder increases.

According to the Joint Commission on Mental Health of Children (1970), 8 to 10% of all children are suffering from a childhood problem serious enough to require professional help. Another 2 to 3% are severely disturbed. These problems range from serious disorders such as childhood psychoses, retardation, and physical abuse to milder disorders such as school phobia, bed-wetting, and extreme shyness. These and other dysfunctions, fully described in abnormal psychology courses, will not be detailed here. Instead we will examine the vulnerability of children in terms of the changing American family. There has been a great deal of recent public discussion about how these sweeping changes have affected children.

Children and the Changing American Family

Historically, children have been cared for at home, in families, by women. It is still true that most of the care of the young is provided by women in their roles of wife, mother, and grandmother. However, the human service workers should be alert to changes in family makeup that may affect the care of youngsters (Bane, 1983). These changes include high divorce rates, a large increase in the number of one-parent (either father or mother) families, and the growing tendency of women to enter the paid labor force. If these trends continue, the traditional, two-parent family will become another minority group. One consequence of these trends is that there is generally less time for parental supervision than there was in the traditional family. In addition, many children are exposed to the stress involved in the breakup of a home. Let's look at the evidence pertaining to the impact of some of these changes on children.

Children of One-Parent Families

A total of 12 million American children are now living in one-parent families (U.S. Bureau of the Census, 1979). Many of them have experienced the loss of a parent either by death or marital discord. There is probably no more painful event in the life of a child. Stress, feelings of insecurity, and self-blame usually accompany this event. Children tend to exaggerate their own role in causing the parent to leave. It is almost inevitable that the insecure home situation will temporarily disrupt the child's functioning. What about long-range effects?

Many human service workers have taken it for granted that the one-parent situation poses serious problems for children. A recent, large-scale study tends to confirm this assumption (National Association of Elementary School Principals, 1980). As a group, one-parent children were found to show lower achievement and to present more discipline problems than two-parent peers in both elementary and high school. They were absent and late more often, and seemed to have more health problems. This and other evidence established children of one-parent families as a target population. In view of the immensity of this population, it is not surprising that helping efforts have been centered around schools.

Although many children handle the adjustment to a one-parent family quite well, it has become apparent to school officials that others need some kind of extra help. One approach that has enjoyed some success is peer counseling in the form of "rap groups" for children. Whether sponsored by the school or a local counseling agency, these groups help the youngster to ventilate strong feelings about the disrupted home life, and also to reduce the sense of isolation that some feel. In the group setting, children realize that their feelings are shared by many others in similar situations.

In some cases, the child may be so disturbed that professional. help is sought. Some community agencies, such as child guidance centers, offer individual or family therapy with a social worker, psychologist, or psychiatrist. Some of these agencies maintain a reference library of books, pamphlets, and films on death and divorce for use by clients and families of clients.

Abused and Neglected Children

It is uncertain if the changes in family pattern just discussed are contributing to the apparent increase in child abuse. Some experts doubt if there has been any real increase, and attribute the apparent increase to intensified case finding and reporting. There is no doubt that there has been a great increase in services for this target population during the past two decades. Presently, about 200,000 child abuse cases are reported every year in this country (Kempe & Kempe, 1979). Between 20 to 40% of the cases involve serious injury to the child. These children may be beaten, mutilated, burned, choked, sexually assaulted, or thrown from windows. The atrocious quality of these assaults is intensified by the fact that the majority of victims are under 3 years of age (Kempe & Kempe, 1979). The remaining cases involve neglect of the child's basic needs for food, shelter, or supervision. As Young (1981) pointed out, neglect is also a form of abuse. For example, a little girl comes to school so dirty that other children ridicule her. Children are locked in an apartment and left alone for days. Although not physically beaten, these children have certainly been abused.

What are the causes of child abuse? It is known that abuse is usually part of a recurring pattern rather than a single incident

4 out of 5 convicts were abused children.

In the United States, an average of 80% of our prisoners were abused children. That is why we are working so hard to help these children today, before they develop into a threat to others tomorrow. With your support, we can have a full staff of trained people available 24 hours a day. Abused children desperately need us. Please let us be there to help. Write for our free brochure, or send in your tax-deductible donation today.

San Francisco Child Abuse Council, Inc.
4093 24th Street, San Francisco, CA 94114

This poster makes a powerful appeal on behalf of abused children.

(Kaplun & Reich, 1976). Abusive parents tend to be young, of lower-class status, frustrated, unemployed, alcohol abusers, and often suffering from marital discontent (Egeland, Clochetti, & Taraldson, 1976). It seems clear that the abusing parents often take out their frustrations on the helpless infant or child.

Treatment Approaches to Child Abuse

In cases of serious child abuse, it was once thought that the best approach was to take the child out of the home. Several types of placement might be considered, including foster homes, institutions for the care of children, or homes with relatives. It was found that these placements often did not work out, because the children were likely to feel rejected by their parents, unwanted by their new care-takers, rootless, and bitter (Coleman, Butcher, & Carson, 1984). Abused children do not necessarily want to get away from their parents. They may love their parents in spite of the abuse, and may be reluctant to get involved in a new, and therefore threatening, situation.

The trend today is to hold the family together if this is at all possible, and to give the parents the support they need to become adequate parents. Rather than punish the parents, the goal is to help them break the cycle of abuse. One approach is to use groups to teach effective parenting to those whose own parents were usually disastrous role models. The abusing parents are encouraged to call staff of the mental health agency when they feel the impulse to hurt their children. It must be understood by all concerned that effective parenting does not come naturally but must be learned in a step-by-step fashion. The study of child abuse makes it quite obvious that maternal and paternal "instincts" cannot be relied upon to produce love and care for a child. Parenting involves a wide range of skills, attitudes, and knowledge that are normally acquired from one's parents. Child abusers often fall into the pattern of imitating their own abusive parents.

Another approach to treatment is Parents Anonymous (PA), a group founded in 1970. Since it is a self-help group, it avoids the angry feelings that are often generated by an outside authority intruding into the home. Often, the abusing parents feel guilty about their maltreatment of their children. They are very sensitive to being shamed and belittled by authorities, however much they may "deserve" it. In the PA meetings, modeled after Alcoholics Anonymous, the abusing parents voluntarily admit their tendencies to others like themselves. With the support of the group, they struggle to control themselves and to find other ways of dealing with their children. While it is too early for a definitive assessment of the effectiveness of this approach, it can be said that PA is growing in popularity. There are now over 100 chapters in this country.

Children are members of many target populations. Additional references to children can be found in subsequent sections on the physically handicapped, the mentally ill, and the retarded.

THE ELDERLY

A White American child born in 1982 can expect to live about 75 years (71.4 for males and 78.7 for females), which is about 20 years longer than a child born in 1920. Members of other racial groups can expect to live about 71 years (66.5 for males and 75.2 for females) (U.S. Bureau of the Census, 1983). Most of this amazing increase in life expectancy is due to reduced death rates for children and young adults. Of special interest to human services workers is the fact that the proportion of elderly persons in the population is growing steadily. There are now 26 million persons 65 or over in the U.S., about 11.4% of the total population (U.S. Bureau of the Census, 1983). By the year 2030, the elderly will probably make up about 20% of the population, and will number nearly 50 million!

This huge increase in the proportion of elderly in the population will have a profound influence on human services because the chances of needing outside help increase sharply with age. About 5% of those between 65 and 75 require help because of serious physical or mental dysfunction. The disability rate then increases sharply at ages beyond 75. Also to be considered is the fact that the elderly suffer higher rates of depression and suicide than the general population (U.S. Bureau of the Census, 1980).

Older persons inevitably undergo physical changes that increase susceptibility to diseases such as cancer, heart disease, arthritis, and diabetes. As the body declines in vitality, it becomes less able to deal with stress and malfunction. The physical problems are compounded by social and psychological difficulties. For example, the elderly person has to face up to the loss of loved ones as well as the possibility of feeling less useful and more of a burden to others. Financial problems are also likely to come along with old age. The majority of elderly persons leave the work force, sometimes pressured to do so by rules and regulations of their employers. With retirement, income drops sharply. This explains why social security benefits are of such vital concern to many elderly Americans.

Social Security

The federal government plays a major role in providing for the needs of the elderly. The Social Security Act, enacted in 1935, provides for a national system of benefits at retirement. About 80% of the aged now receive monthly social security checks. Without these benefits, six out of ten older persons would fall into poverty. Many older persons rely on social security as their sole support. The fact that the average 1981 yearly benefits for a couple was $5684 suggests that many are at or below subsistence levels.

Dependent relatives of covered workers are also eligible for benefits under the Survivors Insurance Program. In addition, Supplementary Security Income (SSI) provides financial help to blind and disabled workers under the age of 65. In recent decades, a program of health insurance, discussed next, was added to social security. In effect, the various programs comprise a vital safety net for many needy older Americans.

Health Care for the Aged

During the late 1950s and early 1960s, there was increasing recognition of the need for some kind of national health insurance. Health costs were rising sharply, and many poor Americans did not have adequate private health insurance. In fact, some had no health insurance at all. Private health insurance is often a fringe benefit of employment and lapses when a person is no longer employed. In recognition of these problems, Congress in 1965 amended the Social Security Act to provide medical care for the aged. This program, called Medicare, provides hospital benefits including a bed in a semiprivate room, operating room charges, regular nursing care, and medical supplies. It also provides for some services at home such as part-time, skilled nursing care for persons convalescing from an illness who no longer needed to be in the hospital. However, the program does not cover routine physical exams, eyeglasses or hearing aids, or immunization. Some critics believe that these limitations, designed to keep the costs of the program to a minimum, effectively deny many older persons access to preventive medical services. Since checkups are not covered, some poor older persons wait until they have definite symptoms so as to ensure coverage. Whether this limitation really saves the government any money in the long run is open to serious doubts.

Despite the major benefits provided by Medicare, there are significant deductibles and limitations in coverage. One million of our elderly are not eligible for Medicare at all. Those who are covered find that the program pays less than half of their health costs in an average year. At the beginning, Medicare paid 80% of what the doctor charged. However, as expenses of the program spiraled, the percentage was reduced to 75%. A decreasing number of doctors are willing to accept "assignment," which means to accept what the insurance pays as full payment. The patient must then pay the difference between the doctor's fee and the insurance allowance. Some elderly Americans simply can't afford to pay this difference. They must go to doctors who accept Medicare. There is an increasing tendency for foreign doctors and others with doubtful credentials to provide services to our poor people, including the elderly poor.

Financing Social Security

There is nationwide concern about the financial solvency of social security. Two factors are responsible for the dire predictions of its impending bankruptcy. One is that the number of recipients has increased to 36 million, making social security the largest social insurance system in the free world. The other factor is the shrinking tax base of the program. Originally, about 7 workers (and their employers) contributed payroll taxes for every beneficiary. Now, there are only 3.2 workers for every beneficiary. The expected increase in the number of elderly recipients in the future will further reduce the tax base. Since payments were exceeding revenues in the early 1980s, it was obvious that something had to be done. In 1983, President Reagan signed into law a $167-billion "rescue package" for social security. For the first time in history, social security benefits were subject to income tax if the gross income exceeded certain amounts. In addition, payroll taxes for employers and employees were raised to 7% beginning in 1985. Persons retiring in the next century may turn out to be the biggest losers of all; the retirement age for receiving full benefits will be gradually raised from 65 to 67 after the year 2000 (Carlson, 1984).

Community Programs for the Elderly

Aside from social security, there are an array of programs that help maintain the elderly in the community. Elderly Americans of low income may be eligible for food stamps and low-cost housing. In addition, many communities have senior centers that offer a range of services including social clubs, counseling, leisure-time skills training, and inexpensive meals. The general thrust of these programs is to reduce the isolation that many elderly persons experience, especially after the loss of a spouse. An attempt is made to connect the person with a lively social group, and to enhance the sense of commitment to the community. For those seniors with problems in getting around, some agencies provide visitors to homebound seniors, or offer escorts to those who need help getting to the doctor, bank, or market. Meals on Wheels provides hot meals to seniors who can't get out of the house.

These programs provide the link between the person and the community, sometimes delaying or preventing institutionalization. However, not all seniors avail themselves of these programs. Some see themselves as extremely capable, not "old" at all, and resent any implication that they need help.

Nursing Homes

Although the great majority of elderly persons are able to live in the community, about 5% are presently living in institutions, including hospitals for the chronically ill, mental hospitals, prisons, and nursing homes (Beaver, 1983). By far the greatest number of institutionalized elderly persons, about 1 million, are living in nursing homes. Nursing homes vary in the amount of skilled nursing care that they provide. Some care for relatively disabled persons, while others cater to those with less severe limitations. It should be made clear that nursing homes are not hospitals in that they do not provide

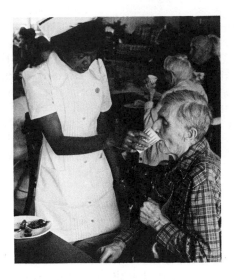

A nurse providing care to a nursing home resident.

service for the acutely ill. Rather, they maintain persons with a chronic condition who do not require active medical intervention. These may be persons with mild brain damage or physical handicaps that limit mobility.

What factors determine the need to place an elderly person in a nursing home? Tobin and Leiberman (1976) identified the following: physical deterioration, lack of supportive services in the community, and the inability of the family to provide the level of care needed by the older person. There is little evidence to support the belief that large numbers of elderly persons are "dumped" into institutions. Usually, American families try to keep their older members in the community if at all possible. In fact, many elderly persons with mild limitations do live with their relatives. However, sometimes the elderly person deteriorates to the point where round-the-clock care is required. As suggested before, the changing patterns of the family, especially the increase in working mothers, makes it increasingly difficult to care for an infirm elderly person at home.

There has been an increase in recent years in the number of elderly living in nursing homes. This may be due in part to changing family patterns but is also related to the increased availability of nursing homes. This increase was spurred by federal funding for this purpose in the 1960s when it became clear that there was a shortage of facilities for elderly Americans. The availability of Medicaid in the mid-1960s also stimulated the growth of nursing homes. Most residents pay for their care through Medicaid. The costs are so high that relatively few persons could afford to pay out of their own resources.

The idea of putting an older person in a nursing home arouses strongly negative feelings on the part of all concerned. Some of this revulsion is due to horror stories about nursing homes that neglect or even abuse patients in their care. Some critics believe that many nursing homes are chiefly concerned with the profit and convenience of management. It is true that the nursing home industry is comprised largely of private, profit-making concerns, many of which are part of larger chains. There is no doubt that abuses do occur, and that some nursing homes seem to be places where patients wait to die. The general trend, however, is that most homes provide adequate custodial care along with token recreation and rehabilitation programs. Even in places where physical care is beyond reproach, the patients seem to spend inordinate amounts of time just sitting around. The patients are often babied to an unnecessary degree because it is faster and easier for staff to feed, bathe, and dress them than to wait for patients to do for themselves. The lack of therapeutic programs is due simply to the fact that it costs money to provide them. Many nursing home administrators are unaware that improvements can be made with no increase in cost by training existing staff to encourage patients to function maximally.

Working with the Elderly

Kahn and Antonucci (1982) reported that older people who are active and in control of life are less likely to be depressed and more successful in coping with problems. Although encouraging older persons to be active is often desirable, it must be kept in mind that older people may have some realistic limitations on their activities. These limitations might be due to irreversible physical deterioration or to loss of loved ones. Older persons often need help in accepting their realistic losses before they can go on to develop new activities and new social relationships.

These realistic limitations only partly explain why some human service workers do not seek to work with the aged. This trend has been observed in social work, psychology, medicine, and other helping professions. The Group for the Advancement of Psychiatry (1971) studied reasons for negative staff attitudes toward older clients and came up with these: the elderly stimulate the workers' fears of their own old age, and also arouse the workers' conflicts with parental figures. Some helpers believe that old people are too rigid to change their ways, while others are concerned about devoting a lot of time and energy to a patient who might soon die.

Those workers who put their fears and prejudices aside find that working with the aged can be very rewarding and enjoyable. The prognosis is not usually as negative as feared, and there are pleasures and delights to be derived from contact with old persons. In our experience, student workers often begin fieldwork training with the aged with distaste but come away from the experience with positive feelings. Often, students are deeply touched by their contacts with elderly shut-ins and nursing home residents. More important is the sense of really making a difference in a client's life.

DISABLED PERSONS

A disabled person is one with a physical or mental impairment that limits one or more major life activities such as seeing, hearing, speaking, or moving. The disabled include not only those who are blind, deaf, physically impaired, mentally retarded, or mentally ill, but also those with hidden impairments such as arthritis, diabetes, heart and back problems, and cancer (Asch, 1984a). Some authors make a distinction between the terms *handicap* and *disability. Disability* refers to the diagnosed condition, such as blindness or deafness, while *handicap* refers to the consequences of the disability. The implication is that the consequences can be greater or lesser depending on various factors such as society's attitude toward the disability in question.

There are no exact estimates of the number of disabled persons, partly because of uncertainty about including people with mild impairments. Bowe (1980) estimated that the total number of disabled in the U.S. is about 36 million, or about 15% of the entire population. Estimates of the disabled population of working age vary from 8.5% to a high of 17% (Asch, 1984a). It has also been estimated that 10% of children under 21 are disabled (Gliedman & Roth, 1980), and that 46% of those 65 and over report a health impairment (DeJong & Lifchez, 1983). By any estimate, the number of persons with serious handicaps is awesome.

Mainstreaming the Disabled

The history of society's treatment of disabled persons can be summed up in two words: segregation and inequality (Burgdorf, 1980). Disabled persons have often been denied their rights, and have not been readily admitted into the mainstream of American life. It is only in recent years that this country has witnessed a wave of activism and accomplishment for handicapped people. Senator

Lowell Weicker (1984) documented some of the social and legal steps that have been taken to help the handicapped. For example, federal courts have issued landmark decisions that state that physical handicap is not a legitimate excuse for denying a person's constitutional rights. Congress passed the Rehabilitation Act of 1973, which prohibits discrimination against qualifed handicapped persons in regard to federal programs, services, and benefits. Perhaps even more important is the Education for All Handicapped Children Act of 1975, which calls for a free, appropriate education for handicapped children in the least restrictive setting. Despite these positive steps, the struggle to admit handicapped persons into the mainstream of social and economic life has just begun.

The disabled person who wishes to participate more fully in community life is often faced with a wide array of barriers. Some of these are physical or architectural in nature. For example, a person in a wheelchair cannot climb stairs or may not be able to open a door without help. A person on crutches may not be able to use certain kinds of public transportation. Governments on all levels have taken steps to eliminate these architectural barriers. To an increasing extent, the handicapped are being provided with ready access to public buildings. Ramps enable the wheelchair-bound person to enter buildings with relative ease. Sidewalks are being modified to allow passage of wheelchairs, and doors and elevators are being changed to permit easier operation by the handicapped. The considerable costs of these alterations have kept them from being instituted in some settings.

Despite legislation calling for the inclusion of handicapped children in regular classrooms, some school systems have not fully complied with the law. In fairness, it must be stated that the special needs of disabled children do impose extra expenses on a school budget that may be tight in the first place. Aside from the costs of physical renovations, there may be additional expenses of providing special equipment and transportation. For example, visually impaired youngsters might need learning materials on tape or in Braille. Turnbill (1982) pointed out that court cases that establish the right of some handicapped children to attend school 12 months a year, of deaf children to obtain interpreters during all aspects of their training, and of handicapped children to obtain psychotherapy at school expense are costly not only in terms of money but also in terms of political capital. What Turnbill implied is that activists who fight for the rights of handicapped children must show some reasonableness in the demands they make. If demands seem excessive to the citizens in a community, there is danger of a loss of public support for services to the handicapped.

The right of disabled persons to equal opportunity in employment is clearly established. However, an important unsolved problem centers around the fact that social security and Medicare regulations tend to discourage disabled people from looking for work. Their support payments and medical benefits often exceed what they could earn after taxes, particularly if their jobs were not steady. If a disabled person earns more than $3000 a year, he or she risks losing government support. There isn't much incentive to work under these conditions.

Psychological Barriers against the Disabled

Negative societal attitudes are another obstacle that limits the acceptance of disabled people into the mainstream. American culture prizes competence, autonomy, and physical attractiveness. Americans are daily subjected to a media barrage of sexy, youthful, healthy people who entertain, sell products, and provide role models. In this atmosphere, it is inevitable that disability, particularly obvious disability, would have a negative impact on a person's sense of self-worth. Some handicapped persons have incorporated these negative cultural attitudes and made them the basis for self-defeating behaviors (Fenderson, 1984). In other words, some disabled persons behave in such a way as to unnecessarily limit their participation in usual life roles and functions. Some may feel that it is no use in trying because they will not be accepted anyway.

There is abundant evidence, reviewed by Asch (1984a), that disabled persons arouse strong negative emotions in able-bodied persons. In particular, handicapped people arouse anxieties about loss, vulnerability, and weakness. The able-bodied person may be repulsed or embarrassed by anything awkward or unusual about the disabled person. It is not surprising, then, that some nonhandicapped persons prefer to avoid social contact with the disabled. When forced to interact, they may behave in unnatural ways. For example, the able-bodied person is apt to go to one of two extremes: one is pretending that the disability doesn't exist and doesn't matter; the other is feeling sorry for the disabled person and being excessively helpful. Richardson (1976) and Goffman (1963) have both written about the rarity of meaningful social interaction between those with disabilities and those without. It is difficult for the able-bodied person to get beyond another's disability and relate on the basis of shared human feelings and desires.

CASE STUDY: Personal Reflections of a Blind Psychologist

Adrienne Asch (1984b) contributed the following reflections about her experiences as a disabled person:

Once, in a group dynamics program, I had to decide under which sign I would stand for an exercise in difference and group identification—white, straight, young, Jewish, woman, or disabled. Because many of the participants had focused on my disability in their dealings with me during the two-week program, because I had already revealed many aspects of myself, including my similarities with others (whether or not they had been seen), and because no other person with a disability was there to convey what it meant to be disabled, I stood under the disability sign.

An acquaintance overheard me say that it had been hard to decide whether to stand under the sign for disabled or that for woman. "If you hadn't identified as disabled," she said, "I would have said you were denying." With more honesty and irritation than tact, I replied, "It's for people like you that I have to stand under that sign. You and your attitudes put me there, not my blindness itself."

Were it not a social problem, disability would require no discussion. In a more just world, disability might not be a social, economic, or political problem. It would not be a topic for meetings and discussions. I write out of conscience, anger, and disappointment—that to live with myself, to better myself and others like me, I had no choice but to speak about what could have and should have been a rather inconsequential part of myself and my life. I write in neither pride nor shame, but simply because I have no other choice.

I long for the day when I, other disabled psychologists, and other disabled people will go into any room in any convention, any meeting, or gathering or job in the world and be greeted, evaluated, rejected, or accepted for who we are as total human beings. We need such a forum not because disabled people are so special, separate, or unique but because we must let people know of our desire and right to be part of the world from which we should never have been excluded [pp. 551-552].

The Rehabilitation Process

The process of helping disabled persons to achieve the highest possible level of productivity and independent functioning is a team effort in which many different professionals play a role. Clearly, the task of physicians, nurses, and other medical specialists is to help the disabled person attain maximum physical use of self. This is one step in the process of rehabilitation. Psychological aspects of the process are of equal importance. In some cases, the disabled person may become so discouraged as to be unresponsive to counseling. Some patients refuse to accept the seriousness of the disability or any limits that it may impose. The rehabilitation counselor helps the patient to deal with psychological obstacles and oversees the patient's progress, and is usually available to the client from the beginning to the end of the process.

In the rehabilitation agency, the patient's school and job history are reviewed in the light of future job or training possibilities. A counseling psychologist may be asked to administer a battery of tests to the patient. The results often provide valuable information about the person's abilities, interests, and aptitudes. Using all of the available information, a plan is developed that involves either training or actual placement on a job. Some large rehabilitation centers are equipped with workshops where patients can try various activities such as carpentry, clerical work, machine operation, and so on. Here, the client is able to gain confidence by achieving success at various tasks. An occupational therapist may be assigned to help the client increase skills and to build up tolerance for sustained work. Even after the client is placed on a job or begins school in the community, follow-up interviews are arranged to resolve any problems that come up in the placement.

The disabled are often perceived by others in a somewhat distorted way. The disability tends to generalize in the minds of others to the whole person—that is, to induce others to see the handicapped as more limited than they really are. In counseling, the disabled person is helped to come to grips with these unrealistic perceptions and the effect of these perceptions on self-image. The effective counselor recognizes that disabled persons are more like able-bodied than otherwise, and work with their real strengths and assets.

THE MENTALLY ILL

Physical illness is easier to define than mental illness because it involves bodily disorders that can usually be observed and measured in precise ways. Mental illness, on the other hand, involves feeling states, perceptions, and behaviors that sometimes depart only slightly from the normal range. To make matters worse, *mental illness* is sort of a catchall term that includes everything from temporary emotional upsets to long-lasting psychological breakdowns. An account of the heated controversies about the nature of mental illness will be reserved for Chapter Four. For the present, the mentally ill will be regarded as persons with emotional and psychological problems who seek help from psychiatric and mental health facilities.

Prevalence of Mental Illness

President Carter appointed a Commission on Mental Health to assess the mental health needs of the nation. The commission's report estimated that as many as 25% of the American population suffer from mild to moderate depression, anxiety, and other indicators of emotional disorder (President's Commission on Mental Health, 1978). It was also reported that about 15% of the population is in need of some kind of mental health service at any given time. In one year, 1975, about 3.6 million people were treated at different types of mental health centers (Rosenstein & Milazzo-Sayre, 1981). Obviously, persons with mental or emotional disorders constitute a sizable target population.

CASE STUDY: The Crisis of Mental Illness

Joan Houghton is a young woman who provided the world with a moving account of her mental illness. She recalled that mental illness, in the form of a psychotic episode, struck her with the force of a nuclear explosion:

> All that I had known and enjoyed previously was suddenly transformed like some strange reverse process of nature, from a butterfly's beauty into a pupa's cocoon. There was a binding, confining quality to my life, in part chosen, in part imposed. Repeated rejections, the awkwardness of others around me, and my own discomfort and self-consciousness propelled me into solitary confinement [Houghton, 1980, p. 8].

Joan remembered sitting with her mother in the waiting room of a mental hospital while her father investigated admission procedures. A young man was seated nearby. Perspiration dripped across his brow and down his cheeks. Joan took a tissue from her purse and gently wiped the moisture from his face. She tried to reassure him that everything would be fine. Presently, Joan was ushered into a small room where she met a social worker and a psychiatrist. After a brief conversation, they presented her with a piece of paper and instructed her to sign. She signed "Saint Joan," without realizing that she had thereby admitted herself to a mental hospital. "My first psychotic episode appeared as a private mental exorcism, ending with the honor of sainthood and the gifts of hope and faith" (Houghton, 1982, p. 549).

Joan was hospitalized for five weeks. Her recovery involved a struggle against her own body, which seemed to be drained of energy, and against a society that seemed to reject her. "It seemed that my greatest needs—to be wanted, needed, valued—were the very needs which others could not fulfill" (Houghton, 1980, p. 8).

Joan eventually recovered and was able to hold a job at the National Institute of Mental Health. An articulate young woman, she wrote eloquent accounts of her struggle with mental illness. It appeared that important, unmet needs played a major role in precipitating her breakdown.

Trends in Mental Health Care

There have been dramatic changes in recent decades in where Americans are treated for mental illness. These changes center around a basic reform in psychiatric care started in the 1950s. The basic idea is to get mental patients out of institutions and to treat them in community-based facilities. In 1955, there were 560,000 patients in state and county mental hospitals. The numbers living in mental hospitals steadily declined to 160,000 in 1978 (Coleman, Butcher, & Carson, 1984). This decline in occupancy reflects increasing awareness among mental health experts that long-term hospitalization is not the best choice of treatment for many patients. For one thing, lengthy hospitalization tends to create a dependence on the institution that hampers the patient's reentry into the community. Another contributory factor has been the introduction of powerful tranquilizing medications. These new drugs help suppress the disturbed and agitated behaviors of some patients, thereby making it possible to treat them on an outpatient basis.

Patients admitted to mental hospitals do not stay nearly as long on the average as in the decades prior to the 1950s. However, soon after this became a trend, it became obvious that many briefly treated patients are not able to live in the community without recurring episodes of acute disturbance. Their symptoms flare up periodically and they have to be readmitted to the hospital. It is not unusual for some mental patients to have 10, 15, or even 20 brief stays at mental hospitals. Critics began to talk about the "revolving door" effect. They also charged that many mental patients were simply being "dumped" into communities that often had not made adequate provisions for their aftercare.

It might be useful at this point to take a closer look at the two parts of the intended reform of mental health care: the first is deinstitutionalization, which means simply getting patients out of long-stay hospitals, and the second is community-based treatment.

Deinstitutionalizing Mental Patients. The 1960s were years of rapid social change. Old ways of doing things were challenged in every area of life, including the mental health field. Social activists charged that large numbers of mental patients were being detained, often against their will, in huge, outmoded psychiatric hospitals. They further alleged that many of these patients were simply being warehoused in custodial wards and not getting much in the way of treatment. Very often, patients were not even asked how they felt about being in the hospital. There was a great deal of merit to these criticisms, especially in regard to the state hospitals. Many of these were located far from the communities they served, making it difficult to reconnect patients with their former community.

Meanwhile, civil rights attorneys were active in championing the rights of mental patients. They argued that mental patients were entitled to due process of law before being committed against their will. If hospitalized, the patients were to receive treatment in the least restrictive environment. These legal efforts finally culminated in the landmark Supreme Court decision *O'Connor v. Donaldson*, which held that it is unconstitutional to confine a nondangerous person in a mental hospital against his or her will unless adequate treatment is provided.

Community Care for Mental Patients. Of course, it was not enough to simply condemn the old approach to mental illness. In response to the pressures of social reformers, mental health experts began to implement a community-based approach to the problem that was designed to achieve certain important goals. One was to prevent mental disability whenever possible by fostering constructive social change. Another was to seek out people in need of help and treat them in the community. Still another goal was to facilitate the reentry of institutionalized people into the community.

The Community Mental Health Centers Act of 1963 was to provide the means of achieving these and other goals. This federal legislation provided for the establishment of a network of mental health centers throughout the nation. Each center was to provide an array of services to the community. Five basic services were to be offered:

1. *Inpatient care.* Each community mental health center was to have a hospital for seriously disordered mental patients. The plan was that patients would be treated as quickly as

possible and returned to the community. Only patients who did not respond to treatment would be referred to long-stay institutions.

2. *Outpatient care.* The center was to provide psychological services through an outpatient clinic.

3. *Partial hospitalization.* A facility was to be provided to treat patients during the day but allow them to return home evenings and weekends. The intent was to prevent patients from becoming dependent on the treatment facility as they might do if confined on a 24-hour basis.

4. *Emergency care.* The center was to maintain a 24-hour crisis center to deal with psychiatric emergencies.

5. *Consultation, education, and information.* The center was to offer consultation, education, and information to others vitally concerned with mental health issues such as teachers, police, city officials, and probation officers. The idea was to facilitate social changes that might help prevent emotional disorders.

The act was subsequently amended to add several other desirable goals in addition to these mandated programs. These included rehabilitation in the form of vocational and physical training for patients as well as research and evaluation. For example, the center was to do research to evaluate its own effectiveness and to explore the causes of psychological disorder.

The plan was a good one but the community mental health centers have not been able to fully attain their goals. The original plan called for the establishment of 2000 centers, each serving a specific catchment or health service area. Only about 600 centers are currently in full operation, which means that only about 40% of the U.S. population is being served.

Current Problems in Mental Health Care

Bassuk and Gerson (1978) wondered how the well-intentioned reform of deinstitutionalization could have created so many problems. These authors asserted that the discharged mental patient was to be supported by a full spectrum of aftercare services, but that communities rarely provided such services. The living arrangements were often very poor. Many patients drifted to substandard inner-city housing that was unsafe, dirty, and overcrowded. There was a lack of vocational training, job referrals, transportation, and recreational facilities. Aftercare agencies complained that they were not given sufficient funds to provide services needed by ex-patients.

Currently, psychiatric facilities in this country are developing into two quite different kinds of settings (Munsinger, 1983). One is the old-fashioned, large, medically-oriented institution in which the primary therapies are drugs, psychosurgery, and shock treatments. The other is the community-based center just described, where the emphasis is on prevention, crisis management, partial hospitalization, and outpatient psychotherapy. One problem is the poor coordination between these two types of facilities. If patients are to get the kind of help they need, it is essential that hospitals improve their linkage with community agencies. This will make it possible to follow patients' progress after discharge and to provide the services they need.

SUBSTANCE ABUSERS

The term *substance abusers* refers to persons who misuse certain substances for the purpose of altering mood or psychological state. The substances used for this purpose range from foods like sugar and carbohydrates to alcohol and hard drugs such as heroin, amphetamines, and barbiturates. Virtually the entire adult population uses some of these substances at one time or another. What is the distinction between using and abusing a substance?

One important criterion is that the abuser employs the substance to avoid facing up to problems. When under stress, he or she "turns on" to the stuff in question in order to feel better without doing anything about the troublesome situation. The abuser runs the risk of becoming addicted; this means that he or she may become both psychologically and physiologically dependent on the substance. Certain drugs, including alcohol, alter body chemistry if taken to excess. Once addicted, the individual must continue to use the substance if unpleasant withdrawal symptoms are to be avoided. It is not practical to review all possible addictions in this section. Attention will be focused on two addictions that have received most attention from human services.

Alcoholics

Some experts believe that alcoholism is the number one public health problem in the United States today. The number of persons who are psychologically dependent on alcohol has been estimated at anywhere from 8 million to 20 million. The lack of precision in the count is due to difficulty in distinguishing between heavy drinkers and alcoholics as well as to the fact that many persons abuse alcohol in secret. The majority of known alcoholics are adult men but the number of adult women who drink to excess has increased in recent years. There is also significant alcohol abuse among teenagers and even among preteens.

Why are so many Americans dependent on alcohol? One important property of alcohol is that it helps the drinker to feel relaxed and uninhibited. Continued use, however, reduces motor coordination and causes a number of deficiencies such as blurred vision, thick speech, and the suspension of normal judgment. This combination of properties explains why the majority of serious auto accidents are alcohol-related. Most individuals are able to use alcohol in moderation to feel at ease in social situations. However, the alcoholic comes to rely on alcohol to help deal with stressful and difficult situations. At some point on the path to addiction, the alcoholic becomes unable to face difficulties without using alcohol as a crutch. Prolonged excessive drinking can lead to a variety of health problems including serious damage to the brain or liver. On a social level, the alcoholic may jeopardize both employment and family life.

Treatment for the alcoholic has changed dramatically in this century. Throughout most of our history, alcoholism was seen as a kind of moral weakness. Drunks were either ignored or treated as criminals. During the first half of this century, it was common practice to jail alcoholics, particularly those of low social status. It became obvious that this punishment had no long-range effect on the alcoholic, who never seemed to learn his "lesson."

Alcoholics Anonymous (AA), founded in 1934, called for an end to punitive, moralistic approaches to the problem. Instead, alcoholism was to be regarded as an illness and treated as such. AA bases its program for helping alcoholics on group meetings during which members confess their dependence on alcohol. One basic tenet of AA is that the alcoholic is not to think of himself as cured at any time. The alcoholic is simply to try to live one day at a time without alcohol. At the same time, the alcoholic gains strength from meeting people who are controlling their desire for alcohol. Added to this is the spiritual emphasis that is one of the pillars of the AA approach. The alcoholic calls upon a higher power to help control the problem. It should be stressed that the organization was founded by and is run by alcoholics. As such, it is a self-help group and a model for similar groups later established by drug addicts. AA seems to be one of the most successful treatment approaches to the problem of addiction to alcohol. One recent study estimated that of the alcoholics who stay in AA, about half are abstinent after two years, 15% drink lightly to moderately, and at least 13% drink abusively (Alford, 1980). Since the remainder could not be traced after two years, it is possible that the failure rate may be higher than 13%.

Psychotherapy by itself has not proved to be of great value in treating alcoholics, nor have strictly medical approaches been of lasting value. For many years, hospitals, both general and psychiatric, were reluctant to undertake treatment of alcoholics. It seemed futile to merely provide the alcoholic with a place to "dry out" when the benefits usually were temporary. Most mental health professionals now believe that treatment must be multifaceted. The first step is primarily medical since it involves detoxification—that is, removing the toxic substances from the body and restoring the body chemistry to normal. Medication is used to control withdrawal symptoms. This may be followed by family and occupational counseling aimed at helping the patient to function better in the community without resorting to alcohol. Follow-up counseling in the community might subsequently be coupled with continued membership in AA. Gradually, hospitals are beginning to establish special units for the treatment of alcoholism along the lines suggested above. Along with this has come a trend to train human services workers in counseling alcoholics.

The most challenging part of the treatment process is not to get the alcoholic to stop drinking but to help maintain sobriety over the long haul. Treated alcoholics and other addicts show a relapse rate of about 60% within three months (Hunt, Barnett, & Branch, 1971). Many alcoholics go through treatment a number of times or through a number of different treatments and still relapse into abusive drinking.

Heroin Addicts

It is even more difficult to determine the number of heroin addicts than the number of alcoholics in the country because of the illegal nature of heroin abuse. Understandably, addicts are not eager to stand up and be counted. During the 1960s there was a great increase in heroin use, so much so that the media began talking about the "heroin epidemic" (Bazell, 1973). Recent serveys show that heroin use continues at a high rate (Coleman et al., 1984). The number of persons who are actually addicted to heroin has been put at 380,000 (Dogoloff, 1980). Of course, many more have tried the drug or use it occasionally.

While alcoholics are widely distributed throughout the range of social classes, heroin addicts tend to be concentrated in the lower socioeconomic classes, particularly among minority group members. Initially, narcotics addiction was seen primarily as a problem of the inner cities. However, during the last two decades, there has been a spread of heroin addiction to White suburban areas as well as to small towns and cities across America. Regardless of area, heroin addiction is most common in persons in their late teens to early twenties. One other group with a high rate of addiction are physicians who have easy access to pure morphine and other narcotics; they typically become involved in drugs at a later age than street addicts, and also seem better able to function on the job than street addicts.

A number of factors account for the appeal of heroin and other opium derivatives. The immediate effect is a sense of euphoria, followed by a state of deep relaxation and contentment. This blissful state, which may last from four to six hours, is followed by the unpleasant return to reality called "coming down." Frequent use of the drug for a month or so is sufficient to addict most people. Addiction is both physiological and psychological in nature. Once addicted, the user feels physically ill if he or she cannot get the drug. Unfortunately, larger and larger doses are needed to achieve the same effect. Drug addiction is then likely to become a way of life, with much time spent getting the money to feed the habit. The addict often turns to illegal means of raising the money, but reports of addicts turning to violence are greatly exaggerated. They are more likely to get involved in theft, burglary, and shoplifting because the income is more reliable. Another major source of income is selling drugs to others, thus perpetuating the problem. Female addicts often turn to prostitution to get money (Rorvik, 1979).

Aside from imprisonment, treatment for narcotics addicts has taken three basic forms: hospitalization, methadone maintenance programs, and self-help groups. Until the 1960s, hospitalization under supervision was usually the only practical alternative. As might be expected, this approach is most successful in helping the addict to "detox"—that is, to overcome the ill effects of withdrawal from heroin. However, the relapse rate is very high once addicts leave the hospital.

Methadone maintenance is probably the most frequently used approach at this time. Methadone is a synthetic narcotic chemically similar to morphine that is itself highly addictive. The presumed usefulness of this drug is derived from its capacity to satisfy or reduce the craving for heroin. Methadone does not produce the stupor associated with heroin, nor does it require ever-increasing doses to be effective. It frees the addict of the necessity of raising money for heroin, and opens the door to normal job and social routines. Unfortunately, most addicts cannot be tapered off to the point where they can go drug-free. In effect, they substitute one addiction for another, but from society's point of view an addiction to methadone is preferable to an addiction to heroin because it decriminalizes the addiction.

In any case, the number of existing treatment programs for heroin dependence is woefully insufficient. Only about 84,000 persons could possibly be treated with methadone at the present time. Even when a methadone program is available, many addicts do not remain in treatment. Many addicts leave methadone programs prematurely every year, and the same tendency is shown in regard to other kinds of treatment programs (Lewis & Sessler, 1980).

The third major approach is based on intense group pressure brought to bear on the addict by his peers—reformed addicts. Synanon is perhaps the best known of these self-help groups for addicts. Founded in the 1960s, it grew to the point where it was able to maintain several residences for addicts in a number of cities. Similar groups began to mushroom in the late 1960s and early 1970s. The general approach is drug-free, and stresses a tough-minded attitude toward the addict, who is seen as a dependent child with few redeeming qualities. In some programs the group assault appears designed to break down the defenses of the addict so completely that new behaviors become a necessity. Drug addicts point out that middle-class professionals are too soft to work effectively with addicts. While this may or may not be true, there is little solid evidence that these self-help groups have found the formula for success. One unsolved problem of such programs is the high dropout rate; the most difficult cases most often simply leave the group.

According to Suinn (1984), the most cautious conclusion that can be drawn from the available data is that treatment programs can have a positive impact on some drug abusers. However, positive gains can be made only if the individual is willing to stay in treatment long enough for improvements to occur—and even then there is no guarantee of success.

Other Addicts

The discussion has focused on alcoholics and heroin addicts because these groups have been the focus of large-scale therapeutic services. It should be kept in mind that there are significant problems in the abuse of amphetamines, barbiturates, cocaine, and other powerful drugs. In addition to drugs that are obtained illegally, tranquilizers and other mood-changing drugs that are legally prescribed by doctors are consumed in immense quantities. Literally millions of prescribed pills, including Valium, Librium, and other antianxiety compounds, are consumed daily in this country. Physicians have been sharply criticized for the free and easy way in which they dispense "minor" tranquilizers such as Librium and Valium. These drugs are potentially dangerous because of possible side effects and because some persons become physiologically dependent on them. Since these drugs may cause drowsiness, it is illegal in some states to drive while under their influence. There is also evidence that mixing mild tranquilizers with other psychoactive drugs, including alcohol, may have undesirable effects on body chemistry. Such mixtures have played a role in many suicide attempts.

THE LAW VIOLATORS

The United States has a very high rate of criminal activity compared to other affluent, industrialized nations. In some years, the number of murders in New York City alone nearly equals the number in all of Western Europe. Almost every yearly edition of the FBI *Uniform Crime Reports* up to 1982 showed an increase in serious crimes. There has been some recent leveling-off of the crime rate, but it continues at a high level. For 1982, the FBI reported that 12.5 million serious crimes were committed in the country including homicide, rape, robbery, aggravated assault, and auto theft (Federal Bureau of Investigation, 1983). It should be kept in mind that these figures refer only to the crimes that were actually reported to enforcement agencies. Many additional crimes simply go unreported.

It is not generally known by the public that juveniles commit a large percentage of serious crimes. In 1981, persons under 18 accounted for one out of every three arrests for robbery, one out of every three arrests for crimes against property, one out of six arrests for rape, and one out of eleven arrests for murder (Federal Bureau of Investigation, 1982). Most of this juvenile crime was committed by males but the rate has risen sharply for females. In 1981, about one in every fifteen juveniles in the nation was arrested. This alarmingly high rate of criminal activity among youngsters is by no means confined to the inner cities. Similarly high rates have been reported for youngsters from suburban and rural areas. In Oregon, for example, one out of four nonurban juveniles had an official record before the age of 18, and many had repeated offenses (National Institute of Mental Health, 1974).

Juvenile Delinquents

A number of factors have been identified as contributing to delinquent behavior patterns. Perhaps most basic is a home life characterized by insecurity and rejection of the youngster. Delinquent youths are likely to come from homes disrupted by divorce rather than by death of a parent. Inconsistent discipline is another contributing factor. Parents are likely to alternate harsh punishment with periods of neglect or disinterest. The delinquent generalizes contempt for the parents to other authority figures including teachers and police. Frequently, delinquents do not receive the kind of parental help and encouragement that is needed for success in school. One study demonstrated quite clearly that inner city delinquents have little confidence that they can achieve success in our society (Institute for Social Research, 1979). They anticipate dropping out of high school and, at best, being stuck in a low-level job. Delinquents sometimes feel justified in breaking the rules because the system is so much against them.

The courts have generally treated juveniles on a different basis from adult offenders. The juvenile court system was designed not so much to punish but to protect the best interests of the child. However, this approach is now under attack by citizens who feel the courts are too lenient with dangerous juveniles. The argument is that teenagers who commit adult crimes—such as rape, assault, and murder—should be treated as adults and dealt with severely. The courts are caught in between the interests of an outraged community and the rights of the youngster.

In general, the courts have several options. The most extreme is to remand the juvenile to an institution or "reformatory," as such places were once called. In the best of the training institutions, the youngster receives psychological counseling along with formal schooling and occupational training. However, most of these places are essentially custodial in nature with some token efforts at rehabilitation. The staff is often inadequate both in numbers and in level of training. The youngster, who spends most of his time with others like himself, is likely to emerge from the school even more antisocial than at time of entrance. Judges and other correctional personnel are aware of the limited benefits of this kind of incarceration and try to find alternative ways of dealing with the problem youngster. One of these alternatives is probation, which is a form of conditional release to the community. A probation officer assigned by the court is supposed to provide close supervision of the juvenile's activities. The offender is expected to pursue serious vocational or career objectives and to get involved in constructive community activities. This approach would have a better chance of success if the probation officer were not overwhelmed with a huge caseload. Generally, probation officers are not able to do the kind of job they feel they could do if they had more time for each child. As it is, probationary programs are not currently as successful as one might hope.

A 5-year study conducted by the California Youth Authority

showed what can be done when caseloads of probation officers are reduced. The 270 youths who participated in the study were granted immediate probation and supervised in their communities. A 15-month follow-up showed that 72% of these offenders had been successfully treated. A comparable group who underwent institutional treatment showed a success rate of only 48% (Coleman et al., 1984). The youngsters in these groups had not committed major crimes such as murder, rape, or arson.

Presently, the police, courts, and training schools are being inundated by huge caseloads. They are being asked to do a job that is difficult under the best of circumstances. It is very difficult for an agency or institution to supply the kind of love, encouragement, and discipline that is provided by a healthy, intact family. Juvenile delinquency is one problem that cries out for preventive approaches. Unfortunately, preventive programs are few in number and limited in scope at the present time.

Some experts believe that only large-scale preventive programs could be successful. They suggest that programs should provide a wide range of educational, occupational, and social opportunities for teenagers. One objective is to involve the community as much as possible in working with the juvenile, who often feels that nobody really cares. Specific programs might include employment for dropouts, group counseling, and various kinds of skills training. At this point, it seems unlikely that government, at any level, is going to increase revenues for comprehensive programs of this type. The immediate trend seems to be toward a reduction of funding for such efforts.

Criminals

Many of the factors that cause juvenile delinquency apply also to criminal behavior. Insecurity, parental rejection, harsh discipline, antisocial attitudes of parents have all been identified as contributing to criminal behavior. In fact, many criminals have records of juvenile delinquency. Other causative factors include drug addiction, emotional problems, and stress associated with poverty and unemployment. It becomes difficult to disentangle cause and effect in the area of maladaptive behaviors. Negative influences in home and community lead to escapist tendencies such as alcoholism and drug addiction, which in turn prevent the appearance of any constructive solutions to problems. Racism, poverty, mental illness, crime, and addictions interact in complex, mutually reinforcing ways.

The rate of criminality is so high in this country that the criminal justice system, which includes police, courts, and corrections, is unable to function in an organized, effective fashion. The courts report crowded calendars, long delays in getting cases to trial, and excessive use of plea bargaining (pleading guilty to a lesser offense) to avoid the expense of a trial. Many prisons are overcrowded, mismanaged, or both. In any case, a number of our prisons have recently exploded into violence and disorder.

The chance of actually being punished for a crime is quite low in the United States. Only about 100 out of every 500 arrestable offenses result in an arrest. Of these 100, only 10 actually appear in court (Brieland et al., 1980). Those offenders who do appear in court have a good chance of being let off on a technicality. For example, the trial of one defendant suspected of robbery and murder ended in a mistrial when it was reported that the jury matron had told jurors her view of the case. Only a tiny majority of criminal cases actually go to full-fledged trial. Of the offenders who are found guilty, the majority are placed on probation. The percentage of crimes that eventuate in an offender actually going to prison is therefore quite small.

Presently, there are over 400,000 persons, including 80,000 women and 74,000 juveniles, in state, federal, and local prisons (U.S. Department of Justice, 1982). In addition, more than 1 million others are on probation. How well do these prisoners represent the criminal population? The answer is probably not very well. The inmates of our correctional institutions are predominantly the "losers" of our society—the poor, the disadvantaged, mostly minority group members (Alexander, 1974). Blacks are understandably bitter about what they feel is a strong bias against them throughout the system. The rich and powerful are often able to evade punishment for offenses that might send a poor person to jail.

At present, it cannot be said that our correctional facilities are serving any purpose very well. They fail to protect the public since criminals are constantly being recycled back into the community, where they are likely to repeat the same crime. Recidivism ranges from 60 to 90%, depending on the type of crime involved (Goldfarb, 1974). Apparently, prisoners are not being rehabilitated in significant numbers. This is not surprising in view of the fact that most prisons provide little more than custodial care with little effort devoted to treatment, rehabilitation, and job training.

In prison, life is routinized, time is structured, and the social system is completely authoritarian. It is not the kind of place in which one can learn to function adaptively in a free society. The longer an inmate remains in prison, the less likely is rehabilitation. Martinson (1974) reported a comprehensive survey of 231 studies involving a variety of programs designed to reduce recidivism. Individual therapy, education, skill development, group therapy, and variations in sentencing and probation all proved to be of little avail. There was some evidence that the personal characteristics of offenders, such as age and type of offense, were more important than the form of treatment in determining future recidivism. Youthful offenders were the best risks. There is an urgent need for pilot studies that would tell us what kinds of prisoners can best be integrated into the community and what kinds of programs would best serve this purpose.

Innovative programs recently introduced at Patuxent Institution show promise of rehabilitating prisoners and provide a slim ray of hope in an otherwise grim picture (Mervis, 1984). Patuxent is home to more than 600 of the most violent criminals in Maryland. A unique feature of this prison is that inmates must volunteer to come there from elsewhere in the prison system. Inmates are selected on the basis of their apparent amenability to treatment, and may be returned to their original setting if they show they are not benefiting from the program. There are over 30 mental health professionals who provide academic, vocational, and recreational instruction along with group and individual therapy. In most other prisons, treatment personnel make up only a tiny percentage of employees.

The main feature of the treatment program is a four-level system. Incoming prisoners start at Level One and can move up to higher levels as they demonstrate an ability to handle greater responsibility. Each higher level provides increased privileges, greater space and privacy, and more freedom. At the highest level, inmates have individual cells that are not locked, and they regulate their own routines to a much greater extent than those at lower levels. Prisoners who show exceptional promise may be sent to Patuxent's own halfway house located in downtown Baltimore. Here the focus is on finding and keeping jobs, and adjusting to life in the community. It is too early for an evaluation of this program but if it is successful other prisons may adopt some of its features.

THE MENTALLY RETARDED

The mentally retarded differ from other target populations in one critical respect: their handicap is defined as subnormal intelligence. It is apparent that some children lack the ability to learn as quickly as their age-mates. In fact, the first intelligence tests were designed to identify children who could not be expected to keep up with their peers. These tests measured the child's ability to memorize, concentrate, grasp verbal abstractions, do arithmetic, and other skills. By definition, the child who is average in ability for a particular age attains an intelligence quotient (IQ) of 100. Those persons who score significantly below average in ability are designated as retarded. The precise cutoff score is arbitrarily selected, and there is variation among scaling systems. However, most authorities consider persons with an IQ below 70 to be retarded.

Retardation can be caused by a variety of factors and conditions. In some cases, a physically healthy youngster may fail to develop normal intelligence because of a destructive home environment or one that offers little intellectual stimulation. Other cases of retardation are due to genetic defects. Down's Syndrome or mongolism, for example, is due to an abnormal number of chromosomes, which results in certain physical abnormalities as well as in subnormal intelligence. Other cases can be attributed to brain injuries occurring in the neonatal phase or at birth. Infectious diseases such as encephalitis or meningitis can also result in intellectual deficiencies. The main point is that retardation is not a specific syndrome. The term simply refers to a state of subnormal intelligence that can be caused by one or a combination of physical or environmental factors.

Retarded persons comprise a significant percentage of the population, numbering about 6.8 million in the United States (Robinson & Robinson, 1976). Within the retarded group, there is wide variation in intellectual ability. The retarded are subdivided into four groups—the mildly, moderately, severely, and profoundly retarded. The great majority of retarded are classified as mildly retarded; these individuals can learn the basic skills of self-care such as dressing and feeding themselves. They can also do many kinds of routine work. As we go down the scale, the retarded are less capable and require more help and supervision. There is also greater probability that the person will show some physical defect or deformity. The profoundly retarded may have limited mobility, and communication is generally limited to some simple gestures and vocal intonations. These individuals usually are cared for in an institutional setting.

The education and training of retarded persons begins with a mapping out of target behaviors. Self-care, social behavior, and basic academic and vocational skills are usually the main areas of concentration. Within each area, specific skills are divided into simple components that the retarded person is capable of learning. Training then proceeds in a step-by-step fashion, gradually building the simple components into skilled performance (Coleman et al., 1984). The advantage of this gradual approach is that the person experiences success frequently in the learning process.

It should be stressed that most retarded persons can learn a

variety of social and vocational skills, and need not be institutionalized. Some mildly retarded persons—the most capable—are taught
in special classes within the public school system. Others are placed
in training schools in the community. They come home after school
just as normal children do. At school, they are taught elementary
reading, writing, and arithmetic to the fullest possible extent, along
with occupational skills. The less capable students may devote most
time to learning the basic skills of daily living—washing, eating,
brushing teeth, buttoning buttons, and so on. Some retardates are
eventually placed in sheltered workshops where they do simple jobs
such as assembling ballpoint pens for modest pay. Often payment is
on a piecework basis. However, the jobs are real jobs and the pay is
real. This means that the worker can experience the satisfaction that
comes from making a contribution to society.

The President's Committee on Mental Retardation (1970) estimated that about 2 million retardates could become self-supporting
if they received the right kind of training. As it is, their potential
contribution is being wasted because of the shortage of adequate
training schools and staff. The majority of retardates living in the
community do not receive the level of service they need. Retardates
who require 24-hour supervision, which only an institution can provide, are even worse off. Many of these institutions are a disgrace to
any decent standards of humane treatment. Many of the large state
facilities provide no more than a low level of custodial care. Salaries
for staff are low, which means that these places often become hav-
ens for inadequate or marginal workers. Periodically, certain of
these institutions are exposed by the media, but they usually return
to their customary low level of care after the uproar dies down. It
seems that the general public would prefer not to be confronted with
conditions in our institutions for the retarded. This attitude results in
a tragic waste of human potential.

SUMMARY AND CONCLUSIONS

This description of some target populations gives an idea of the
magnitude of the task facing human services today. Of course, one
cannot add up the number of persons included in each population
since there is overlap among the groups. An individual may be poor,
physically disabled, elderly, *and* an alcoholic. In fact, there is a strong
tendency for poverty and advanced age to be disproportionately
associated with both mental and physical disorders. A member of a
low-income family is twice as likely to become disabled as a member
of a middle-class family. It is also true that nearly half of the adult
disabled population is at or near the poverty level. Even considering

this overlap between groups, it has been estimated that one of every six Americans, or 36 million, is disabled in some way (Bowe, 1980). Even more alarming is the increase in the number and percentage of Americans who are chronically ill, over 65, or disabled.

It is not known how the U.S. will respond in the future to this greatly increased need for services. It is apparent that there has been a distinct shift in national priorities during the past decade. The earlier commitment to solve social problems, particularly those associated with poverty and racism, has given way to a focus on national defense and other priorities. The prevailing trend is to hold down or reduce spending for social programs. In one sense, the pattern is a familiar one. Historically, periods marked by concern for the less fortunate members of society have alternated with periods of relative neglect. No one knows how long the current trend will continue. Certainly, many programs have been cut, and the impact has been keenly felt by human services workers and the populations they serve.

One possible approach to reducing costs of human services involves the increased use of prevention programs. Millions of dollars are spent on facilities and services for criminals, mental patients, alcoholics, and drug addicts. Yet relatively little money is invested in programs designed to prevent individuals from joining these target groups in the first place. Similarly, larger sums are spent on welfare benefits than on programs that might keep some persons off the rolls. Obviously, a person who has been trained for a well-paying job is unlikely to need long-term welfare support. The initial cost of a successful prevention program would be more than made up in the long run. Unfortunately, politicians and others concerned with funding have proved very resistant to investing in prevention programs. These issues will be discussed in more detail in Chapter Eight.

It is likely that new approaches to target populations will increase proportionately with the growth of population. However, some groups, particularly the elderly and disabled, will increase at a disproportionate rate. The net effect is that a greater percentage of the population will be in need of services, which will be provided by a relatively smaller number of human services workers. This is the dilemma that will face human services in the near future.

ADDITIONAL READING

Beaver, M. L. (1983). *Human service practice with the elderly.* Englewood Cliffs, NJ: Prentice-Hall.

Bloom, B. L. (1984). *Community mental health: A general introduction* (2nd ed.). Monterey, CA: Brooks/Cole.

Bowe, F. (1980). *Rehabilitating America.* New York: Harper & Row.

Burgdoff, R. L., Jr. (Ed.). (1980). *The legal rights of handicapped persons.* Baltimore, MD: Paul Brookes.

Julian, J., & Kornblum, W. (1983). *Social problems* (4th ed.). Englewood Cliffs, NJ: Prentice-Hall.

Robinson, N. M., & Robinson, H. B. (1976). *The mentally retarded child* (2nd ed.). New York: McGraw-Hill.

Szasz, T. (1973). *The myth of mental illness* (rev. ed.). New York: Harper & Row.

Wilson, J. Q. (1977). *Thinking about crime.* New York: Vintage.

REFERENCES

Alexander, S. (1974, July 8). Under the rock. *Newsweek,* p. 35.

Alford, G. S. (1980). Alcoholics Anonymous: An empirical outcome study. In *Addictive behaviors* (Vol. 5, pp. 359–370.). Oxford: Pergamon Press.

Asch, A. (1984a). The experience of disability: A challenge for psychology. *American Psychologist, 39,* 529–536.

Asch, A. (1984b). Personal reflections. *American Psychologist, 39,* 551–552.

Bane, M. J. (1983). Children and the welfare state: The changing role of families. *American Educator, 7,* 14–20.

Bassuk, E. L., & Gerson, S. (1978). Deinstitutionalization and mental health services. *Scientific American, 238,* 46–53.

Bazell, R. J. (1973). Drug abuse: Methadone becomes the solution and the problem. *Science, 179,* 772–775.

Beaver, M. L. (1983). *Human service practice with the elderly.* Englewood Cliffs, NJ: Prentice-Hall.

Bethel, T. (1980, October). *Treating poverty: Wherein the cure gives rise to the disease* (Reprint Paper 16). Los Angeles: International Institute for Economic Research.

Bowe, F. (1980). *Rehabilitating America.* New York: Harper & Row.

Brieland, D., Costin, L. B., & Atherton, C. R. (1980). *Contemporary social work* (2nd ed.). New York: McGraw-Hill.

Burgdorf, R. L., Jr. (Ed.). (1980). *The legal rights of handicapped persons.* Baltimore, MD: Paul Brookes.

Carlson, E. (1984). Social security fix: A look at what lies ahead. *Modern Maturity, 27,* 28–33.

Coleman, J. C., Butcher, J. N., & Carson, R. C. (1984). *Abnormal psychology and modern life* (7th ed.). Glenview, IL: Scott, Foresman & Company.

DeJong, G., & Lifchez, R. (1983). Physical disability and public policy. *Scientific American, 48,* 240–249.

Dogoloff, L. I. (1980). Prospect of the 1980s: Challenge and response. *Drug Enforcement, 7,* 2–3.

Egeland, B., Clochetti, D., & Taraldson, B. (1976). Child abuse: A family affair. *Proceedings of the N. P. Masse Research Seminar on Child Abuse,* 28–52.

Federal Bureau of Investigation. (1982). *Uniform crime reports.* Washington, DC: U.S. Government Printing Office.

Federal Bureau of Investigation. (1983). *Uniform crime reports.* Washington, DC: U.S. Government Printing Office.

Fenderson, D. A. (1984). Opportunities for psychologists in disability research. *American Psychologist, 39,* 524–528.

Gliedman, J., & Roth, W. (1980). *The unexpected minority: Handicapped children in America.* New York: Harcourt Brace Jovanovich.

Goffman, E. (1963). *Stigma: Notes on the management of spoiled identity.* Englewood Cliffs, NJ: Prentice-Hall.

Goldfarb, R. L. (1974, July). American prisons: Self-defeating concrete. *Psychology Today,* pp. 20, 22, 24, 85, 88–89.

Group for the Advancement of Psychiatry, Committee on Aging (1971, November). *The aged and community mental health: A guide to program development* (Vol. 8, Series #81). New York: Author.

Houghton, J. F. (1980). One personal experience: Before and after mental illness. In J. G. Rabkin, L. Gelb, & J. B. Lazar (Eds.), *Attitudes toward the mentally ill: Research perspectives.* Rockville, MD: National Institute of Mental Health.

Houghton, J. F. (1982). First person account: Maintaining mental health in a turbulent world. *Schizophrenia Bulletin, 8,* 548–552.

Hunt, W. A., Barnett, L. W., & Branch, L. G. (1971). Relapse rates and addiction programs. *Journal of Clinical Psychology, 27,* 455–456.

Institute for Social Research. (1979, Winter). *Newsletter.* Ann Arbor: University of Michigan.

Joe, T., & Yu, P. (1984, May 11). Black men, welfare, and jobs. *The New York Times,* p. A-31.

Joint Commission on Mental Health of Children. (1970). *Crisis in child mental health: Challenge for the 1970s.* New York: Harper & Row.

Julian, J., & Kornblum, W. (1983). *Social problems* (4th ed.). Englewood Cliffs, NJ: Prentice-Hall.

Kahn, R. L., & Antonucci, T. C. (1982). Applying social psychology to the aging process: Four examples. In J. Santos & G. R. Vandenbos (Eds.), *Psychology and the older adult: Challenges for training in the 1980s.* Washington, DC: American Psychological Association.

Kaplun, D., & Reich, R. (1976). The murdered child and his killers. *American Journal of Psychiatry, 133,* 809–813.

Kempe, R., & Kempe, H. (1979). *Child abuse.* London: Fontana/Open Books.

Lewis, D., & Sessler, J. (1980). Heroin treatment. In Drug Abuse Council, *The facts about drug abuse.* New York: Free Press.

Martinson, R. (1974). What works?—Questions and answers about prison reform. *The Public Interest, 35,* 22–54.

Mervis, J. (1984, June). Patuxent remains unique after 30 years. *APA Monitor, 15,* 1, 26.

Munsinger, H. (1983). *Principles of abnormal psychology.* New York: Macmillan.

National Association of Elementary School Principals. (1980, September). One-parent families and their children: The school's most significant minority. *Principal, 60,* 31–37.

National Institute of Mental Health. (1974). *Teenage delinquency in small town America* (Research Report 5, DHEW Publication No. [AdM] 75–138). Rockville, MD: Alcohol, Drug Abuse, and Mental Health Administration.

O'Connor v. Donaldson, 422 U.S. 563 (1975).

Patterson, J. T. (1981). *America's struggle against poverty 1900–1980.* Cambridge, MA: Harvard University Press.

Pear, R. (1984, August 3). *Rate of poverty found to persist in spite of gains. The New York Times,* pp. A-1, B-8.

President's Commission on Mental Health. (1978). *Report to the President.* Washington, DC: U.S. Government Printing Office.

President's Committee on Mental Retardation. (1970). *The decisive decade.* Washington, DC: U.S. Government Printing Office.

Richardson, S. A. (1976). Attitudes and behavior toward the physically handicapped. *Birth Defects: Original Article Series, 12,* 15–34.

Robinson, N. M., & Robinson, H. B. (1976). *The mentally retarded child* (2nd ed.). New York: McGraw-Hill.

Rorvik, D. M. (1979, April 7). Do drugs lead to violence? *Look*, pp. 58–61.

Rosenstein, J. J., & Milazzo-Sayre, L. J. (1981). *Characteristics of admissions to selected mental health facilities, 1975*. Rockville, MD: U.S. Department of Health and Human Services.

Suinn, R. M. (1984). *Fundamentals of abnormal psychology*. Chicago: Nelson-Hall.

Tobin, S. S., & Lieberman, M. A. (1976). *Last home for the aged*. San Francisco: Jossey-Bass.

Turnbill, H. R. (1982, August). *Oversight on Education for All Handicapped Children Act, 1982*. (Testimony before the Senate Subcommittee on the Handicapped, 97th Congress. Available from the Senate Committee on Labor and Human Resources, Washington, DC.)

U.S. Bureau of the Census. (1979). *Statistical abstract of the United States* (100th ed.). Washington, DC: U.S. Government Printing Office.

U.S. Bureau of the Census. (1980). *Statistical abstract of the United States* (101st ed.). Washington, DC: U.S. Government Printing Office.

U.S. Bureau of the Census. (1981). *Statistical abstract of the United States* (102nd ed.). Washington, DC: U.S. Government Printing Office.

U.S. Bureau of the Census. (1982). *Statistical abstract of the United States* (103rd ed.). Washington, DC: U.S. Government Printing Office.

U.S. Bureau of the Census. (1983). *Statistical abstract of the United States* (104th ed.). Washington, DC: U.S. Government Printing Office.

U.S. Department of Justice. (1982, October/November). Prisoners at mid-year 1982. *Bureau of Justice's Statistical Bulletin*, 1–4.

U.S. Department of Labor, Manpower Administration (1970). *Win for a change*. Washington, DC: U.S. Government Printing Office.

Weicker, L., Jr. (1984). Defining liberty for handicapped Americans. *American Psychologist, 39*, 518–523.

Young, L. (1981). *Physical child neglect*. Pamphlet put out by National Committee for Prevention of Child Abuse.

HUMAN SERVICES IN HISTORICAL PERSPECTIVE

INTRODUCTION

Who is responsible for helping the disadvantaged within a society? The family? Religious organizations? The government? Is helping to be viewed as a basic human right or as a societal gift? Throughout history societies have responded to these questions in various ways. If a society does accept some responsibility for helping its disadvantaged, additional questions quickly emerge. Which groups of people and types of problems should be helped, to what extent, and how?

How a given society answers these questions is based on its dominant values, attitudes, and beliefs. If a society believes that its poor or elderly members should be helped, then it will develop some system or method to provide the needed care for these target populations. Another society may give priority to its physically or mentally disabled members and develop services focused on these groups with others excluded.

The present range and diversity of human services is quite large. Throughout history many people and events have influenced the development and direction of the field. As societies have changed through the ages, values and beliefs have often been replaced or at least modified by new ones. The developing human services systems of today are to some extent an outgrowth of our previously held societal values and beliefs concerning helping. It is likely that the quality, methods, and availability of human services in the future will be greatly influenced by current attitudes toward helping. Through knowledge of the past we can better understand the present and also be in a more favorable position to shape the future.

For clarity and to help you understand more fully the historical development of the interrelated aspects of the human services field, this chapter is divided into several sections. The first section provides a general overview of the historical roots of the human services field by tracing the development of early societal beliefs and helping practices. The next section traces changing societal attitudes and helping practices that have contributed to the development of human welfare services. The following section examines the historical development of mental health services. The chapter concludes with a brief discussion of future trends in the human services field.

PREHISTORIC CIVILIZATIONS

The earliest records of helpful treatments can be traced back to the Stone Age of approximately half a million years ago. Through cave drawings and the remains of primitive skulls, scientists know about a medical treatment called trephining. In this procedure a small section of the skull was bored out, probably by means of sharp stones or other such crude instruments. This hole cut from the skull was supposed to allow the evil spirits that were believed to inhabit the afflicted person's body a route of escape, thereby curing the person. Scientists have surmised that this treatment was administered to people who evidenced certain forms of observable deviant behavior. It should always be remembered that what constitutes deviant behavior is a product of what the norm for behavior is at a given point in time.

In this early era, most human problems were attributed to devils, demons, or other evil spirits. Belief in the supernatural or demonology was the dominant belief system of the age, and various procedures or rites were used to exorcise evil spirits. The belief in the supernatural arose from early man's attempt to explain the universe. All natural phenomena such as earthquakes or floods were attributed to the work of evil spirits. These ancient people also accepted the related belief, called animism, that spirits inhabit various inanimate objects such as rocks, trees, or rivers. The shaman, or medicine man who performed rites of exorcism, can now be viewed as the earliest human services worker. It was commonly believed that these individuals understood the secrets of the supernatural and possessed certain religious or mystical qualities that enabled them to help afflicted individuals.

Life during prehistoric times was at best a matter of pure survival against the hostile environment. Human problems centered around gathering food and having a relatively safe place to sleep. Poverty meant not being able to locate or secure food, and sometimes the weaker persons were simply left to perish. In situations involving the physically disabled or infirm elderly, the tribe or extended family unit would usually share or provide for these individuals. However, how important afflicted persons were to the tribe often determined the amount of assistance they received. In some instances, individuals separated from other tribes were taken in and befriended. Newcomers usually had to prove their worth in some manner in order to be allowed to stay with the tribe. The family was the primary source of help, but religion played an increasing role in the evolution of human services.

EARLY CIVILIZATIONS

Prior to 450 B.C. the world was believed to be governed by supernatural spirits. There were no major organized attempts to understand human problems and behavior from a scientific point of view. However, significant changes in beliefs were about to emerge that would alter the earlier supernatural explanations for human behavior.

During the Golden Age of Greece, a number of philosophers began to put forth new beliefs concerning human nature. One of these was the Greek physician Hippocrates (460–377 B.C.), who disagreed with the belief that supernatural spirits were the sole cause of human disease. He believed rather that most diseases were chiefly physiological or organic in origin. He shared the point of view earlier postulated by Pythagoras that the brain was the center of intelligence and that mental disorders were due specifically to the malfunctioning of the brain (Coleman, 1976).

Another contribution made by Hippocrates was his development of a system of psychiatric labels for patterns of deviant behavior. These labels included melancholia, mania, and epilepsy. To more clearly appreciate the radical change in belief advocated by Hippocrates, one must consider that the previous explanation for epilepsy was that it was a sacred or divinely ordained disease. Hippocrates claimed this disease was caused by a blockage of air in the veins due to secretions of the brain (Hoch & Knight, 1965). The treatments advocated by Hippocrates differed considerably from the earlier skull-cutting procedures. His treatments often involved vegetable diets, exercise, and pursuing a tranquil lifestyle.

Whether Hippocrates had the correct physiological explanation or treatment is not of critical historical importance here. The theory that diseases could be explained by natural—as opposed to supernatural—causes is of major importance. This change in belief systems regarding the origin of diseases influenced another significant change. Since deviant behavior or psychological problems could now be viewed as diseases of organic origin, they could now be considered part of the domain of medicine (Rimm & Somervill, 1977). As such, physicians performed the necessary treatments rather than priests, medicine men, or other religious healers. This separation of treatment responsibilities was one of the first steps toward developing the system of specialization that has continued to the present time in human services.

In the ancient Rome of 150 B.C., another physician, Asclepiades, advocated treatment procedures for mental disorders that stressed a medical and humane approach. His recommended treatments often involved massages and baths, to soothe excited or nervous patients, and wine to calm the nerves. He actively denounced cruel and severely harsh treatments still popular at this time, such as housing patients in totally dark cells, beatings with chains, bloodletting, castration, and subjecting patients to prolonged periods of starvation.

Galen (130–200 A.D.), a Greek medical writer, was able to compile, systematize, and integrate a considerable amount of material from many complementary fields. His topics included medicine, anatomy, physiology, and logic. In addition, he made a major contribution to the understanding of abnormal behavior by developing a system of classifying the causes of mental disorders. He believed all disorders were either physical or mental. He felt these causes could originate from such things as injuries to the head, fear, shock, or emotional disturbances.

The early civilizations presented some striking contradictions in helping attitudes and services. While many advances were being made and many individuals were attempting to struggle against fear, ignorance, and superstition, the use of cruel treatment procedures was still prevalent. As many advocated more humane and philosophical beliefs concerning the nature of man, the practice of buying and selling slaves existed. The poor and disabled often begged for alms along city streets. Although physicians were available for the sick, only those who could pay had access to them. The Romans and the Greeks viewed physical weakness or disability with little tolerance. Often the physically ill were taken out of towns to uninhabited areas or deserted islands where they were left to struggle by themselves or die. Of course, this pertained predominantly to the poor or those without resources or family protection. As in most societies, the rich were treated one way and the poor another.

The period of 200–475 A.D. marked a steady decline for civilization. As major plagues killed thousands upon thousands of people between the first and the fourth centuries A.D., intense fear and anxiety spread throughout Europe and the Mideast. In this climate of fear, Christianity emerged and developed a large and zealous following. Medicine could not stop the plagues, so people turned to the comfort and solace offered by Christianity, which became the prime religion of the Western world. Religious figures replaced medical figures as the saviors from illness. The causes of disease were again explained in terms of loss of faith to demons. Evil spirits were viewed as the cause for most human misfortunes.

THE MIDDLE AGES

The Middle Ages date from the collapse of Rome at the hands of the advancing barbarians from the East in the fifth century. During this time exorcism reemerged as the prevalent treatment for most disorders. The medical advances achieved by Greece and Rome were mostly forgotten (Fisher, Mehr, & Truckenbrod, 1974). Christianity became the dominant power throughout the Middle Ages.

As the Church became steadily more powerful and organized in the early part of the Middle Ages, it developed and provided a variety of human services. Monasteries often served as sanctuaries, refuges, and places of treatment for the mentally ill. The Church established institutions for the poor, provided residences for the handicapped, sponsored orphanages, and founded homes for the aged. Initially, these services were housed within church facilities but later other nonreligious sites were founded.

In its earliest beginnings, the Church espoused the belief that the wealthy or those with adequate resources had a duty or responsibility to help the less fortunate. The less fortunate, in turn, began to expect assistance as an obligation or duty from the wealthy. Both the rich and the poor developed social roles and expectations for one another, and a clear distinction between the two classes was evident. It is, however, important to note that assistance given to the poor was set at the lowest subsistence or survival level. Much of contemporary human services philosophy can, in fact, be traced back to these early interpretations of religious values and teachings.

During this period there was little interest in finding out why the disadvantaged were disadvantaged. The causes of poverty, for example, were of little interest to those providing such services. The rights and obligations for each class of society were clearly spelled out, and no further understanding was needed.

Initially, people believed that giving to the disadvantaged was important simply because others were deserving of and needed help. The Church gradually began to lose this emphasis on helping out of humanitarian concerns and replaced it with the notion that helping had to be done if one wanted to ensure a peaceful afterlife and means to salvation. The Church preached that giving was a means of salvation, a means to an end. People would be rewarded in an afterlife for fulfilling their obligations in this life. Giving was seen as a necessary responsibility or duty of the wealthy that they often fulfilled reluctantly.

As the Church developed human services, the overall climate of the Middle Ages was marked by extreme cruelty and chaos. Between the period of 1200 to 1400 there was a strong increase in belief in witchcraft, and mass outbreaks of flagellation (whipping) rituals occurred (Russell, 1972).

Although the Church tried to control all opposing beliefs and alternative religious movements, it was not completely successful. As people became disillusioned with the ability of the Church to protect them from misfortune, a variety of fanatical sects emerged throughout medieval Europe, and fear of witchcraft became a mass obsession. As Rimm & Somervill (1977) pointed out,

> Witches were viewed not only as degenerate beings in league with devils, but also as causes of sickness, disease, personal tragedies, and the stealing and killing of children. They were perceived as

vicious instigators of terror, highly dangerous to a threatened and unstable society [p. 16].

In the Middle Ages the growth of fanatical sects represented a form of extremism, an impulsive act often characteristic of youth. In fact, the Europe of the Middle Ages was a youthful society. The death rate was extremely high and people did not often survive past 40 years of age.

Beginning in the 13th century under Pope Innocent III, a religious tribunal was established. This tribunal, referred to as the Inquisition, was given the responsibility of seeking out and punishing any and all crimes associated with witchcraft or other forms of heresy. The methods employed by this ecclesiastical body to obtain confessions for accused crimes included intimidation, burnings, boiling suspects in oil or cutting their tongues out, and other inhuman forms of torture. The Inquisition, although utilizing cruel and inhuman measures, espoused the belief that the Church was providing service to society by getting rid of the causes of disease and famine. It also served as a means for the Church to exert its power and encourage loyalty by threatening those who did not conform with stated policies and beliefs.

Throughout the Middle Ages a major power struggle existed between church and state. Each faction wanted more power to govern without interference from the other. The Church developed a steady source of income by demanding that its parishioners donate approximately 10% of their income for church-related activities. The State viewed this steady source of income as a threat to its own base of power and sought many times to make it illegal to give money or services to those who could work.

Gradually, the disadvantaged came to be classified according to whether they could physically work or were unfit for work, such as the disabled, elderly, and children. Those individuals deemed legitimately unfit for work came to be known as the worthy poor while the others were looked upon as being lazy and unworthy of assistance. Even though this steady clash for power existed, the Church was successful through most of the Middle Ages at preserving its domain, especially as far as providing human services to "worthy" individuals.

THE RENAISSANCE

As Europe emerged from the Middle Ages, it entered a period of rapid and turbulent change marked by the end of a feudal system, the birth of industrialization, and a decline in the power of the

Church. As the government became more powerful and influential, individual states, cities, and towns developed more power. The middle class, comprised mainly of tradespeople, grew and prospered and became a more visible and distinct part of society.

By the 16th century, change had significantly altered the previously established religious, social, and economic order. The government, the Church, and newly emerging business leaders shaped the nature and direction of societal change. Unfortunately, the rationale for change is often based upon the priorities and complex concerns of those in power and does not necessarily benefit all in society. These changing societal forces had a tremendous influence upon the direction and quality of human services. It is important to realize that what has become today a system providing an enormous range of services for the welfare of human beings from birth until death originally started out as simply providing food or shelter to people as a form of social welfare.

Having now provided a general overview of the early development of human services philosophy and practice, we will next examine the subsequent growth of human welfare services, and then of mental health services.

HUMAN WELFARE SERVICES SINCE THE RENAISSANCE

During the 16th century the Protestant Reformation escalated the many struggles for power between Church and State. By the end of the 16th century the State had finally established authority over the Church. As a result of diminished Church power, it became incumbent upon the State to take over many services formerly provided by the Church, which included providing for human services.

Under Henry VIII of England, the government formally took over the human services functions of the Church to provide for people who were not self-sufficient, and established a system of income maintenance and public welfare. The official policy mandating this transition of power was outlined in the Statutes of 1536 and 1572. In 1601 the Elizabethan Poor Law established a system that provided shelter and care for the poor. This law also specified local responsibility for the poor and disadvantaged. It was first the responsibility of the family to provide for all human services. If the family could not provide such services, it then became the responsibility of the State to provide for disadvantaged individuals within their communities.

Although there were people with good motives and intentions, the poor laws were not initially created as a generous humanitarian gift from the State to aid its disadvantaged citizens; the poor laws were a means of social control following an era of mass frenzy, disease, famine, and economic instability that threatened to break apart the existing social structure.

As a result of these poor laws in England, a system for classifying the disadvantaged was established. This system classified the disadvantaged into three categories: (1) the poor who were capable of work, (2) the poor incapable of work due to age, physical disability, or motherhood responsibilities, and (3) orphaned or abandoned children who became wards of the State. The poor who could work were forced to work in State-operated workhouses. Massive overcrowding, filth, and inadequate food and sanitary conditions made these workhouses barely tolerable. If the individual was incapable of work and in need of food and shelter, he or she could be sent to an almshouse (poorhouse). The living conditions here were similar to those of the State workhouses. By comparison to the almshouse or workhouse, a more tolerable alternative was available for the more "fortunate" of the disadvantaged. In certain communities it was possible for a person or family to remain in their own dwelling and receive contributions of food and other items from their community. This circumstance was far less common than the other methods of providing services. Money was never given directly to the poor family, and any other essential services such as medical care were not generally available.

As this early, often crude, human services system evolved, procedures and rules were more clearly established and defined. Policies were established to decide who would be eligible for available services, and who would have the authority to decide who got what and who went where. As the programs became more complicated, the government created a subsystem with sole responsibility for overseeing its public welfare system. Each community had its specified government welfare administrator, who made the local decisions regarding a person's eligibility for services. As the number of individuals who were in need of assistance increased, the more impersonal the local community bureaucracy became. Indeed, this is still a problem with modern welfare systems. The form of welfare bureaucracy created in England during this period became the early forerunner of our modern welfare system in the United States.

The Industrial Revolution

By the 1800s the Industrial Revolution was developing momentum. The Industrial Revolution began with the invention of a few basic machines and the development of new sources of power. The advent of industrialization created the mechanization of manufacturing and agriculture, changed the speed and methods of communication and transportation, and began the development of factory systems of labor. These events, in turn, caused dramatic changes in economic systems (Perry & Perry, 1983).

Large populations of unemployed individuals moved from rural areas to urban centers in search of work. Although new forms of labor were needed and work was available for some, the great majority of people still found themselves in poverty conditions. As a result of the swell in the disadvantaged population within urban areas, many public institutions were created. The majority of poor found themselves facing worse conditions than those left behind. Adequate living space was scarce, producing overcrowded and unhealthy conditions. Food was in short supply and the urban environment provided little room to grow crops. Families often found themselves separated as members left in search of work.

Workers were generally seen by businessmen as commodities, to be used only when needed and disregarded when work was not immediately available. It was during this time that workers started to band together to share and provide what they could for one another. This banding together for the collective benefit of all resulted in the development of the early guilds and unions. In an effort to deal with the perceived threat to the social order brought on by these large numbers of disadvantaged people in urban areas, the government created more workhouses, debtor's prisons, houses for delinquents and orphans, and mental institutions.

The period of the Industrial Revolution brought about a new social philosophy that had a strong influence upon society's attitude toward the poor and disadvantaged. This new social philosophy, known as the Protestant work ethic, reinforced a set of values supporting the virtues of industrialization while condemning idleness as being almost sinful.

Hard work and thereby the accumulation of wealth was interpreted as God's reward for leading a virtuous life. On the opposite end of this philosophy, poverty was often viewed as some form of punishment from God. This philosophy, as most notably preached by John Calvin, supported the notion that poverty-ridden individuals should remain in their disadvantaged conditions because God had divinely ordained this condition for them.

It was during the 1830s in England that the concept of "less eligibility" was established. This concept set forth the guideline that any assistance given to the disadvantaged must be lower than the lowest wage given to any working person. Working was seen as an ultimate good and not working, for any reason, was to be looked down upon. In theory, this concept sought to provide an incentive for all to work.

Another corresponding influence on society's attitude toward the disadvantaged was the introduction of the concept of laissez-faire economy by the Englishman Adam Smith in 1776. His book *The Wealth of Nations* argued for an economy where government was to have virtually no influence and place no restrictions upon the free marketplace. Without government control, society would grow and prosper by itself based on people's individual merit and hard work. Supporters of this concept did not see human services as a right, but instead as a misguided societal gift—a gift that they perceived would actually hinder overall economic production.

As previously described, many of these events and philosophies that were developing in England and Europe had a strong influence upon societal attitudes toward helping in the United States. In the United States, the economic value system emerging from England was again reinforced by the writing of another Englishman, Herbert Spencer. It was Spencer who interpreted Charles Darwin's writings on evolution in a provocative manner. His ideas, which came to be known as Social Darwinism, applied theories of animal behavior to human behavior. Using Darwin's biological premise in regard to natural selection, and coupling it with an economic argument, Spencer espoused that those disadvantaged people unfit for society should not be helped because it was the natural order of things for them to help themselves or perish, as in nature. This, it was felt, would provide another incentive for people to work. Of course, this theory did not take into consideration those individuals who, for physical or other reasons, were unable to work. Additionally, this theory did not consider the many individuals who wanted work but for whom no work was available. In essence, Social Darwinism only served to foster an attitude of indifference toward the poor.

Early Reform Movements in the United States

As the many institutions for the disadvantaged grew in size, workers were needed to supply the various types of helping services. One positive effect of the growth of these public institutions was that it helped formalize the system of "professional" helpers. Conditions within institutions were intolerable. The large number of people housed in small spaces created unbearable overcrowding. Lack of heat in winter, instances of brutality, inadequate food, and many other examples of inhuman treatment generated a good deal of concern by private citizens over these conditions and led to a series of attempts at social reform.

Many of the social reformers of the mid-19th century did not focus their efforts on a single injustice, but instead called for a voice of reason and human concern in every area of human welfare. In the late 1800s and early 1900s the movement toward human welfare made great advances. In this period of heavy immigration to the United States, many thousands of newly arrived immigrants found themselves homeless and displaced in their new country. It was during this time that settlement houses were developed to provide immigrants with the essentials of life and to help them to get a foothold in American society.

The settlement house movement was a reflection of early human services philosophy. Settlement house workers embraced the view that it was the responsibility of society to help. They also advocated a major shift in helping attitudes and human services thinking, to the belief that many of the problems confronting individuals are created by environmental circumstances rather than by personal inadequacy. This point of view has recently come to be known as the human services perspective. The founders of the movement expressed the idea that one must work toward improving the social conditions existing within society. To accomplish this goal, a system providing for basic human services must be created to facilitate an adequate quality of life. It was further believed that a truly successful human services system should provide opportunities for all people to improve their lives and realize their potentials.

One notable early settlement house was Hull House, founded in Chicago by Jane Addams. It was here, many authorities believe, that contemporary social work was born. Using Hull House as the primary hub of her human services activity, Addams managed to create a small but comprehensive network of human services in her Chicago neighborhood that included basic adult education classes, kindergartens, and an employment bureau. In the following years many other settlement houses were founded throughout the country. They served as a training ground for those providing social work services.

The early 1900s in the United States marked the resurgence of another significant human services movement. Often referred to as the progressive or social justice movement, its aim was to bring about social change through political action and legislative reform. This movement, which reflected liberal reform ideas, was embraced by many factions of society including the unions. Accepting the earlier idea that the social environment is a major factor in creating peoples' problems, the reformers advocated a series of economic reforms, including the setting of a minimum wage, a pension system for older workers, an eight-hour day and a six-day work week, as well as laws providing for unemployment insurance and regulation of child labor. Many successful changes occurred despite the prevailing conservative outlook. The government began to assume greater responsibility for the provision of human services. During this period, a growing number of Americans became aware that a system of human services is integrally connected to the economic system and the role of the government. A comprehensive system providing for human services requires the support and interconnectedness of all institutions within society.

The Depression and World War II

The stock market crash of 1929 and the Great Depression changed dramatically the lives of many Americans. With huge numbers of unemployed workers and a depressed economy, the need for expansion of human services was evident. With millions of people unemployed, the relationship between environmental circumstances and human problems could not have been made any clearer.

As pointed out in Chapter One, the federal government under the direction of President Franklin Delano Roosevelt established a series of government aid programs, the New Deal. These programs attempted to make work available where possible and to provide direct assistance to those people incapable of work. Examples of such programs were the Works Progress Administration, which provided jobs, the Civilian Conservation Corps, which provided training, and Aid to Dependent Children, which provided for direct government aid.

In 1935, a major governmental response to the existing social conditions was to create the Social Security Act. This legislation established a form of social insurance and protection for individuals against an unpredictable economy. This measure not only helped to alleviate the current social conditions but was also calculated to aid and protect future generations. This human services legislation subsequently provided for a wide array of health and social welfare services.

It has happened throughout history that peoples' attitudes change but sometimes have a difficult time being completely erased. There are always those who cling to previous ideas and attitudes for both good and bad motives, as well as those who advocate change for similarly varied reasons. The 1940s in the United States witnessed a reemergence of the trend toward conservatism. Public criticism was again heard denouncing the governmental system of providing for human services as helping to create a form of "welfare state." Conservatives felt that too much aid would rob people of the incentive to help themselves. However, as conservatives and liberals debated how much assistance is beneficial, returning World War II veterans created a further need for a variety of human services. As

Chapter One has indicated, this clash between conservative and liberal thinking is still very evident today.

The Sixties

The 1960s were characterized by social unrest in the United States. While the Vietnam War was being waged overseas, many Americans at home participated in marches and demonstrations to protest the ills they felt existed within the system. This was a turbulent, sometimes violent, period marked by protests at many college campuses across the country. Widespread and organized efforts of this kind resulted in an eventual end to the war, and advanced the civil rights movement and the War on Poverty. These latter movements were successful in bringing national attention to the plight of minorities and the poor. New legislation was enacted that resulted in the establishment of many programs and services. Although the civil rights movement and the War on Poverty did create increased economic and educational opportunities for the disadvantaged, they did not eliminate poverty and discrimination in the United States.

In the 1970s and 1980s, human welfare services in the United States have grown considerably. A massive number of programs exist that provide for human services throughout the life cycle. In the midst of such an array of services, the need for services of these types still remains great. Debates continue to rage over which programs are truly helpful and worthy of funding and which should be trimmed from our federal or state budgets. This controversy over social policy is discussed in more detail in Chapter Seven. Having reviewed the development of human welfare services, we can now examine the corresponding growth of mental health services.

MENTAL HEALTH SERVICES SINCE THE RENAISSANCE

The historical development of our system of mental health services in certain instances paralleled the development of our system of human welfare services, as previously described. It is now apparent that having an adequate food supply, shelter, income, and other necessities of life has a direct bearing on one's mental health. Of course, our contemporary knowledge and understanding of how environmental factors influence human problems is much better than it was in the past. Previously, individuals deemed mentally ill faced a grim future without any substantial alternatives. In the section that follows, we examine the people and events that have helped to shape our societal attitudes and treatment of the mentally ill.

Early Mental Asylums

Early institutions created to house the behaviorally deviant were commonly referred to as asylums. The word *asylum,* when used in this context, refers to a place of refuge that provides protection, shelter, and security. Although many mental patients did view the asylum as a place of refuge or safety, a good number probably did not. It was society that viewed the asylum as a form of protection and shelter from those people labeled as deviants.

The early public mental institutions in Europe and the United States were located within communities, with the community being primarily responsible for the governance and maintenance of the institution. As communities tend to be different from one another, so too did these institutions differ from one another. No universal guidelines for patient care or procedures were established among this broad network of community mental institutions, and mistreatment and abuse frequently occurred.

One noteworthy exception, among others, to the generalized inhumane treatment and lack of concern towards the mentally ill was the mental hospital established in 1409 in Valencia, Spain. This hospital is probably the oldest mental hospital still functioning today (Andriola & Cata, 1969). As a rule, patients were readily discharged after they were seen as able to return to society. Patients were treated with relative dignity and a system of voluntary admissions was established. The example set by this hospital is even more striking when one considers that the Inquisition and witch-hunting mania was also prevalent during this era.

One of the earliest public asylums and the one most typical of the overall character of these institutions was St. Mary's of Bethlehem (Bedlam), created in 1547. Although originally intended to be humanitarian in nature, this institution, as well as others to follow, was little more than a dungeon in which the behaviorally deviant were locked up and subjected to cruel, often ghoulish, treatment. Inadequate food, insufficient clothing, filth, infectious disease, and overcrowding were commonplace. The more difficult patients were subjected to treatments that consisted of days, weeks, or months spent in mechanical restraints or chained to the walls and denied food or water. The majority of patients were either mentally retarded, aged, physically ill, or accused or convicted of crimes. Little attention was given to individual cases, and the patients could just as easily have been sent to a prison or poorhouse as a mental institution.

The Era of Humanitarian Reform

During the next two hundred years, similar conditions existed in institutions for the insane in this country such as Pennsylvania Hospital, founded in 1752, and Williamsburg Hospital, founded in 1773 (Bloom, 1977). During the late 1770s and early 1780s, a reform movement began that would alter significantly, although briefly, the previously existing conditions within mental institutions. This movement towards humane treatment of the insane has been referred to as the era of humanitarian reform and the moral treatment movement. This movement, which had its earliest beginnings in Europe, had great influence upon institutions in the United States in the late 18th and early 19th centuries.

Following the French Revolution in 1792, a physician, Phillipe Pinel, became the director of La Bicétre, a mental institution in Paris. It was here that Pinel, inspired by the idea that the insane might be curable, unchained some prisoners, and provided adequate food, clothing, and other necessities of life to all. Although reform was clearly evident, Pinel and other early reformers still advocated the use of harsh measures as sometimes useful tools of treatment. However, the reforms of Pinel are considered by many to be the first major revolution in mental health care (Wahler, Johnson, & Uhrich, 1972).

This reform movement, begun in France, spread to England. In 1813, the British physician Samuel Tuke, the director of the York Retreat, initiated a similar series of reforms. In the United States, other physicians also advocated similar improvements. It was during these early years of reform that physicians gained most in prestige and prominence in their evolving interest and later specialization in treating the behaviorally deviant.

Even though the early reforms advocated by Pinel, Tuke, and others had an impact upon the institutions of the day, by the middle 1800s in the United States public awareness and interest in the plight of the mentally ill had waned. Without such interest, the institutions once again fell back into a period characterized by neglect and widespread mistreatment. It was in the mid-19th century that Dorothea Dix was to become a prominent figure in the evolution of human services. Through her efforts, the earlier reform movement that began in Europe and lost temporary impetus in the United States was again revived and gained its greatest foothold in the United States. Dorothea Dix was instrumental in gathering enough public support to make greatly needed changes in the inhuman conditions existing within the asylums as well as within prisons and many poverty-related shelters.

Following a personal investigation of asylums and prisons

throughout the country, Dix wrote many articles for newspapers outlining the plight of the disadvantaged. She contacted legislators and began a successful lobbying effort to inform and educate the public concerning these conditions within the institutions. As Bloom (1977) indicated,

> Before [Dix's] career came to an end, 32 state mental hospitals had been built in the United States, care of the mentally ill had been removed from the local community, and the professional orientation toward the insane had been changed from seeing them as no different from paupers or criminals to seeing them as sick people in need of hospital care [p. 11].

The creation of a system of large state psychiatric hospitals to replace predominantly poorly run smaller community institutions was seen as an improvement in care for the mentally ill. However, this progress was followed by new problems. Believing the large psychiatric hospital to be the answer, the public seemed to lose concern for this population. In the following years, a gradual and steady rise in new admissions to these hospitals once again resulted in overcrowding, mismanagement, and mistreatment.

During the early 1900s, advocates of the social justice movement, who had been active earlier in other areas of human welfare, turned their attention to abuses within mental institutions. Having no desire to dismantle these institutions, they sought rather to change the system of patient treatment and procedures. New policies creating individual treatment plans were established. This appeared to be a more humane and responsible way to administer treatment. Each patient would be treated individually, taking into consideration his or her prior history. This policy seemed a step in the right direction, but it unfortunately created other abuses within the system. Too much arbitrary power and authority was given over to the professionals and bureaucrats overseeing these systems. Of course, there were patients who benefited from more individualized consideration, but generally the large and unchecked state system often ignored individuals' rights and denied the possibility that the state could be wrong in certain instances.

Freud's Influence

By the 1920s and 1930s, Sigmund Freud's classic theories concerning human behavior were well established and widely accepted. Having had to endure considerable criticism in the earlier years of his developing work due to his emphasis on human sexuality, his later refined theories had a major impact upon most facets of society. Although Freud did not work directly in institutions, he had a strong influence on the prevailing treatment approach. His theories were so publicly accepted that the mental institutions of the 1930s adopted his approach to treatment and became psychoanalytically oriented. His contributions were so influential that many consider the second mental health revolution to have begun with public acceptance of his work (Wahler et al., 1972).

As we will discuss in Chapter Four, many criticisms of certain aspects of Freud's theories still continue today. One such criticism by those who employ a human services perspective is that Freud's psychoanalytic theories focus too narrowly on the inner person, excluding the environmental factors that impact upon and influence human behavior.

Freud's impact, though considerable, did not lead to significant changes in the institutional system of care for the mentally ill. Steady deterioration in this system continued. Although there were exceptions, generally most hospital staffs were overworked, understaffed, and poorly trained. Patients were often neglected and many remained in hospitals for years.

The Trend toward Deinstitutionalization and Decentralization

Beginning in the early 1950s, certain changes began to develop in several hospitals due to growth in the field of psychopharmacology. It was now possible through the use of drugs to effectively reduce a patient's bizarre behavior, thereby affording other opportunities for treatment. Many patients previously viewed as untreatable were now able to return to the community while continuing with drug treatments at home (Pasamanick, Scarpitti, & Dinitz, 1967). Many controversies surfaced regarding the alleged widespread misuse or abuse of such drugs. Critics claimed that patients who were not in need of such drugs were given them routinely to keep them under control. Others pointed out that drugs may cause side effects that are as bad as the illness being treated.

Deinstitutionalization became a major policy in institutions during this time. There was a growing belief that people could be more successfully treated in familiar community settings. It appeared to some that deinstitutionalization was implemented more because of financial concerns than for treatment reasons. It was felt that it was just too expensive to keep people institutionalized on a round-the-clock basis and treatment was initially thought to be less expensive in community settings.

Another change appearing at this time in the large state hospitals was geographic decentralization. This procedure, which initially began as a change focused on administrative admissions procedures, was to eventually have a significant effect upon the role of mental patients and their communities. Through this new administrative procedure, patients were placed in hospital wards based upon their place of residence prior to admission. Patients were housed and treated with other patients from their own community rather than being dispersed throughout the hospital system. Prior to this change, state hospitals generally remained isolated and removed from the communities they served. Through geographic decentralization, communities became more aware of the patients residing therein. Many problems have surfaced regarding this issue as many communities have openly voiced fear and dissatisfaction with having mental health facilities or programs located in them.

The Community Mental Health Movement

The 1960s was an important era for the field of mental health. Many professionals have in fact referred to this decade as the third mental health revolution (Hobbs, 1964; Wahler et al., 1972). The changes occurring in this period marked another significant shift in human services philosophy as characterized primarily by the community mental health center movement.

The Joint Commission on Mental Illness and Health (1961, p. 2) evidenced the thrust of the community mental health movement as they recommended that the objective of modern treatment should be the following:

1. To save the patient from the debilitating effects of institutionalization as much as possible.
2. If the patient requires hospitalization, to return him to home and community life as soon as possible.
3. Thereafter to maintain him in the community as long as possible.

In 1963, the Community Mental Health Act was signed into law. This legislation reflected a growing philosophy that mental health services should be located in the community with the government allocating funds for the creation of these comprehensive community mental health centers. In Chapter Two we examined the specific services offered by these centers. Deinstitutionalization was encouraged, resulting in a major shift of mental patients from the large mental hospitals to these community mental health centers.

The community mental health movement has its advocates

and its opponents. There are those who assert that while the number of patients in the large institutions has decreased and the average length of stay has been reduced considerably, the tendency to re-admit patients again and again to the institutions has correspondingly grown (Wahler, 1971). Other watchful observers of the movement have pointed to instances in which patients have been placed in community settings without adequate supervision. Opponents of the movement indicate that the initial community centers often resembled the traditional hospital organization. The difficulty of developing new mental health services grew out of a situation where the workers were already socialized into and evolved from the old hospital system (Perlmutter & Silverman, 1972).

Advocates of the movement point to the healing power of the community and the need to normalize the method of treatment as much as possible. If the goal of treatment is to eventually return the patient to a functioning life in the community, the community must be an integral part of treatment.

The Advent of Paraprofessionals

Another important development in the decade of the 1960s was the formal recognition of the role of paraprofessionals, as reflected in the paraprofessional or new careers movement. The 1964 Economic Opportunity Act and the Schneuer Subprofessional Career Act of 1966 provided the impetus and the government funds to recruit and train entry-level workers for a range of positions within the human services field. These related pieces of legislation coupled with other antipoverty amendments created approximately 150,000 jobs for paraprofessionals (Reissman, 1967).

The rapid growth of the paraprofessional movement arose from a perceived manpower shortage as the new community mental health centers sought initially to utilize personnel in more innovative ways. Albee (1960) pointed out the critical shortage of trained mental health professionals. He predicted an even greater shortage in the future and advocated the creation of a new kind of mental health generalist worker who could be educationally prepared in a shorter period of time. Through the creation of two- and four-year training programs based in colleges, it was believed that aspiring workers could receive enough broad-based education and general human services skills to enable them to function on a generalist level alongside the more highly trained professionals. Many of the basic tasks previously performed by psychologists, psychiatrists, or social workers—such as intake interviewing and setting of fee schedules—could be delegated to the paraprofessional, thus freeing the professional to focus selectively on more advanced clinical aspects of treatment and diagnosis often requiring more extensive graduate preparation. Chapter Six provides a closer examination of the diverse functions of paraprofessionals.

Since the 1960s, new and expanded roles have been created for paraprofessionals. Gartner (1971), Wahler et al. (1972), and Alley, Blanton, and Feldman (1979), among others, have traced the evolving functions and roles of these workers. The role of the paraprofessional, once narrowly defined as merely custodial in nature, had grown by the 1970s to include a large range of therapeutic activities. As Minuchin (1969) noted, the paraprofessional movement initiated a reexamination of professional roles and tasks, which resulted in a renewed interest in environmental factors as opposed to the intrapsychic view of maladaptive behavior. As a result, the human services field of the 1970s and 1980s emphasizes the use of paraprofessionals in roles reflecting the importance of a patient's social and environmental needs.

THE EIGHTIES AND BEYOND

The many tasks and problems facing our human services system today are similar to those faced in previous times. Poverty, unemployment, and mental illness still exist. What is different, however, is that new methods and approaches are needed to deal with the problems that are now a part of our highly complex contemporary society. As Alvin Toffler (1970) described, the civilization of today is unlike any other in history. The rate of change is so rapid and the changes themselves so complex that it is almost impossible for anyone to keep pace with the developments occurring in a field. Societal change, although beneficial in certain respects, has also created significant stress, anxiety, and insecurity for many. As the trend toward specialization increases, more and more people find that their previously acquired skills become rapidly obsolete. While scientific achievements have increased the life span, the threat of global nuclear war has given rise to widespread concerns about what type of future awaits us.

In an effort to keep pace with the society of today, the human services system has also become highly complex, specialized, and at times fragmented. As the need for human services appears evident, the conservative trend of the 1980s is toward reduced federal spending for such services. As Chapter Seven examines further, the shortage of funds is becoming an increasingly large issue in the 1980s and will presumably be so in the 1990s. The same questions consistently appear: Whom do we help? How much? What individuals or institutions should decide these questions? How much have we learned from the examples set by history and to what extent will history repeat itself? The need and the challenge certainly remain for contemporary human services workers.

ADDITIONAL READING

Dana, R. H. (1981). *Human services for cultural minorities.* Baltimore: University Park Press.

Green, J. W. (1982). *Cultural awareness in the human services.* Englewood Cliffs, NJ: Prentice-Hall.

Hofstadter, R. (1944). *Social Darwinism in American thought.* Boston: Beacon Press.

Komisar, L. (1974). *Down and out in the U.S.A.: A history of social welfare.* New York: New Viewpoints.

Leacock, E. B. (1971) *The culture of poverty: A critique.* New York: Simon & Schuster.

Morales, A., and Sheafor, B. W. (1980). *Social work, a profession of many faces.* Boston: Allyn & Bacon.

Nash, K. L., Jr., Lifton, N., & Smith, S. E. (1978). *The paraprofessional: Selected readings.* New Haven, CT: Advocate Press.

Reich, C. A. (1970). *The greening of America.* New York: Random House.

Trattner, W. (1974). *From poor law to welfare state.* New York: Free Press.

Ward, M. J. (1946). *The snakepit.* New York: Random House.

Weinberger, P. E. (1969). *Perspectives on social welfare.* New York: Macmillan.

REFERENCES

Albee, G. W. (1960). The manpower crisis in mental health. *American Journal of Public Health, 50,* 1895–1900.

Alley, S., Blanton, J., & Feldman, R. (Eds.). (1979). *Paraprofessionals in mental health: Theory and practice.* New York: Human Sciences Press.

Andriola, J., & Cata, G. (1969). The oldest mental hospital in the world. *Hospital and Community Psychiatry, 20,* 42–43.

Bloom, B. L. (1977). *Community mental health: A general introduction.* Monterey, CA: Brooks/Cole.

Coleman, J. (1976). *Abnormal psychology and modern life.* Glenview, IL: Scott, Foresman.

Fisher, W., Mehr, J., & Truckenbrod, P. (1974). *Human services: The third revolution in mental health.* New York: Alfred.

Gartner, A. (1971). *Paraprofessionals and their performance.* New York: Praeger.

Hobbs, N. (1964). Mental health's third revolution. *American Journal of Orthopsychiatry, 34,* 822–833.

Hoch, P. H., & Knight, R. P. (Eds.). (1965). *Epilepsy: Psychiatric aspects of convulsive disorders.* New York: Hafner.

Joint Commission on Mental Health Illness and Health. (1961). *Action for mental health.* New York: Basic Books.

Minuchin, S. (1969). The paraprofessional and the use of confrontation in the mental health field. *American Journal of Orthopsychiatry, 34,* 722–729.

Pasamanick, B., Scarpitti, F. R., & Dinitz, S. (1967). *Schizophrenics in the community.* New York: Appleton-Century-Crofts.

Perlmutter, F., & Silverman, H. A. (1972). C.M.H.C.: A structural anachronism. *Social Work, 17,* 78–84.

Perry, J. A., & Perry, E. K. (1983). *The social web* (4th ed.). New York: Harper & Row.

Reissman, F. (1967). Strategies and suggestions for training nonprofessionals. *Community Mental Health Journal, 3,* 103–110.

Rimm, D. C., & Somervill, J. W. (1977). *Abnormal psychology.* New York: Academic Press.

Russell, J. B. (1972). *Witchcraft in the Middle Ages.* Ithaca, NY: Cornell University Press.

Toffler, A. (1970). *Future shock.* New York: Random House.

Wahler, H. J. (1971). What is life all about or who all needs paraprofessionals? *The Clinical Psychologist, 24*(3), 11–14.

Wahler, H. J., Johnson, R., & Uhrich, K. (1972). *The Expediter Project: Final report to National Institute of Mental Health.* State of Washington: Department of Social and Health Services.

THEORETICAL PERSPECTIVES

INTRODUCTION

A theory is a statement that attempts to explain connections among events. It is not, in itself, a fact, but a concept that brings facts together into a sensible overall picture. There is nothing mysterious about the process of making, testing, and using theories. Even quite young children construct useful theories about events in their daily lives. These take the form of ideas such as *If I say I'm sorry, Mommy won't hit me* or *If I do good at school, my parents will give me a present.* These ideas are based on observations of previous events. On a simple level, they enable the child to understand, predict, and sometimes control the environment.

The process of theory making goes on throughout life. The fact is that the individual is constantly being bombarded with incoming stimuli. Without mental structures to classify and organize these events, the individual would be overwhelmed and unable to function in an organized way. In this sense, theory making is absolutely essential to successful living.

Just as personal theories enable the individual to function effectively, so scientific theories enable the human services worker to function effectively. In this chapter, we look at a number of major theories that help workers to understand the causes of disorders and to plan effective action to either prevent or treat these disorders. We begin by discussing the nature of scientific theory. We then examine two general theoretical frameworks for helping: the medical model and the human services model. This is followed by a detailed look at three more specific theoretical viewpoints that can be applied within the broader frameworks. These are the psychoanalytic, the humanistic, and the behavioristic systems of therapy. The chapter includes a brief look at some nontraditional paths to personal fulfillment, and closes with an account of systems theory, which some believe holds great promise as a theoretical viewpoint for the future.

SCIENTIFIC THEORY

There is no hard and fast distinction between personal and scientific theories. All theories are intended to help us make sense of the world around us. The distinguishing features of scientific theories are that they are consciously formed, tested, and shared with other researchers. One purpose of scientific theories is to serve as a guide to future research. Ideally, theories should be continually tested and modified to fit newly discovered facts.

Of course, scientists often fall short of this ideal. Many theories once accepted by reputable authorities are now completely discredited. Sometimes incorrect theories are based on faulty, or limited, observations. For example, a number of early investigators attributed criminal behavior to inherited tendencies (Lombroso-Ferrero, 1911). In this view, the criminal was a "born type" who could be distinguished from normals by certain physical traits such as a low forehead, an unusually shaped head, eyebrows growing together above the bridge of the nose, and protruding ears. Modern investigators found this theory did not account for criminals who lacked these physical characteristics, and that it ignored data that linked criminal behavior to poverty and certain social conditions.

Theories can be no better than the facts on which they are based. Some investigators are not above faking data to "prove" a point. It was recently reported, for example, that a distinguished British psychologist had falsified—actually made up—data that supported his contention that intelligence is inherited. We can only hope that this kind of gross faking is rare. On the other hand, it is by no means unusual for a scientist to be biased in favor of cherished beliefs. In fact, everyone shows this sort of bias at times. People are more likely to accept evidence that supports their beliefs than evidence that goes against these beliefs. Since theories often serve as guides to action, the blind acceptance of an incorrect theory may have harmful consequences. The only remedy against the hazards of bias is to be receptive to *all* of the relevant facts in a situation.

THEORIES ABOUT HUMAN DISORDERS

Now that you have a general idea of what theories are and what purposes they serve, our focus shifts to the main concern of this chapter—theories about human disorders. Very simply, these are theories that try to explain why and how certain disorders come about. Based on this understanding, each theory proposes certain treatments designed to alleviate the disorder in question. Theories, then, are not merely matters for dry academic discussion, but have a powerful impact on what the helper does for or to the client.

Traditionally, human disorders are divided into two main types: physical, and mental or psychological. The latter will be emphasized since these are of main concern to the human services worker. All of the major theories to be reviewed offer reasonable explanations of how and why psychological disorders occur. However, the explanations are quite different one from the other. Why are there so many different explanations? There are several possible answers to this question. One is that human behavior is so complex that no single theory can explain every disorder. Another answer is that each theory tends to focus on certain kinds of abnormal behavior. A third point, related to the other two, is that different theories tend to focus on different levels of observation. Before proceeding to the specific theories, it is necessary to clarify what is meant by the latter term.

Three Levels of Observation

Each theory tends to focus on one of three general levels of observation: the biological, the psychological, or the social level. In other words, researchers tend to specialize in the study of events at one particular level.

From the *biological* point of view, an organism is viewed as a physical or biochemical system. Disease, physical damage to the body, and/or inadequate development of internal organs may all hamper an individual's ability to get along in the outside world. For example, some forms of mental retardation are due to abnormal development of the brain and nervous system. It is also known that one form of senility is due to a breakdown of the blood vessels of the brain. Physical abnormalities are the main province of medical science. The medical approach to treatment, to be described, employs medication, surgery, and other physical methods to cure, or at least ameliorate, disorders.

From the *psychological* point of view, the individual attempts to gain gratification of needs and goals by interacting with the outer environment. In order to adapt successfully, the person must behave in ways that suit the immediate situation. The person's skills, motives, needs, emotions, and ways of handling stress all play a role in this adaptive struggle. Obviously, some individuals are more successful than others in attaining satisfactions. Some of the psychological problems familiar to the human services worker are clients' low self-esteem, lack of skills, and self-defeating ways of trying to achieve stated goals in life.

The *social* level refers to the powerful influences of family, schools, neighborhood, and society. To the human services worker, one of the most important social variables is socioeconomic status. This includes specific factors such as income, level of education, and the prestige value of one's occupation. High-level executives, administrators, and professional persons rate higher on this scale than do blue-collar workers and welfare recipients. The majority of those who receive help from human services are concentrated in the lower income levels.

There is controversy, and some confusion, about applying these three levels of observation to specific disorders. There are biological, psychological, and social theories about alcoholism, schizophrenia, criminality, and many other disorders. Various investigators proclaim that one level is more important than the other two in causing these disorders. There is, for example, intense debate about the relative importance of inherited physical traits in predisposing an individual toward one disorder or another. The fact is that all three levels may be involved in the development of a certain disorder.

Multiple Causes

In both medical and social sciences, it is now generally accepted that many disorders have more than one cause. For example, on the biological level, the immediate cause of tuberculosis is infection by a certain bacterium. Since this is a common bacterium, the following question arises: Why do some people come down with the disorder while others do not? The answer is that the victim is often in a physically run-down state in which the body's normal defenses against infection have been depleted. Further investigation usually shows that a number of psychological and social factors play a role in getting the victim into this state. For example, the lifestyle of the patient often seems to have a frantic, overactive quality. Social factors are implicated by the fact that the incidence of tuberculosis is far higher in poor than in affluent communities. Obviously, then, biological, psychological, *and* social factors may all be involved in causing a particular disorder.

Political Implications of Theory

The controversies among theories are not merely matters of factual evidence but also involve underlying political and economic factors. For example, it makes a difference if the behavior problems associated with poverty are attributed to (1) psychological defects such as laziness or lack of intelligence, or to (2) the impact of society, which has stacked the cards against the poor. In the first case, the individual is held fully responsible for his or her poor circumstances. In the second, the person is seen as the victim of social and economic factors beyond his or her control. Obviously, a more sympathetic response goes along with this second point of view.

MODELS OF DYSFUNCTION

This brief introduction to theory paves the way for discussion of two general models of dysfunction: the medical model and the human services model. The term *model* in this context refers to a general theoretical point of view about the causes of disorders. Perhaps the earliest model was the religious or magical perspective, which emphasized evil spirits as the cause of illness. The medical model with its scientific emphasis gradually replaced the spiritual notion of causation. The medical model emphasizes biological factors, such as bacterial, viral, or genetic agents, in causing diseases. More recently, the human services model with its focus on social factors has challenged the medical model. We will first take a detailed look at the medical model.

THE MEDICAL MODEL

As applied to mental or psychological disorders, this model stresses the causative role of factors *within* the individual. Adherents of the medical model do not claim that all so-called "mental" disorders are due to biological or organic factors. In fact, they make a distinction between *organic* and *functional* disorders.

The organic disorders are caused by physical abnormalities of the brain, nervous system, and other internal systems. Epilepsy, senility, some kinds of retardation, and certain psychotic states are examples of disorders in which some physical abnormality has been found to play a role. Organic disorders may be caused by inherited defects, chemical imbalances, viral infection, malnutrition, and various drugs and poisons. Those associated with physical damage are likely to be long-standing, while those associated with drugs may represent temporary disorders of brain function.

The functional disorders, in contrast, are due to psychological factors operating within the individual. These might include poorly controlled drives and impulses, unrealistic ideas, and unresolved conflicts. Addictions, antisocial tendencies, neuroses, and some psychotic reactions are classified as functional disorders. This means that the major causes are presumed to relate to the personality of the individual rather than to any physical defects. There are some disorders, such as the schizophrenias, that cannot be classified with great confidence because of doubt about the causes.

Medical Procedure

Regardless of whether a disorder is organic or functional, the procedures of medical practice can be applied to it. This means that a certain psychological disorder can be approached as though it were a physical disorder like measles or tuberculosis. The first step in medical and psychiatric practice is to arrive at a *diagnosis*, which means to classify and label the disorder according to the presenting symptoms. Next comes the formulation of a *treatment plan*, which may include medication, shock therapy, psychotherapy, and/or confinement to a mental hospital. The treatment is related to the *prognosis*, which is an educated guess about what degree of recovery can be expected for the patient.

For example, a young man became despondent over losing his fiancee to someone else. He made the rather dramatic suicidal gesture of threatening to jump from the roof of an apartment building but let himself be talked down by the police. He was taken to a community mental health center and admitted to a ward for observation and treatment. He was diagnosed as suffering from a depressive reaction. The treatment plan included brief counseling sessions to help him ventilate his feelings of hurt, loss, and anger. In addition, he was put on a mood-elevating drug. In view of his history of good functioning, the prognostic outlook was favorable. This is the medical model in action: a psychological or emotional reaction is handled with the basic procedures of medicine.

Treatment Approaches of the Medical Model

Since the medical model is accepted by many professionals employed in mental hospitals, prisons, schools, mental retardation centers, and other settings, the human services worker needs to understand something about the treatments derived from this model.

By far the most common treatment approach is drug therapy, sometimes called chemotherapy. Recent years have seen the development of a wide variety of powerful drugs that are capable of modifying mood and emotional states. The major tranquilizers, for example, are a class of drugs first introduced to this country in the 1950s. They quickly became a major treatment modality in psychiatric clinics and hospitals when it was found that they suppress or cover over some of the disturbed behavior of psychotic persons. They are likely to be used when a patient shows extreme tension, aggressiveness, delusions, hallucinations, or insomnia. Without producing a cure, they often make the patient more manageable by staff. Thorazine, Mellaril, and Stelazine are the trade names of three of the most frequently used drugs of this type.

Another popular therapy involves the use of minor tranquilizers to reduce tension and anxiety. They are so frequently prescribed by physicians in private practice that one of seven Americans is estimated to use them on a frequent basis (Mehr, 1983). These drugs, which include the familiar Valium and Librium, are often effective in reducing anxiety but have been criticized on the grounds they really do not help the person get at the source of the problem.

Another relatively recent drug therapy is the use of lithium carbonate for persons suffering from manic-depressive disorders. It is particularly useful in controlling the excessive elation, irritability, and talkativeness of the manic phase. Another group of mood-altering drugs are the antidepressants, which have been effective in combating certain types of severe depressive states.

Drugs are only one type of medical model treatment. A number of convulsive therapies have been developed for use with psychiatric patients. The most common of these in current use is the famous, or infamous, electroconvulsive therapy (ECT). Used extensively in private psychiatric hospitals, it involves administering an electric shock at the patient's temples for a brief (.1 to .5 second) duration. Treatments are given several times a week and may continue for five or six weeks. It is used mainly to treat persons who are depressed, especially when there is no obvious external stress such as loss of job or divorce. Probably no other form of therapy evokes such negative feelings as this one. Despite modern trappings, it appears to many like some kind of medieval torture. During the 1950s, there were many reports of abuse and sloppy administration of the procedure. It was used with a wide variety of disorders, and results were often unfavorable. Recent refinements of the technique have reduced side effects and increased its effectiveness.

Another medical-type treatment called psychosurgery has also been sharply criticized by human services workers. The most frequently used procedure of this type is the lobotomy, which involves cutting nerve fibers connecting the frontal lobes to other parts of the brain. Literally thousands of these operations were performed on mental patients during the years before the introduction of major tranquilizers. It was used mainly with patients who were so aggressive that they presented severe management problems. Unfortunately, the procedure often produces serious irreversible side effects such as lethargy, childish behavior, and mental dullness. Although positive results have sometimes been reported, many critics believe these are not impressive enough to justify its continued use.

Other therapies related to medical approaches, such as rehabilitation and occupational therapy, are described in Chapter Six.

Criticism of the Medical Model

A number of authors have cried out against the injustices that arise from the medical/psychiatric approach to mental illness. Szasz (1973), for example, charged that his psychiatric colleagues were guilty of persecuting mental patients under the guise of treating them. In particular, he questioned the validity of labeling certain persons as mentally ill when, in fact, they were merely suffering from problems in living. Mental illness, he went on, is a myth, not a genuine disease at all. The underlying purpose of labeling (diagnosing) certain persons as mentally ill is to provide society with a convenient means of getting rid of undesirable deviates. These are typically persons who have committed no real crime but are bothersome, annoying, or frightening to other people.

Along the same lines, Kovel (1980) charged that psychiatry's focus on the psychological aspects of the patient "is a handy way of mystifying social reality" (p. 73). The same author argued that psychiatrists exert social control over social misfits by telling them they have a case of this or that, and imposing a treatment plan. What is left out of the process is acknowledgment of the damaging role of poverty, poor housing, lack of opportunity, unemployment, and other social ills.

Those who endorse the human services model, to be discussed next, would probably agree with these criticisms of the medical model.

THE HUMAN SERVICES MODEL

The human services model received its major impetus during the 1960s. It was closely associated with social movements devoted to bettering the lives of oppressed minority groups. Human services workers thought of themselves as warriors, and sometimes even as revolutionaries. Impatient with the medical model and its emphasis on the inner person, these workers wanted to bring about great social changes by improving the environment. In particular, they focused on the harsh external conditions that oppressed the lives of the poor. These workers were not interested in formulating complex theories. Their attitude was pragmatic—that is, based on a spirit of practical problem solving (Fisher, Mehr, & Truckenbrod, 1974). The idea was if something worked, use it.

The basic assumption of this model is that maladaptive behaviors are often the result of a failure to satisfy basic human needs. The first step in intervention is not diagnosis but an assessment of the victim's life situation with a view to discovering what needs are not being met. The person may be in need of decent housing, medical attention, a job, or a more adequate diet. Other persons may not lack for these essentials but may be extremely lonely and in need of social interaction. It is not surprising that emotional problems are intensified by such factors as unemployment, loneliness, and low social status. Society, not the individual, is seen as the culprit. Therefore, society must be prodded to provide the needed goods and services.

Hansell's Theory

One of the most elaborate theories used by human services workers is Hansell's (1970) motivation theory. He theorized that persons have to make seven basic attachments in order to meet their needs. If a person does not make each attachment, he or she goes into a crisis or state of stress. Here is a list of the seven basic attachments, along with signs of failure of each one:

1. Food, water, and oxygen, along with informational supplies. Signs of failure: boredom, apathy, and physical disorder.
2. Intimacy, sex, closeness, and opportunity to exchange deep feelings. Signs of failure: loneliness, isolation, and lack of sexual satisfaction.
3. Belonging to a peer group such as social, church, or school group. Signs of failure: not feeling part of anything.
4. A clear, definite self-identity. Signs of failure: feeling doubtful and indecisive.
5. A social role that carries with it a sense of being a competent member of society. Signs of failure: depression and a sense of failure.
6. The need to be linked to a cash economy via a job, a spouse with income, social security benefits, or other ways. Signs of failure: lack of purchasing power, possibly an inability to purchase essentials.
7. A comprehensive system of meaning with clear priorities in life. Signs of failure: sense of drifting through life, detachment, and alienation.

Human Services Interventions

Hansell's scheme lends itself readily to the task of helping the client in practical ways. The worker needs to find ways to satisfy some of the client's unmet needs. The client's complaints are related to the signs of failure described above. Sometimes the nature of the unmet need is blatantly obvious, but at other times may be quite subtle. The client is not always able to cooperate with the helper. For example, the client may deny having a certain need, or may feel demeaned by accepting the kind of help available. The aim of human services counseling is usually to link the client with sources of satisfaction. This might involve helping the client secure welfare benefits, find a job, join a club or social group, return to school, or locate a temporary shelter. The focus is on solving problems here and now. Past problems and bad experiences may be discussed but they are not the main focus of counseling.

The human services worker is usually a generalist trained to work in a variety of agencies to provide across-the-board services to clients and their families (S.R.E.B., 1978). By definition, a generalist is familiar with a variety of therapeutic approaches rather than specializing in one or two areas. The main goal of intervention is usually to identify the needs and problems of the client and then to provide resources to meet the needs and solve the problem. Of course, the worker is not usually able to meet needs in a direct, personal sort of way but is familiar with service providers in the community. These include doctors, ministers, lawyers, police, parole officers, mental health professionals, and just about anyone else who may be able to help the client. If needed services are not available, the worker may be able to influence the community to set up new programs. More of this is discussed in Chapter Eight.

A wide variety of roles may be played by the human services worker, each calling for special skills. The worker may be an advocate, a mobilizer, a teacher, or an administrator. The skills required by these activities are discussed in further detail in Chapter Five. The immediate point is that the underlying purpose is usually the same: identifying and meeting the needs of clients.

Human services workers have sometimes criticized mental health professionals (psychiatrists, clinical psychologists, and social workers) for overlooking obvious practical solutions to human problems. One reason for this oversight is that these professionals are often trained in intricate psychological theories and treatment methods. They often see problems as reflecting deep emotional conflicts rather than poverty and other external factors. Psychoanalytic theories in particular confer status and prestige on therapists. One author suggested that the mundane problems of poverty hold little fascination for the middle-class professional who would prefer to psychologize about the poor and prescribe the latest fashion in psychotherapy (Pelton, 1978).

ISSUES UNDERLYING CONFLICT BETWEEN MODELS

The conflict between adherents of the medical and human services models goes far beyond disputes over theory. A host of issues related to power, money, and licensing have not been fully resolved. For example, human services workers maintain that the criteria for delivering service should center around competence to do the job. They point out that indigenous workers who live in the community served are often more effective in helping residents than highly educated professionals. They also point out that paraprofessionals are often able to perform counseling and therapy just as effectively as highly trained personnel. Without denying the usefulness of indigenous workers and paraprofessionals, traditional mental health professionals are likely to emphasize the importance of advanced academic training, degrees, and licenses in determining job duties, salaries, and responsibilities. They see themselves as supervising workers with less academic training. Each side accuses the other of basing claims on narrow self-interest rather than considering the needs of clients.

Although this topic is discussed further in subsequent chapters, we can state here that human services workers are increasing steadily in numbers and assuming more and more responsibility for delivery of services. With this growth has come an increased desire for professional training and status. What is emerging is a new breed of professional, trained not in medical model disciplines but in human services.

SCHOOLS OF THERAPY

The two models just discussed can be regarded as general theoretical frameworks for helping. A number of other more specific theoretical viewpoints can be applied within the broader frameworks. This section highlights three perspectives most commonly used in group and individual approaches to psychological problems. These are psychoanalytic, the humanistic, and the behavioristic schools or systems of therapy.

A "school" in this context is a group of workers who study certain disorders and use similar methods of study. Although the members of a school may disagree about various points, they share certain basic ideas about the causes of psychological disorders. These basic beliefs, in turn, dictate their approach to helping.

New schools typically arise when a group of young researchers begin to question established beliefs. The early psychoanalysts, for example, challenged the prevailing psychiatric opinion of the 1800s that mental disorders were always due to physical defects of the brain or nervous system. The pioneers of analysis studied disorders known as neuroses that seemed to be due to emotional rather than physical factors. The psychoanalytic movement, which grew out of this early work, eventually became the dominant approach to mental health during the middle decades of this century. More recently, the psychoanalytic school itself has been challenged by adherents of opposing schools. These later developments cannot be fully appreciated without understanding the basic ideas of psychoanalysis.

THE PSYCHOANALYTIC VIEWPOINT

The development of psychoanalysis is very much associated with Sigmund Freud and his followers. Actually, many of Freud's insights, such as the idea of the unconscious mind, had already been discovered by others (Schultz, 1975). There is no doubt, however, that Freud was responsible for shaping psychoanalysis into a coherent system of thought. Under Freud's direction, psychoanalysis became one of the influential movements of modern times.

Major Freudian Concepts

The major idea that evolved from psychoanalysis was that neurotic symptoms are due to a conflict within the patient. Neurotic symptoms include *phobias,* which involve an intense fear of a specific stimulus such as enclosed places; *obsessions,* which involve the repeated intrusions of certain unwanted thoughts into consciousness; and *compulsions,* which require the patient to repeatedly perform some ritualistic act such as hand-washing. These and similar complaints are the result of a conflict between a person's sexual and aggressive urges, on the one hand, and society's demands for control of these impulses, on the other (Maddi, 1972). The neurotic symptoms represent attempts to resolve the conflict. For example, a patient may suffer from a compulsion to wash hands many times a day. This may be an attempt to reduce guilt about urges to masturbate or perform some other "unclean" act. The person is not consciously aware of the underlying desire. According to Freudian theory, the desire must be made conscious and the conflict resolved before the symptom will go away.

In Freudian terms, the personality is made up of three subsystems: the id, the ego, and the superego. The *id* is the seat of primitive instincts such as sexual and aggressive drives. This part of the personality wants what it wants—now. It is the first system to appear in the development of the child. The *ego* is gradually developed to help the child attain gratification in a realistic and socially acceptable manner. The ego employs reason and logic, and is concerned with helping the person survive in the world. The *superego*, similar to the conscience, is an outgrowth of the taboos and moral values of the society as interpreted by the parents. It aims to inhibit desires that are regarded as wicked or immoral. These three forces are in constant interaction, one factor that makes the theory very complex.

When the ego, the "executive" of personality, is confronted with id impulses that are threatening to get out of control, anxiety and guilt feelings are aroused. In some instances, the anxiety is reduced by coping with the impulses in a satisfactory way. A young person may, for example, decide to gratify sexual urges in the context of marriage. When a realistic resolution of conflict is not available, the ego employs a defense mechanism to reduce tension. For example, the entire conflict may be repressed—that is, blocked from awareness. Or the desire may be expressed in some disguised or symbolic way. For example, aggressive urges may be discharged in sports and games, while erotic feelings may be expressed in artistic pursuits.

Therapeutic Concepts

Early in his career, Freud began to work with Josef Breuer, a Viennese physician who pioneered in treating neurotics. Breuer treated a number of patients whose symptoms were "hysterical" in nature— that is, due to emotional rather than physical factors. Some of these patients suffered memory losses or paralysis of certain organs but had no physical defect that could account for the symptoms. Breuer treated them with hypnosis, the method used by earlier therapists. Under hypnosis, patients were often able to recall painful experiences, called traumas, associated with the onset of the symptoms. Breuer found that if the patient could relive the painful emotions associated with the trauma, the symptoms often disappeared. This was the beginning of the "talking cure," a method based on uncovering feelings and experiences buried in the unconscious.

Free Association.   Freud carried on the "talking cure" with new patients. He gradually developed the technique of free association, in which the patient lies on a couch and is encouraged to say anything that comes to mind, no matter how embarrassing it may seem. The basic aim was to bring into conscious awareness any memories or thoughts that had been repressed—that is, pushed into the unconscious because of their threatening nature. While free associating, clients sometimes "blocked"—that is, became unable to bring emotionally charged thoughts into conscious awareness. Freud regarded this as a sign of resistance, which can be defined as any tactic or behavior that works against the production of unconscious material. All clients resist therapy at one time or another. Freud recognized that resistances must be approached with caution since they protect the patient from unbearable anxiety. Overcoming resistances became a regular part of analytic therapy.

Transference.   Freud found that during therapy his clients sometimes experienced feelings, attitudes, and defenses toward him that were derived from previous significant relationships. It seemed as if these feelings and attitudes had been transferred from the past to the present. The client reacted to him as though he were mother, father, or some important figure. Occasionally, patients seemed to fall in love with him, and wanted very much to please him. Or sometimes the client would be very hurt if strong feelings were not reciprocated.

According to Freud's theory, transference reactions imply that the client is generalizing from past experience. If the mother was warm and overprotective, the client assumes that the analyst will also behave in this way. Over the years, analysis of transference became a central feature of analysis because it provided a vehicle for resolving old conflicts. Analysis of transference made it possible for analysts to work toward a radical change in the personality of the client.

The goals of psychoanalytic therapy have changed greatly over the years. The aim of the early work was simply to relieve neurotic symptoms, while later analysts aimed to bring about significant personality change. In this sense, psychoanalysis is the most ambitious system of therapy, one reason why therapy may take many years.

Psychoanalytically Oriented Psychotherapy

The form of treatment developed by Freud came to be known as classical or orthodox psychoanalysis. It required three, four, or even five sessions a week, and could go on for many years. Free association, dream analysis, and analysis of transference were the major technical methods. As the analytic movement grew and its practitioners emigrated to America and other parts of Europe, the treatment was adapted to different cultures. Psychoanalysis became very popular in this country during the 1930s and 1940s, but it was streamlined to suit American needs and tastes. The number of sessions was reduced to one or two a week, an armchair was usually substituted for the couch, and there was relatively greater emphasis on solving present-day problems as opposed to delving into the past. Many psychiatric clinics and mental hospitals employed this modified analytic approach in treatment and training.

Early Revisionists: Adler and Jung

Due in part to his forceful personality, Freud gained many followers during the early decades of this century. However, some of them found themselves unable to accept critical aspects of his theory. For example, two of his early followers, Alfred Adler and Carl Jung, disputed Freud's claim that repressed sexual drives were the primary cause of neurotic symptoms. To Freud's dismay, they both advanced major revisions of his theory and went on to organize psychoanalytic schools of their own. Both argued that Freud had not fully realized the importance of social and cultural factors in shaping personality. Beyond this area of agreement, Adler and Jung went on to construct widely divergent theories.

Adler's Individual Psychology. Adler firmly believed that human beings are social beings first and foremost, that personality is formed by patterns of relationships with others. Adler's best known concepts are those of *inferiority* and *compensation.* He taught that everyone suffers inferiority feelings to some degree because each of us was, in fact, inferior to adults during childhood. In addition, some individuals feel inferior to peers and siblings because of real or imaginary deficiencies. Some children are smaller, weaker, or uglier than others, while others compare themselves unfavorably in regard to intelligence or material possessions. The greater the intensity of inferiority feelings, the greater the need to compensate by striving to be superior. The person may seek power, strive for perfection, or develop some special skill or talent to the utmost. The ways in which a person strives for mastery become part of his or her style of life.

Adler developed an approach to treatment that was more direct than the classic approach. He sat opposite the patient and focused the discussion on the patient's attitude toward other people and society. He believed that most people who needed treatment were excessively selfish in their outlook on life. Neurotics, criminals, pampered children, and various social misfits had one feature in common: they thought only or primarily about themselves. The path to psychological health was to develop a strong "social interest." This meant being helpful to others, seeing them as worthy, and controlling one's urge to compete irrationally against others for power. In general, Adler's approach is very congenial to those with a human services orientation. He was very much interested in improving the lives of ordinary people, and is credited with being one of the first to set up child guidance centers for the benefit of working class families.

Jung's Analytical Psychology. Jung is regarded as the most complex and difficult of the analysts, some of his concepts verging on mysticism. More than any other analyst, he stressed the importance of the religious and spiritual side of human nature. He delved into occult writings and sought insights into the nature of man by studying the dreams and myths of primitive peoples. *Man and His Symbols,* edited by Jung (1964), is a good introduction to this mysterious world.

Jung agreed with Freud that behavior is often influenced by ideas buried in the unconscious mind. He went on from there to suggest that the unconscious mind is made up of two layers. The first is the *personal unconscious,* which contains personal experiences that have been repressed or forgotten. The second layer is the *collective unconscious,* which contains experiences inherited from our ancestors. All share this collective unconscious, which includes images and ideas never experienced on a personal level. These ancient experiences are embodied in *archetypes,* which are significant racial memories passed from one generation to the next. Some of the archetypes include the Great Mother, the Hero, the Wise Old Man, and God—images that recur in every human society. These archetypes are based on common human experiences such as birth, love, conflict, and death. They can be recovered through dreams and fantasies, and can be tapped to enhance creative abilities and to provide insights about our personal development.

Jung's approach to treatment stressed the client's need for personal growth. He observed that many of his patients, particularly those of middle years, complained of a sense of stagnation in their lives. They had completed certain of life's tasks, such as raising their children, and now found themselves without any clear sense of direction. Jung used dream analysis and fantasy to help clients get in touch with their true selves. The images that appeared in fantasy productions were sometimes derived from personal experience, sometimes from the deeper layer of the collective unconscious. Each could provide clues about what was needed to get the personality moving toward growth and fulfillment. Jung's ideas about growth of personality influenced the humanistic theorists, to be discussed later.

Later Revisionists: The Neo-Freudians

The next generation of psychoanalytic thinkers included Karen Horney, Erich Fromm, Erik Erikson, and Harry Stack Sullivan. Though they remained in the psychoanalytic tradition, they each departed considerably from the Freudian model. The theories of these neo-Freudians are too complex to be presented in detail. However, some of their major ideas can be briefly reviewed.

The neo-Freudians highlighted social factors in the development of personality. Horney, for example, believed that the child's dominant motive is not gratification of instincts but a striving for security and acceptance by others. When important persons in the family are perceived as hostile and ungiving, the child experiences painful feelings of anxiety. Horney discerned three major trends or tactics that children use to reduce this anxiety and increase security. Some children find themselves in a situation in which moving toward others makes them feel safe; these children may become submissive and self-effacing in their dealings with others. The second pattern shown by some youngsters is a moving away from others; these children seem to act on the premise that if they don't get too close to others, they won't get hurt. The third pattern is moving against others, which may take the form of rebellious and antisocial behavior. The other neo-Freudians developed somewhat different ideas but agreed with Horney's emphasis on social interaction.

The new revisionists all doubted Freud's assumption that the adult personality was shaped by early childhood experiences. For example, Sullivan, who founded the interpersonal theory of psychiatry, believed that experiences during the juvenile and adolescent phases could have a profound impact on personality. He felt it was crucial for a youngster to have some chums and confidants during these difficult periods of life. Without close friends, the isolated child runs the risk of sexual difficulties and even serious psychiatric illness in early adulthood. Sullivan attributed his own serious psychological problems to loneliness and isolation during his juvenile years (Perry, 1982). He identified strongly with the young schizophrenic patients he treated at psychiatric hospitals. His treatment approach emphasized the creation of a therapeutic ward environment, and he was one of the first to train ward attendants and other paraprofessionals in the daily treatment of these patients. His approach is therefore of considerable interest to human services workers who are treating patients in mental hospitals.

Along with the other neo-Freudians, Erikson (1963) stressed the social aspects of human development. He taught that at each stage of life, the person tries to establish an equilibrium between the self and the social world. At each phase of development, the person is faced with a task or a crisis to be resolved. For example, the infant's basic task is to develop a sense of trust in self, others, and the world. Obviously, the infant is totally dependent on others for survival. In an atmosphere of insecurity, the child may develop a sense of mistrust that can retard progress and color later relationships with others. At each later phase, the person is faced with another crisis. Obviously, it would be helpful for the human services worker to have an understanding of the developmental tasks faced by clients at various stages. It is sometimes important to examine the choices a client made at previous stages of life, and to consider how these are affecting current functioning.

Criticisms of Psychoanalysis

No other psychological theory has been subjected to such intense criticism as has psychoanalysis. Some of the early attacks were harsh and highly emotional in tone, and may have been triggered by Freud's exposure of sexual problems in Victorian Europe. The day is past when professionals are shocked by frank discussion of sexual matters. However, certain other criticisms are not based on outraged sensibilities but on serious doubts about the scientific credibility of psychoanalysis.

Many critics have noted that analysts often base conclusions on what patients remember about their past experience. As Freud himself discovered, there is no way to be sure if these anecdotal reports represent real events, fantasies, or some combination of fact and fancy. There is rarely any independent verification of the events reported by patients. Thus, there is some basis for the criticism that psychoanalysts have built a huge theoretical structure on a weak foundation.

Another serious criticism is that analytic theory lacks predictive value, and relies on after-the-fact explanations (Hall & Lindzey, 1978). For example, it is not very helpful to be informed that a client attempted suicide because of a strong death wish, since the "explanation" is circular. In other words, the strong death wish is inferred from the behavior itself. Other behaviors are explained in terms of complex interactions between id, ego, and superego. If a patient gives in to sexual impulse, this might be interpreted as a victory for the id over the superego. If the impulse is repressed, the superego has won. The problem is that psychoanalysis does not provide clear rules for predicting *in advance* if one or another part of personality is going to dominate future behavior.

Another type of criticism centers around the general failure of analysts to report on the effects of their therapy. Considering the popularity of analytic thinking during the 1920s to the mid-1950s, there were very few reports of the outcome of the treatment. Those reports that did surface usually did not include a control group —that is, a comparison group of patients who received no treatments or some other treatment. Prochaska (1979) reviewed some of the relevant studies and concluded that there is still insufficient evidence to judge the effectiveness of analytic therapy. Certainly, there is little to support the claim that psychoanalytic therapy is superior to briefer forms of therapy. The failure of analysts to provide objective evidence about the effects of their therapy was one of the factors that led to its partial eclipse after the 1950s.

Perhaps the most scathing denouncements of Freudian theory have come from those with a human services orientation. Certain implications of Freudian theory can be seen as harmful to the interests of disadvantaged persons. For example, Freud's idea that the child develops an irrational, unconscious mind early in life seems to imply that behavior is largely determined by these unconscious forces. Maladaptive or antisocial behavior is seen as the outcome of internal forces beyond rational control, thus downplaying the role of here-and-now environmental events. As Fisher et al. (1974) pointed out, mental health workers with an analytic point of view focus their efforts on "curing" patients, a process that involves a long search into the past history of the patient. It is also accepted that diagnosis and treatment are lengthy and complicated, requiring considerable expertise and training. The therapy itself tends to require considerable verbal and intellectual skills on the part of the patient. Those who do not possess such skills or a capacity for reflection are looked upon as uninteresting and possibly untreatable cases. These and other aspects of the analytic approach were simply unacceptable to the social activists of the 1960s. They wanted to help people now, and they wanted to do it primarily by changing the environment—rather than changing the person.

Some Useful Applications of Psychoanalytic Concepts

Now that the turbulent sixties and seventies are behind us, human services workers can examine psychoanalysis in a more dispassionate light. There seems no doubt that psychoanalysis is here to stay. Although no longer predominant, it is one of several therapeutic approaches actively competing for students, adherents, and clients. Certain analytic ideas have withstood the test of time and may be useful to human services workers.

The concept of defense mechanisms is probably the most widely used concept in psychotherapy. It is often useful to consider how a client reacts to anxiety and guilt feelings, and perhaps to discuss some alternative ways of dealing with these painful emotions. It is also helpful to the client to review those unpleasant past experiences that may be interfering with present functioning. Without becoming bogged down in the past, it may be important for both worker and client to understand how the client got into his or her current predicament. This review of the past may reveal some self-defeating behaviors that the client needs to modify in the future.

Regardless of theoretical bias, counselors and therapists acknowledge that certain Freudian themes come up again and again in therapy. These include the client's desire to be preferred by the parent of the opposite sex, sibling rivalry, guilt feelings about sex, and fear of closeness or intimacy with another. The therapist can benefit from psychoanalytic insights about these issues without accepting them as doctrine. Regardless of its faults, psychoanalytic theory is probably the most comprehensive available for the study of complex human relationships.

THE HUMANISTIC PERSPECTIVE

The humanistic perspective is not a school with definite organization and clearly established leaders. It represents a kind of informal association of persons who share certain basic philosophical notions. Some of these ideas were derived from existential philosophy, which focuses on the meanings a person gives to his or her experience in the world. The existential approach to therapy is sometimes regarded as a separate school in its own right. However, the humanistic and existential approaches are so closely related that, for present purposes, we will consider them together.

Philosophical Underpinning

The humanist orientation emphasizes the unique qualities of humans, especially their capacity for choice and their potential for personal growth. A major assumption is that the individual is free to choose alternatives in life. Humanists deny the psychoanalytic belief that human behavior is dominated by animalistic drives. There is always a capacity for free will and choice even if the person *feels* trapped by circumstances or compulsive drives. A related assumption is that the person strives toward the highest possible fulfillment of human potentialities. There is potential for growth, for some kind of forward movement, in every human being. In this sense, humanists share a generally optimistic view of human nature.

Carl Rogers, American psychologist and humanist.

The existential/humanist position is to some extent a reaction against the methods of modern science. Existentialists, in particular, argue that science tends to dehumanize people by regarding them as mechanical devices. In this view, science tends to pull people apart in a misguided attempt to see how they work. The person is divided into sensations, feelings, drives, perceptions, thoughts, physical systems, and so on. In this process of analysis, the unique quality of the individual is lost.

Furthermore, humanists maintain that this unique person cannot be understood by a distant objective observer. Real understanding requires getting into the frame of reference of the other person—that is, understanding how the other experiences and perceives the world. Some sort of dialogue between two persons is necessary for the understanding to come about. It is also assumed that both persons engaged in a dialogue are likely to influence and change each other. The human being is never seen as a finished product but as always changing.

The following sections go into more detail about some of the concepts and treatment applications devised by humanistic theorists. Some of the major figures associated with the humanistic approach are Abraham Maslow, the psychologist cited in Chapter One; Carl Rogers (1951, 1961), who founded client-centered therapy; Eric Berne (1964) and Thomas Harris (1967), who developed transactional analysis; and Fritz Perls (1969), the major pioneer of Gestalt therapy. Victor Frankl (1963) and Rollo May (1969) are prominent existential psychologists. We cannot go into detail about the ideas of each of these authors, but we can examine some of the basic concepts related to helping that most of them would endorse.

The Humanistic Approach to Helping

Humanists take a *holistic* view toward understanding their clients. This means that they want to understand the person as a whole, as opposed to breaking the personality into its components. The focus is on this person's private view of the world rather than on objective reality. What a person believes to be true influences behavior whether it is really so or not. If you are convinced that a person dislikes you, this belief governs how you relate to that person even though the other person may not really dislike you.

The humanistic therapist helps the client to clarify feelings, to think more deeply about problems, and to explore all important aspects of the current life situation. The helper provides an atmosphere in which this kind of exploration can safely take place. Unlike other significant persons in the client's life, the therapist has no desire to push the client in one direction or another. In other words, the helper does not want to mold or shape the client into some preconceived image. Clients are therefore free to search for their own special meanings and directions in life.

Implied in what has been said is that humanists are not sympathetic toward the therapist who plays the role of doctor/expert. The humanistic counselor does not study, direct, or analyze the client. Nor does the humanist assume a superior position from which to look down on the client. Counseling is a dialogue between two persons, each with his or her unique experiences and perceptions. The helper does not have instant remedies or solutions to life's problems but helps clients struggle toward their own answers.

Self-Actualization. The humanistic approach to helping is based on the concept that self-actualization is a primary motivating force in human behavior. Rogers (1959) defined this motivational force as "the inherent tendency of the organism to develop all its capacities in ways which serve to maintain or enhance the organism" (p. 196). Crystals, plants, and animals grow without any conscious fuss; the same kind of natural ordering process is available to guide the development of the person (Whyte, 1960). Very often, however, the forces of self-actualization bump up against conditions that other persons impose (Meador & Rogers, 1979). In other words, the child may be loved and approved only when behaving in certain specified ways—for example, when good, cheerful, productive, successful, or competitive. These conditions begin to warp the natural process of self-actualization. Often, the child totally accepts these conditions since he or she has no basis on which to question them. In therapy, the person has the opportunity to resume growth in the atmosphere of acceptance provided by the therapist.

Maslow's (1954) concept of self-actualization is contained in this sentence: "What a man *can* be, he *must* be" (p. 46). This means that individuals must do what they are best equipped to do. One can maximize one's potential as a secretary, administrator, artist, politician, or mechanic. Skills, interests, background, and inherited tendencies all need to be considered in determining areas of maximal fulfillment. Serious difficulties may arise if the drive for self-actualization is thwarted. For example, if a person who wants to help disadvantaged people must work as an accountant, or someone with artistic ability is employed as a sales clerk, the need to fulfill potentials is not being satisfied. The individual may feel out of place and may be haunted by a sense of self-betrayal.

Responsibility.   Many people who seek counseling have been thwarted in their push for self-actualization by a tendency to live for others. All too often, they have been influenced by parents, teachers, or peers to pursue goals that are uncongenial to their true natures. Often, the growing child seeks approval from elders by living up to their demands and expectations. Some adults who seek help remain stuck in patterns of childish dependency. They have not fully accepted responsibility for finding their own path in life. Perls (1969) suggested that a prime goal of therapy is "to make the patient *not* depend upon others, but to make the patient discover from the very first that he can do many things, much more than he thinks he can do" (p. 29). He added that frustration is essential for growth because it helps people to muster their own resources and to discover that they can do well on their own. The therapist has to be alert to the manipulations of clients who may try to get the therapist to tell them what to do. The general thrust of humanistic therapy is to get the client to assume responsibility for thoughts, feelings, and direction in life. Only then is the person really free to pursue self-actualization.

The Self-Concept.   The self-concept is the core or center of the personality around which experiences are organized and interpreted. The "I" or the "self" includes how we see ourselves, how we think others perceive us, and how we would like to be. The self-concept begins to develop early in life. The child begins to evaluate certain experiences as good and bad, and, quite naturally, takes on the values of parents, teacher, and peers. However, values imposed from the outside may require the child to ignore inner feelings. For example, if the child learns that anger or sexual urges are bad or not valued, the child may block these urges from awareness.

Rogers (1951) suggested that maladjustment occurs when the person denies to awareness significant experiences that do not fit the self-concept. When one's behavior and experiences do not mesh with the way one sees oneself, there is a lack of "congruence," which may lead to tension and anxiety. One goal of therapy, then, is to help the client experience and accept these denied experiences. The client may, for example, come to accept hostile feelings as OK in some situations. The hope is that this acceptance will reduce the tension and conflict.

Criticisms of the Humanistic Approach

Some critics believe that humanists exaggerate the benefits of the therapists' accepting attitude. It may take more than an attitude of positive regard to transform the client into a self-actualizing person. When Carl Rogers attempted to treat schizophrenics with this approach, the results were not especially impressive (Rogers, 1967). It may be unrealistic to expect one caring relationship to overcome years of negative life experiences.

Nor is it always helpful to emphasize that people have choices. Many poor, discouraged people do not see themselves as having many choices, and they really do not have the range of options available to affluent persons. They may need some practical kinds of help and some new opportunities before they can experience their potential for growth.

The humanistic approach does not seem to apply to patients who are not intellectually capable of making their own decisions. Young children and many retarded persons and mental patients are not really able to make decisions about direction in life. The major decisions must be made by the persons responsible for their care. Although every client can be treated in a respectful way, it often doesn't make sense to treat the client as an equal. The behaviorist approach, to be discussed, seems to lend itself more effectively to treatment of people with limited potential.

Positive Aspects of the Humanistic Approach

The most useful aspect of the humanistic perspective is that it provides the human services worker with a sophisticated understanding of the helping relationship. Humanistic therapists have gone far beyond armchair speculation on this issue. Credit must be given to Rogers, his associates, and other humanists for providing solid research evidence about qualities in a relationship that facilitate positive change. Since this evidence is discussed in Chapter Five, there is no need to review it here. Suffice it to say that humanists have contributed significantly to improving the tools and skills of the counselor.

THE BEHAVIORISTIC MODEL

Unlike psychoanalysis, behaviorism did not begin as a method of treating psychological problems, but has its roots in experimental studies of animal and human behavior. Dating back to the previous century, it began as a reaction against psychological studies in which human subjects were asked to report on their sensations and perceptions. The early behaviorists felt that psychology wasn't getting anywhere by gathering vague reports of conscious experience. They argued that there was no way to verify a person's private experiences. They proposed, instead, that psychology be put on a firm scientific footing by studying overt behavior under such conditions that two or more observers could agree that a particular action or response had taken place. Psychology, they said, should focus on the effect of the environment on the behaving organism, and should provide precise measurements of both the stimulating conditions and the resulting behavior. Private events such as dreams, fantasies, and thoughts would be ignored until techniques were invented to measure them in some verifiable fashion.

The early behaviorists believed that important laws governing behavior could be revealed by studying the behavior of animals—cats, dogs, rats, pigeons—in carefully controlled experimental situations. The emphasis was on conditioning, which involved situations that brought about a change in the behavior of the organism. Two general kinds of conditioning were identified, and were designated as *classical* and *operant* conditioning. It is important for the counselor/therapist to understand both types since therapeutic approaches have been derived from each.

Classical Conditioning

Classical conditioning involves the study of reflexes—that is, responses elicited by certain stimuli in an automatic fashion. Such responses do not have to be learned or acquired by the individual. For example, an animal or person will respond with an eye blink if a puff of air is applied to the eye. Another automatic response in some creatures is to salivate when eating or chewing. Ivan Pavlov's (1927) studies of this salivary reflex in dogs are among the best-known experiments in the field of psychology. The basic experimental approach was as follows. Before conditioning, surgery was performed on the dog's cheek so that the saliva could be collected and measured precisely. During training, a bell, buzzer, or some other neutral stimulus was sounded just before food was given to the dog. As it ate, saliva would naturally begin to flow. The neutral stimulus and the food were presented over and over on subsequent feedings.

Eventually, the dog salivated to the neutral stimulus even when no food was presented. Pavlov had succeeded in conditioning the response to a stimulus that would not elicit it before training. He also observed that this conditioned response would eventually fade away—became extinguished—if the food were no longer presented.

Classical conditioning would be of limited interest if it applied only to dogs or salivary responses. Its importance stems from the fact that conditioning occurs in many real-life situations. In particular, the laws of classical conditioning seem to underlie the fear response. Many of us have been conditioned by life events to fear certain objects and situations such as dogs, water, examinations, snakes, or enclosed spaces. Fears can also become associated with social situations involving persons of the opposite sex, authority figures, crowds, and so on. Once a fear has become associated with a particular situation, it may not help very much to be told that the fear is irrational or exaggerated. Behaviorists have developed some useful techniques, to be discussed, for helping people to overcome their fears.

Operant Conditioning

The other major type of conditioning, called either operant or instrumental, usually involves responses that are under voluntary control. This is in contrast to the involuntary reflex involved in the classical method. In the operant approach, the animal or person is moving freely in the environment. American psychologist E. L. Thorndike (1913) studied ways in which the behavior of animals could be influenced by certain environmental inputs. He found that if a response is followed by a pleasant or satisfying consequence, the response is likely to be repeated or strengthened. Similarly, if a response is followed by an unpleasant or punishing event, it is less likely to occur. These simple principles were called the *law of effect*.

In more recent times, B. F. Skinner is probably the best-known investigator of operant behavior. The basic principles can be demonstrated in the lab by means of the Skinner box. This is nothing more than a chamber with a lever and a food tray. A hungry rat placed in the box first explores its surroundings. Eventually it pushes down on the lever, which causes a pellet of food to drop into the cup. The rat soon begins to press the lever more and more frequently because this response is reinforced—that is, followed by a desirable or gratifying outcome.

In everyday life, our behavior is constantly influenced by patterns of rewards and punishments. Children are trained by parents and teachers by means of good things to eat, grades, and expressions of approval. "Bad" or socially unacceptable behaviors may be fol-

B. F. Skinner, a major spokesman for the behavioristic tradition.

lowed by either punishment or taking away desired rewards. The general pattern continues into adult life when others shape our behavior by rewarding certain performances with paychecks, promotions, or verbal praise while discouraging other actions with various punishments and deprivations. The principles of operant conditioning have been applied to a number of therapeutic goals. Some will be reviewed in a subsequent section, but first we look at the beginnings of applying behaviorism in therapy.

John B. Watson and Little Albert

John B. Watson was an American psychologist who coined the term *behaviorism* and did much to make the new approach known to the general public. In his book *Psychology from the Standpoint of a Behaviorist*, which appeared in 1919, and in numerous magazine articles, he argued that the social environmental was a powerful factor in conditioning personality and behavior. He boasted that given control over a child's early environment he could produce a lawyer, doctor, Indian chief, criminal, or just about any kind of adult.

The immediate importance of Watson is that he advanced the idea that behaviorism could be applied to the understanding and treatment of psychological disorders. His experiment with Little Albert, an 11-month-old boy, attracted a good deal of attention (Watson & Rayner, 1920). The purpose of the experiment was to show that an irrational fear, or phobia, could be acquired through conditioning. The experimental procedure was designed to condition a fear of a white rat in Little Albert, who previously was fond of this and other animals. The experimenter, standing behind the boy, struck a steel bar with a hammer when Albert reached out to touch the white rat. The loud noise frightened the child and made him cry. After this procedure was repeated a few times, Albert became very fearful at the sight of the animal even without the loud noise. This newly acquired fear of white rats generalized to rabbits and other furry animals as well as to white furry objects such as a lady's muff.

Later, one of Watson's asociates devised a method of treating such fears. Mary Cover Jones (1924) first conditioned a fear of a white rabbit in a child named Peter. She then presented the white rabbit at a distance when Peter was enjoying something to eat. Gradually, she brought the animal closer and closer, taking care not to evoke the fear response. The boy's fear was gradually eliminated, presumably because the once-feared stimulus was progressively associated with pleasant feelings.

The Behavioristic View of Abnormal Behavior

The experiments just described, and similar ones, demonstrated that phobias, irrational fears, and other types of abnormal behavior might be the result of learning and conditioning. The implications of these discoveries had a profound impact on the way in which behaviorists viewed abnormal behavior and "mental illness." They concluded that there is no basic difference between abnormal and normal behaviors, since all behaviors are acquired by the same processes of learning and conditioning. The terms *abnormal* and *maladaptive* are simply labels applied to behaviors that are ineffective, self-defeating, or unacceptable to society. For example, one person may have learned through painful experience that stealing is followed by unpleasant consequences. Another person may have learned that stealing pays because the rewards are immediate and the punishment uncertain, absent, or tolerable. It merely clouds the issues to label some behaviors as antisocial or maladaptive. It is even worse to label certain persons as mentally ill or sick because it implies that they suffer from some mysterious defect of mind or spirit. Rather than labeling people, it might be more constructive to help them unlearn undesirable patterns of response and substitute new, more adaptive patterns.

The Growth of Behavior Therapy

In addition to Watson and his associates, a number of other workers began to apply behaviorist ideas to treatment. By and large, however, behavior therapies remained in the shadow of analytic approaches until about the mid-fifties. Since that time the behaviorist approach has shown extraordinary growth and may soon become the dominant psychological approach to therapy.

Behavioral techniques have been employed in almost every kind of human services facility, including mental hospitals, community mental health centers, correctional facilities, family service agencies, child welfare agencies, schools, and community settings (Sundel & Sundel, 1982). Behavioral therapies have been developed to treat a variety of problems including obesity, smoking, substance abuse, speech difficulties, bed-wetting, tics and similar nervous habits, sexual dysfunctions, and a variety of psychosomatic problems such as ulcer and high blood pressure. Before describing some of these techniques, we need to tell about the assessment procedure that precedes treatment.

Behavioral Assessment. Behavioral treatment begins with a careful assessment of the problematic behavior rather than with the formal diagnosis required by the medical model. The origin of the behavior is considered along with the factors that currently maintain the behavior. This leads to the establishment of *behavioral objectives*—in other words, to specifying the behaviors to be changed and the new behaviors to be acquired. Behaviorists ridicule the pursuit of vague goals in therapy. For example, if a client complains of lacking self-confidence, the behaviorist attempts to pin down exactly how the client behaves in specific social situations. The therapist might ask how the client would behave if he or she were a self-confident person. These behaviors then become the target behaviors and a program is set up to help the client acquire these behaviors. One advantage of this approach to therapy is that the therapist and client have a clear idea of what they are trying to do.

The following sections describe some of the treatment methods devised by behavior therapists.

Systematic Desensitization. Systematic desensitization is probably the most widely used therapy based on classical conditioning. As currently practiced, it is an elaboration of the previously discussed method of treating fears and phobias developed by Watson and his associates. Of modern investigators, Joseph Wolpe (1958, 1969) did the most to refine the technique and to establish its therapeutic usefulness.

Treatment begins with an assessment of the stimuli or situations that evoke the fear response in the client. Water, open spaces, dogs, spiders, snakes, high places, or enclosed areas are some of the specific things or situations that may cause intense fear. The method can also be applied to social fears such as being rejected or criticized by certain persons.

During initial sessions, the client is taught some variant of the progressive relaxation technique originally developed by Jacobson (1938). This technique helps the client to learn to relax by alternately tensing and relaxing the major muscle groups of the body. The next phase of treatment involves making up an anxiety hierarchy—a series of scenes related to one of the client's fears. The scenes are graded in terms of how much fear they evoke. For example, a student who is fearful of examinations might use a hierarchy in which the first scene involves being told by the professor that an exam is scheduled in two weeks. Further scenes bring this dreaded event closer and closer, until the final scene in which the student imagines receiving the exam itself. In treatment, each scene is imagined and paired with the relaxation procedures. When the client can imagine the least threatening scene without tension, the next scene is presented. Eventually, the client is able to imagine every scene in a relaxed manner.

The results of systematic desensitization have generally been quite positive, showing that the treatment generalizes to real-life situations. In some applications, the therapy takes place in real-life situations rather than in the therapist's office. For example, clients who are afraid to fly in an airplane may be taken through a real-life hierarchy of situations that ends with their actually getting into a plane and flying. Regardless of where treatment takes place, the basic aim of this approach is to substitute a desirable response (relaxation) for an undesirable response (tension/anxiety) in a gradual, step-by-step way.

Aversive Therapies. Aversive therapies attempt to reduce an undesirable behavior by means of punishment. The undesirable behavior is followed by electric shock or another unpleasant stimulus. Aversive methods have been used to control head-banging, self-mutilation, and other self-destructive behaviors. Applications have also been developed to treat sexual perversions such as child molestation, incest, and exhibitionism.

The basic approach is to associate the undesirable behavior with pain or extreme discomfort. For example, a 12-year-old retarded girl living in an institution was in the habit of hitting her ear with her arm and shoulder. Her ears were badly battered and needed frequent medical attention. She was referred to a behavior intervention ward, where any attempt to bang her ears was followed by a one-second electric shock to the upper portion of her arms. She was connected to shock apparatus by means of wires that allowed immediate delivery of the shock. This procedure was effective in reducing the behavior. With further training, she was able to do without the machine, and she was eventually reassigned to another ward (Schaefer & Martin, 1975).

Aversive methods do not always work as well as in the above example. Sometimes their effect is temporary and the treatment has to be repeated. In other instances, they may generate rage or excessive fear in the patient. Whenever possible, most therapists prefer to use positive reinforcers to influence behavior.

Token Economies. Perhaps the most ambitious use of positive reinforcement of voluntary behaviors is the token economy used in some mental hospitals and other institutions. The aim is to encourage desirable behaviors by following them with some gratifying reward. Undesirable behaviors are usually discouraged by depriving the patient of a reward. As usual in behavior therapy, the first step is the establishment of target behaviors. These might include self-care, grooming, and housekeeping behaviors as well as socializing with others and satisfactory performance on various jobs around the institution. A certain number of tokens can be earned for each behavior. Typically, the task and rewards are shown on a chart prominently displayed on the ward or section. The tokens can be redeemed at a commissary for cigarettes, candy, magazines, personal articles, and so on. In some settings, the patient can exchange tokens for a rental TV or even the freedom to leave the ward. Ayllon and Azrin (1965) described a token economy at a state mental hospital that was highly effective in modifying social and work behaviors in the patients. There is evidence that longer-term benefits also occur. Another reason for the increasing popularity of the approach is that the principles underlying the treatment are easy to understand. Workers and therapists can learn to apply the methods after a brief training program.

Recent Trends in Behavior Therapy

The methods described so far are based on traditional theories of learning and conditioning. Several new approaches have been put forth in recent decades. These include techniques based on social learning theory, cognitive behavior therapy, and biofeedback. The following sections provide brief summaries of these approaches.

Social Learning Theory and Modeling. Social learning theorists point out that people can learn new responses simply by watching others perform them. For example, everyone has acquired some language and social skills by imitating others. A kid brother might learn something about how to approach girls by watching his older brother in action. Probably all of us have acquired certain actions or mannerisms by watching performers in movies or TV programs. This process of learning by imitation is called modeling by behaviorists.

Modeling has been used in a variety of clinical situations and has been found to be especially effective with children. One important benefit of certain modeling procedures is the reduction of fear in the observer. An example is the use of models to alleviate children's fears of surgery. Seeing a person do well in a difficult situation is encouraging to another who is faced with the same situation.

Assertion Training. Social learning is also involved in the currently popular assertion training. This is designed to help people who have difficulty standing up for their rights in social situations. Some cannot say "no" in a firm, polite fashion, and may end up being manipulated, pushed around, or abused by other people. Assertion training is not only for meek or shy people but may also benefit those who become so aggressive in social situations that they invite counterattack. Both the shy and overly aggressive types need to learn to assert their rights and interests in a socially acceptable way.

The main technique of assertion training is behavioral rehearsal. The client, usually in the context of a group, rehearses responses to social situations such as declining a date, saying no to the salesperson, or correcting a waiter. In the safety of the therapy situation, the client has the opportunity to rehearse various responses while getting feedback from the therapist and group members.

The Cognitive Trend in Behavior Therapy. In recent decades, some behaviorists have departed from the tradition of sticking with the overtly observable aspects of a learning situation. These cognitive behaviorists argue that much human behavior is influenced by thinking, particularly by expectations of future reinforcements. Humans think about past experiences, reach conclusions, and plan future behavior in terms of complex goals (Munsinger, 1983). The environment influences thinking, which in turn influences what the person does in specific situations.

The cognitive/behavior approach to treatment owes a great deal to Albert Ellis's (1973) rational emotive therapy. He maintained that our thoughts and beliefs have a powerful effect on how we behave and feel in certain situations. If one's thoughts about a particular event are irrational, it is likely that one is going to react in a foolish or maladaptive way. For example, if a student believes it is *crucial* to be extremely competent in every one of life's tasks, then failure on an examination may be experienced as some sort of catastrophe. The therapist helps the client by proposing a more rational belief to substitute for the irrational one. The therapist may, for example, suggest that it is desirable to do well on tests but one failure is not the end of the world. This might be followed by an exploration of the reasons (such as poor study habits) for the poor performance, with suggestions for improvement.

Biofeedback. Biofeedback is another relatively recent application of behavior theories. Based on a mix of operant and classical conditioning, biofeedback makes it possible for persons to gain increased control over certain physiological responses not previously under voluntary control. Research has shown that humans and animals can learn to control some of their internal functions, such as heart rate and blood pressure, if given feedback about these responses. The feedback is provided by a machine that measures a certain physiological response in a precise way and converts the information into a signal that the person can see or hear. The feedback may, for example, take the form of a clicking noise, a tone, or a visual display such as deflection of an indicator dial.

Here is an example of how biofeedback might be applied in a clinical setting. A client complains of severe tension headaches that are due to excessive contraction of muscles in the forehead. The therapist attaches to the client's forehead electrodes that register the amount of activity or tension of these muscles. These signals are amplified by the biofeedback device and transformed into a tone of varying pitch. The pitch goes higher as the muscle tension increases, lower as tension is lessened. The client's task is to lower the pitch, and keep it low. As muscle tension is reduced, the tension headache goes away. In subsequent training sessions, the client learns to reduce muscle tension without the biofeedback machine. Just how this learning takes place is still a subject for debate. The immediate point is that the technique often works.

Biofeedback has been used with some success to treat certain cardiac disorders, asthma, insomnia, migraine, speech problems, sexual dysfunction, and chronic anxiety. It is too early for any serious assessment of the effectiveness of biofeedback treatment. New techniques and improvements of older ones are constantly being reported. It can be said that the results so far have been promising and warrant further study. One significant advantage of biofeedback is that it does not carry the risk of side effects.

Criticisms of Behavioristic Approaches

Behavior therapy has been sharply criticized by civil rights advocates who point out that prisoners and mental patients have sometimes been subjected to behavior modification programs against their will. In some instances, inmates in institutions have been pressured to "volunteer" for such programs, while being given the distinct impression that noncompliance would be viewed as a failure to cooperate. This kind of threat must be taken very seriously when authorities have the final say about matters of parole or discharge. Even when participation is truly voluntary, the goals of treatment—the desired behavioral changes—are selected by staff often with little or no input from the "subjects." Humanists doubt that a person can grow toward maturity and self-responsibility by being treated like a robot. Behaviorists view the matter of choice and free will in a quite different way than humanists. B. F. Skinner's (1971) *Beyond Freedom and Dignity* elaborates his view that freedom is an illusion.

Positive Aspects of Behavioristic Approaches

Despite these and other criticisms, behavior therapy is growing rapidly in popularity, is the object of intensive research efforts, and has produced useful treatments for a variety of human illnesses and problems. Certain behavioristic ideas can be usefully applied by human services workers dealing with different kinds of problems. One useful idea is simply the notion of establishing clear-cut behavioral objectives for the helping process. What is the goal of a session with a client? What objectives is a community organization trying to attain? What would have to happen to solve the problem or meet the need? If an unproductive situation seems resistant to change, it may be worthwhile to discover the reinforcing agents that maintain the situation. Once clear-cut objectives are established and a strategy for meeting these goals is decided upon, it is relatively easy to measure progress toward the goal. Whenever possible, it is helpful to gather solid facts and data that indicate progress toward the goal.

WHICH THEORY IS BEST?

Instead of asking which theory is best, it might be better to ask which theory and treatment is the most useful in regard to a particular human problem. Theories are conceptual tools designed to help us understand complex situations. The tool is selected to suit the task to be done. Most helpers agree that certain theories seem to fit a particular client better than others. Probably the majority of skilled helpers are eclectic in approach. This means that they make use of several theories or parts of theories in their work, rather than being firmly devoted to one approach. From the eclectic point of view, it is acceptable to use the concept or treatment that seems appropriate to a particular situation. There is no requirement to be consistent in approach from case to case.

You may now feel somewhat bewildered by the variety of theoretical approaches that can be used in the helping process. Table 4-1 provides a condensed overview of the theories discussed in this chapter. It compares the five major theoretical perspectives along certain dimensions. In other words, it highlights, perhaps exaggerates, the differences between theories. It should help clarify the main points of comparison between these approaches.

ALTERNATIVE PATHS TO PERSONAL FULFILLMENT

This chapter has focused on what might be called the traditional approaches to psychological helping. These are the relatively well-established approaches that enjoy backing from governmental agencies, universities, and other organizations. You may be aware that there are also a number of unusual or alternative routes to psychological well-being. During recent decades, for example, there has been an explosion of interest in Eastern religions such as Buddhism and Hinduism. Spiritual leaders of these faiths, called gurus, have enjoyed considerable popularity, especially in large cities such as New York and San Francisco. Weiten (1983) suggests that this development is due to a need of Americans to turn inward in a quest for peace and serenity. We Americans live in an action-oriented society in which we tend to race about, fulfilling materialist goals. The Eastern religions place relatively greater value on contemplation, intuition, and spirituality than on action and materialism. They offer the possibility of making contact with the inner self, and perhaps experiencing oneself as part of a spiritual universe.

Transcendental meditation is one application of meditative technique that has become popular in this country. The technique has been divorced from its Hindu religious base, simplified, and aggressively marketed to Americans. The meditator sits with eyes closed and focuses attention on a mantra, a specially assigned Sanskrit word. The exercise, which involves repetition of the mantra, is practiced twice daily for 20 minutes. There is evidence that meditation helps a person enter a relaxed state with calming of emotional responses (Wallace & Benson, 1972). Others maintain that these benefits can be achieved by simply resting or relaxing (Holmes, 1984).

A great many other approaches to self-realization have been proposed in recent years. Erhard Seminars Training (est), Scientology, and Silva Mind Control are three examples that have received nationwide attention. All have aroused intense controversy. Some graduates of these programs proclaim that their lives have been positively transformed. Others are less extravagant in their claims

Table 4-1
A Comparison of Major Theoretical Approaches

	Medical Model	Human Services Model	Psychoanalytic Model	Humanistic Model	Behavioristic Model
Complexity of Theory	Complex	Simple	Very complex	Moderately complex	Relatively simple
Past/Present Emphasis	History used to arrive at diagnosis	"Here and now" solutions sought	Strong historical emphasis	"Here and now" emphasized	Present relearning
Assumed Causes of Disorder	Physical, bodily malfunctions	Unmet human needs	Internal conflict/ instinct vs. morals	Experiences that blocked self-actualization	Determined by previous conditioning
Therapeutic Approach	Medication, surgery, and physical treatments	Connect person with source of need satisfaction	Make conflict conscious	Create climate for growth, self-exploration	Change specific behaviors, habits, and thoughts
Length of Treatment	Varies depending on diagnosis	Short-term preferred	Very long-term (years)	Short to intermediate (months)	Usually short-term

and say only that they received valuable insights and gained certain skills from participation. Critics, including Weiten (1983), believe that they are money-making operations based largely on "meaningless psychobabble" (p. 478) rather than on scientific evidence. We leave it to you to delve further into these controversies if you are interested.

SYSTEMS THEORY: THE MODEL OF THE FUTURE?

A major development in recent years has been the widespread application of systems theory to scientific problems. A system, living or nonliving, can be defined as a group of related parts having some function or purpose in common. Miller (1978), in applying systems theory to living organisms, proposed that living systems are part of a sequence of larger systems—such as family, community, and nation —and are also composed of a series of smaller subsystems such as organs, tissues, and cells. Each system has a measure of independence from the larger system of which it is part, but it is also dependent on the larger system in some ways. For example, an individual has some independence from family but also remains part of the family in important ways. Each system has a boundary, transfers energy and information across the boundary, and is controlled by some decider system such as parents in a family (Baruth & Huber, 1984). Feedback mechanisms adjust the behavior of the system in somewhat the same way as a thermostat regulates temperature in a heating system. By these mechanisms, individuals interact with one another so that each influences the other.

Perhaps the major application of systems theory to psychological treatment has been in the field of family therapy. It became apparent to the family therapists of the 1950s and 1960s that traditional theoretical approaches were of limited use in understanding family interactions. It was sometimes observed, for example, that when one member of the family showed improvement, another got worse. The traditional therapies, which had been developed largely in one-to-one treatment, did not provide clear explanations for these kinds of complex interactions. Systems theory was applied to the study of the family and soon became the dominant approach in this field. Systems therapists began to question the prevailing view that the member of the family with the presenting complaint or symptom was the sick one. They also doubted that this symptomatic member, usually a child or adolescent, should be the major focus of treatment. They came around to the view that the identified patient reflects disturbances in the entire family system. Rather than focus on a disturbed family member, these therapists treated the entire family and sometimes even brought in members of the extended family. It was found that present-day conflicts in the family sometimes reflected unresolved issues of previous generations.

One important application of systems theory to the understanding of family dynamics is the notion of circular causality in the family system. This means that interactions between members take place in a circular manner: the behavior of one influences a second, which, in turn, may influence a third, which may return to affect the first (Baruth & Huber, 1984).

The usefulness of systems theory is by no means confined to family therapy. Glasser (1981) is one of several authors who have applied systems to individual therapy, and there have been numerous applications of this approach to specific clinical problems (for example, Schmolling, 1983). Human services workers should also be aware that systems theory can illuminate their understanding of large organizations. After all, many human services workers spend much of their professional time as part of a service delivery system. An instructive and amusing introduction to understanding organitions from a systems point of view was provided by John Gall (1977).

Systems theorists are inclined to believe that their model will eventually come to dominate the behavioral sciences. This remains to be seen. There is no doubt that the influence of this new approach is spreading rapidly.

ADDITIONAL READING

Corey, G. (1982). *Theory and practice of counseling and psychotherapy* (2nd ed.). Monterey, CA: Brooks/Cole.

Guerin, P. (Ed.). (1976) *Family therapy: Theory and practice.* New York: Gardner Press.

Horney, K. (1950). *Neurosis and human growth.* New York: Norton.

Ivey, A. E., & Simek-Downing, L. (1980). *Counseling and psychotherapy: Skills, theories, and practice.* Englewood Cliffs, NJ: Prentice-Hall.

Jung, C. (Ed.). (1964). *Man and his symbols.* Garden City, NY: Doubleday.

Ornstein, R. E. (1976, October). Eastern psychologies: The container vs. the contents. *Psychology Today,* pp. 36–43.

Rogers, C. R. (1977). *Carl Rogers on personal power.* New York: Delacorte Press.

Rosen, R. D. (1977). *Psychobabble.* New York: Atheneum.

Schmolling, P. (1984). Schizophrenia and the deletion of certainty: An existential case study. *Psychological Reports, 54,* 139–148.

Skinner, B. F. (1971). *Beyond freedom and dignity.* New York: Knopf.

Sullivan, H. S. (1953). *Interpersonal theory of psychiatry.* New York: Norton.

Yalom, I. D. (1980). *Existential psychotherapy.* New York: Basic Books.

REFERENCES

Ayllon, T., & Azrin, N. H. (1965). The measurement and reinforcement of behavior of psychotics. *Journal of the Experimental Analysis of Behavior, 8,* 357–383.

Baruth, L. G., & Huber, C. H. (1984). *An introduction to marital theory and therapy.* Monterey, CA: Brooks/Cole.

Berne, E. (1964). *Games people play.* New York: Grove Press.

Ellis, A. (1973). *Humanistic psychotherapy: The rational-emotive approach.* New York: Julian Press.

Erikson, E. H. (1963). *Childhood and society* (2nd ed.). New York: Norton.

Fisher, W., Mehr, J., & Truckenbrod, P. (1974). *Human services: The third revolution in mental health.* New York: Alfred.

Frankl, V. (1963). *Man's search for meaning.* New York: Washington Square Press.

Gall, J. (1977). *Systemantics: How systems work and especially how they fail.* New York: Quadrangle/New York Times Books.

Glasser, W. (1981). *Stations of the mind: New directions in reality therapy.* New York: Harper & Row.

Hall, C. S., & Lindzey, G. (1978). *Theories of personality* (3rd ed.). New York: Wiley.

Hansell, N., Wodarczyk, M., Handlon-Lathrop, B. (1970). Decision counseling method: Expanding coping at crisis in transit. *Archives of General Psychiatry, 21,* 462–467.

Harris, T. (1967). *I'm O.K.—You're O.K.* New York: Avon.

Holmes, D. S. (1984). Meditation and somatic arousal reduction: A review of the experimental evidence. *American Psychologist, 39,* 1–10.

Jacobson, E. (1938). *Progressive relaxation.* Chicago: University of Chicago Press.

Jones, M. C. (1924). A laboratory study of fear: The case of Peter. *Journal of Genetic Psychology, 31,* 308–315.

Jung, C. (Ed.). (1964). *Man and his symbols.* Garden City, NY: Doubleday.

Kovel, J. (1980). The American mental health industry. In D. Ingleby (Ed.), *Critical psychiatry.* New York: Pantheon Books.

Lombroso-Ferrero, G. (1911). *Criminal man.* New York: Putnam's.

Maddi, S. (1972). *Personality theories: A comparative analysis.* Homewood, IL: Dorsey Press.

Maslow, A. H. (1954). *Motivation and personality.* New York: Harper & Row.

May, R. (Ed.). (1969). *Existential psychology* (2nd ed.). New York: Random House.

Meador, B. D., & Rogers, C. R. (1979). *Person-centered therapy.* In R. J. Corsini (Ed.), *Current psychotherapies* (2nd ed.). Itasca, IL: F. E. Peacock.

Mehr, J. (1983). *Human services: Concepts and intervention strategies* (2nd ed.). Boston: Allyn & Bacon.

Miller, J. G. (1978). *Living systems.* New York: McGraw-Hill.

Munsinger, H. (1983). *Principles of abnormal psychology.* New York: Macmillan.

Pelton, L. H. (1978). Child abuse and neglect: The myth of classlessness. *American Journal of Orthopsychiatry, 48,* 608–617.

Pelton, L. H. (1978). Child abuse and neglect: The myth of classlessness. *American Journal of orthopsychiatry, 48,* 608–617.

Perls, F. (1969). *Gestalt therapy verbatim.* Moab, UT: Real People Press.

Perry, H. S. (1982). *Psychiatrist of America: The life of Harry Stack Sullivan.* Cambridge, MA: Belknap Press.

Prochaska, J. O. (1979). *Systems of psychotherapy: A transtheoretical analysis.* Homewood, IL: Dorsey Press.

Rogers, C. R. (1951). *Client-centered therapy.* Boston: Houghton Mifflin.

Rogers, C. R. (1959). A theory of therapy, personality, and interpersonal relationships, as developed in the client-centered framework. In M. S. Koch (Ed.) *Psychology: A study of a science* (Vol. 3). New York: McGraw-Hill.

Rogers, C. R. (1961). *On becoming a person.* Boston: Houghton Mifflin.

Rogers, C. R. (Ed.). (1967). *The therapeutic relationship and its impact: A study of psychotherapy with schizophrenics.* With E. T. Gendlin, D. J. Kiesler, C. Lovax. Madison, WI: University of Wisconsin Press.

Schaefer, H. H., & Martin, P. L. (1975). *Behavioral therapy* (2nd ed.). New York: McGraw-Hill.

Schmolling, P. (1983). A systems model of schizophrenic dysfunction. *Behavioral Science, 28,* 253–267.

Schultz, D. (1975). *A history of modern psychology* (2nd ed.). New York: Academic Press.

Skinner, B. F. (1971). *Beyond freedom and dignity.* New York: Knopf.

S.R.E.B. (1978). Staff roles for mental health personnel: A history and rationale for paraprofessionals. Atlanta: Southern Regional Education Board.

Sundel, M., & Sundel, S. S. (1982). *Behavior modification in the human services* (2nd ed.). Englewood Cliffs, NJ: Prentice-Hall.

Szasz, T. (1973). *The myth of mental illness* (rev. ed.). New York: Harper & Row.

Thorndike, E. L. (1913). *The psychology of learning: Vol. 2. Educational psychology.* New York: Teachers College.

Wallace, R. K., & Benson, H. (1972). The physiology of meditation. *Scientific American, 226,* 84–90.

Watson, J. B., & Rayner, R. (1920). Conditioned emotional reactions. *Journal of Experimental Psychology, 3,* 1–14.

Weiten, W. (1983). *Psychology applied to modern life: Adjustment in the 80s.* Monterey, CA: Brooks/Cole.

Whyte, L. (1960). *The unconscious before Freud.* London: Tavistock Publications.

Wolpe, J. (1958). *Psychotherapy by reciprocal inhibition.* Stanford, CA: Stanford University Press.

Wolpe, J. (1969). *The practice of behavior therapy.* New York: Pergamon Press.

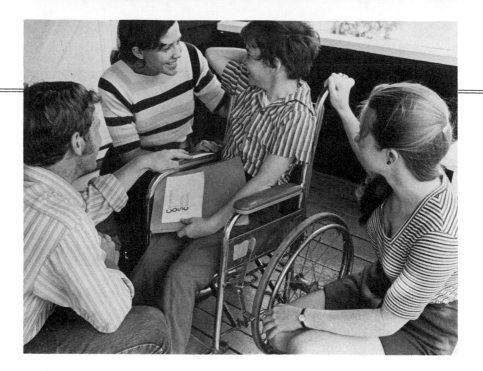

INTRODUCTION

CHARACTERISTICS OF
  EFFECTIVE HELPERS
Empathy
Genuineness
Objective/Subjective Balance
Self-Awareness
Acceptance
Desire to Help
Patience

BASIC HELPING SKILLS
Listening
Communicating
Giving Feedback
Observing
Confronting
Clarifying
Report Writing

THE HUMAN SERVICES WORKER

INTRODUCTION

Chapter Four discussed the major theories of the human services/ mental health field. This chapter begins with the premise that theoretical knowledge alone is not sufficient for effective helping. Some workers know their theory but are ineffective in applying it. Other helpers seem to work well with clients but have very little theoretical background. In short, there is no definite relationship between the effectiveness of helpers and their knowledge of theory. Besides, it often happens that workers using the same theoretical approach vary greatly in effectiveness. What makes one more effective than the other?

We explore this question in terms of the characteristics that have been shown to contribute to successful helping. These characteristics, attitudes, and skills have been identified mainly by humanistic psychologists, who have done a great deal of research on the nature of the helping relationship. Empathy, genuineness, and self-awareness are some of the helper characteristics that contribute to a good relationship with a client. In addition, this chapter reviews some of the basic skills, such as the ability to listen and communicate effectively, that are vital to the helper's success. The chapter closes with a discussion of the special skills required in group and community settings. Throughout this chapter the terms *worker, helper,* and *counselor* are used interchangeably to familiarize you with the many ways in which these terms are presently used.

CHARACTERISTICS OF EFFECTIVE HELPERS

Although research has not yet indicated a "correct" method of helping, it has identified certain characteristics of helpers that are associated with successful helping. For example, the findings of Avila, Combs, & Purkey (1978), Brammer (1973), Truax & Carkhuff (1967), and Rogers (1961) indicated that effective workers possess certain personal characteristics that contribute to success. The discussion that follows examines these characteristics that contribute to the development of helping relationships.

Empathy

Empatheia is the Greek word that refers to affection plus passion touched by the quality of suffering. In Latin, the word *pathos* is analagous to the Greek *patheia* with the added dimension of "feeling." Through the years, this somewhat vague meaning has evolved into a more comprehensive definition. For example, Brammer (1973) views empathy as the ability to appreciate and understand the client's perspective. More simply, empathy is the ability to see things from another's point of view. Empathy is viewed by many professionals as the most important characteristic in a helping relationship. It serves as a basis for relating and communicating. For example, when clients feel deeply understood they are generally more willing to risk disclosure of their inner feelings. Carkhuff & Berenson (1967) concluded that "the therapist's ability to communicate at high levels of empathic understanding involves the therapist's ability to allow him or herself to experience or merge in the experience of the client" (p. 109).

Empathy is often viewed as conveying sensitivity to the client and trying to understand what "walking in the other guy's shoes" may feel like. The helper does not necessarily have to have had the experiences of a client in order to understand the client's feelings. Feelings are universal. Different experiences often generate similar feelings. For example, death of a loved one and divorce may both generate feelings of loss and anguish.

For empathy to be constructive and worthwhile, it must be demonstrated, as in the following example:

Client: I just recently lost my father, who had cancer.
Helper: It must be a very painful experience, causing you to feel angry, sad, and abandoned.

Genuineness

Genuineness is the degree to which the helper can express true feelings. To be a genuine helper, one must avoid role playing or feeling one way and acting another. Genuine helpers do not take refuge in any specific role, such as counselor or therapist. Genuineness involves self-disclosure. It implies a willingness to be known to others.

In most types of helping relationships, a certain degree of modeling behavior takes place. The client sometimes tries to emulate the characteristics of the helper. If the helper is genuine, free, and expressive, the client is also free and able to express authentic feelings.

Shulman (1982) adds two dimensions to our examination of this characteristic by introducing parallel elements: "Two words are closely related in explaining the meaning of genuineness—*congruence* (when one's words and actions correspond) and *authenticity* (when one is him- or herself, not a phony)" (p. 307). Being genuine, however, is not free license to do or say anything to the client at the whim of the helper. Helpers are not "free spirits" who inflict themselves on others. Being genuine does not necessarily mean expressing all one's thoughts to the client.

Helpers can be genuine without being hostile or hurtful to the client. For example, a client may ask the helper, "What do you really think of me?" Assuming the helper has negative feelings at the moment toward the client's behavior, these feelings could be openly expressed in a variety of ways without appearing as a direct attack on the client. The helper might express disappointment at the client's unwillingness to attempt to change this behavior. In other words, one can dislike a person's rigidity but can still respect the person as an individual.

Sharing personal experiences with the client can sometimes be helpful. For instance, the counselor may be helping someone come to grips with problems generated by a recent divorce. The helper may have been divorced and can therefore understand the range of the client's feelings on a personal level. In this instance, it may be appropriate to share experiences with the client and disclose how one worked toward resolving and understanding those feelings. Of course, it is possible for the helper to share emotions and feelings without discussing specific events or circumstances in one's life.

Objective/Subjective Balance

Subjectivity refers to private, personal, and unique ways of experiencing situations. Being subjective means one's experience is unique and not directly observable by another person. It is a private reaction or feeling to someone or something. This reaction tends to be biased since it only pertains to the individual's experience.

Objectivity emphasizes verifiable aspects of an event. Objectivity involves the noting of facts without distortion by personal feelings or prejudices. It stresses description of what can be seen, heard, touched, and so on. An objective statement based on verifiable evidence might be "Bill is 5 feet 6 inches tall, weighs 145 pounds, and has blue eyes," while a subjective statement of these same conditions could be "Bill is too short, overweight, and has unattractive weird-looking eyes."

Subjectivity and objectivity represent opposite ends of a continuum. In the helping process there are disadvantages to each quality when carried to extremes. The helper who is too subjective can become overly emotionally involved with the client, as in the case of taking sides in marital counseling. In this sense the helper can run the risk of losing the ability to make appropriate decisions or judgments.

Pure objectivity alone is also not a desired quality. Objectivity refers to a detachment from one's personal feelings. The purely objective helper can run the risk of being viewed by the client as cold, uncaring, aloof, and uninterested in the client's well-being. This can cause obvious difficulties in communication and build up feelings of resentment on the part of the client.

Either quality, when carried to extremes, can lead to difficulty in understanding people. The quality to be desired is an objective-subjective balance. A helper must have the ability to stand back and view a situation accurately but without becoming detached from personal feelings. Human services helpers need a blend of both qualities.

Self-Awareness

Self-awareneses is the quality of knowing oneself. It includes knowl-edge of one's values, feelings, attitudes and beliefs, fears and desires, and strengths and weaknesses. The self is comprised of one's thoughts about oneself. This means that there are literally hundreds of ideas and images that make up the sense of self. One's values, beliefs, ideas, and images become clear when one asks questions such as: What's important to me? Which aspects of myself do I like or dislike? The self-concept can be regarded as the inner world in which one lives. In the helping process, the helper often expresses this inner world and makes it visible to the client.

The effective helper must be aware of what messages are being transmitted to the client through both word and action. It is only through self-examination that we can begin to understand what aspects of ourselves would be most beneficial to the helping process. Combs, Avila, and Purkey (1978) stressed the following:

> **Professional helpers must be thinking, problem-solving individu-als. The primary tool with which they work is themselves. This understanding has been referred to as the self as instrument or self as tool concept. In the human services a helping relationship always involves the use of the helper's self, the unique ways in which helpers are able to combine knowledge and understanding with their own unique ways of putting them into operation [p. 6].**

It is generally accepted among many professionals that if one wants to become more effective as a helper, it is necessary to start with self-awareness. Helpers who aspire to utilize self in an effective way must be aware of their patterns of personality and their needs. Helpers have a responsibility to be conscious of the ways in which their personalities and behaviors affect others. The helper's beliefs, values, and attitudes can have a powerful effect on the helping process.

Acceptance

Acceptance is demonstrated by viewing the client's feelings, attitudes, and opinions as worthy of consideration. The accepting helper sees each person as having a fundamental right to think, act, and feel differently. From the humanistic perspective, communicating acceptance of the other person is vital to developing and maintaining the helping relationship. Communication of acceptance leads to feelings of psychological safety on the part of the client. In this setting, the client believes that no matter what he or she discloses, the counselor will react in an accepting manner. As an accepting person, the helper recognizes the uniqueness in each human being. Brill (1973) suggested

> **The basis of any relationship is acceptance of the individual's right to existence, importance, and value . . . . Out of acceptance should come freedom to be oneself—to express one's fears, angers, joy, rage, to grow, develop, and change—without concern that doing so will jeopardize the relationship [p. 48].**

A major problem with understanding the quality of acceptance is that one can confuse acceptance of a client with approval of the client's behavior. Accepting a person does not imply that one likes or approves of all the values or behaviors of that person. For example, a counselor may be working with a heroin addict who is attempting to kick the habit. The counselor may accept the client's feelings, experience, and beliefs, but not approve of heroin addiction. Thus, when a helper says of a client, "I can accept anyone except a child abuser," the helper is judging the behavior as a total representation of the client. Individuals are made up of numerous values, attitudes, and behaviors. No single value, attitude, or behavior represents the total individual.

Desire to Help

Many proponents of the humanistic perspective believe that effective helpers have a deep interest in other people and a desire to help, which causes them to receive satisfaction in promoting the growth and development of others. The feelings of self-satisfaction derived from seeing others make positive changes in their lives are a basic reward to the helper. This sincere desire to help is displayed and becomes readily observable in the helper's attitude toward his or her work. Just as people respond more favorably to a salesperson who evidences enthusiasm and interest in the product he or she is selling, so clients respond more favorably to a helper who is enthusiastic about and interested in helping. One caution should be noted in this regard: sometimes the helper's desire to help can extend too far, creating unnecessary client dependency on the helper for various tasks clients should take care of themselves.

Helpers accept as a social value the belief that people should help one another. When one devotes a considerable amount of time and energy to helping others, it demonstrates a basic belief that those being served do have the fundamental ability to change (Cowen, Leibowitz, & Leibowitz, 1968). Many professionals agree that a desire to help people is a basic value for those entering the human services field.

Patience

Patience is the ability to wait and be steadfast. It is refraining from acting out of haste or impetuousness. As a helper, one may often feel that it would be beneficial to a client to do a particular thing, confront a situation, and so on. Patience is based on the understanding that different people do things at different times, in different ways, and for different reasons, according to their individual capacities.

Frequently, a helper must wait for a client to be ready to take a next step toward resolving a particular problem or toward achieving a desired goal. For example, a helper might be helping a retarded individual to use eating utensils, a task that often involves a lot of repetition over a long period of time. People do not always proceed on a prescribed timetable. Human beings can be awesomely frustrating creatures who often resist change even though the change is recognized as ultimately beneficial. An effective helper must have the patience to allow for the client's development and growth according to the client's needs and abilities.

BASIC HELPING SKILLS

Human services professionals must master certain basic skills to be successful. A skill is an ability to perform a particular task in a competent fashion. Many individual skills make up the helping process.

Individuals are not born with the skills that are essential for relating effectively to other human beings. These skills are learned through training. Some helpers do, however, have more natural abilities than others. Effective helpers continue to acquire additional skills and strive to refine already existing skills. Since each individual is different, each helper must develop his or her own style and way of using these skills, which become the "tools of the trade." In this section we discuss seven basic helping skills.

Listening

To listen means to pay attention to, to tune into, or to hear with thoughtful consideration. Skillful listening is equally as important as talking and acting. It is through listening that the helper begins to learn about the client and how the client sees the world and him- or herself. The helper needs to listen attentively to all messages from the client about such matters as how the client views his or her problems and what the client expects the helper to do about them. Without listening, all forms of potential help may become misguided.

To be effective as a listener, one must become aware of more than just the words that are spoken. There is a basic difference between hearing words and listening for the full meaning and message of the words. It is often not what the client says but how it is said that is important. A client's body posture, tone and pitch of voice, silences and pauses, and speech patterns are all significant in understanding what a client is trying to communicate. A phrase has different significance if spoken in a sarcastic tone than if spoken in a voice filled with cheer and lightness. You probably often ask friends, "How are you?" When a friend responds "fine," you can either accept it at face value or suspect that there is something beneath the surface that contradicts the message. In other words, you may sense a negative feeling that contradicts the overt statement. Effective listening requires sensitivity to inconsistencies between a person's words and actions. The client who says "I'm fine" while tears begin to well up in his or her eyes is obviously communicating a contradictory message.

When listening to clients, the helper must recognize both the cognitive and affective content of what is being communicated. Cognitive content refers to thoughts and ideas. Affective content refers to the feeling tone of the message. When we watch a mime perform on stage, no words are spoken but the mime's actions convey a full range of feelings and behaviors. The affective content sometimes differs from the cognitive content and is often less apparent. Responding accurately to a client's statement depends on the helper's ability to hear and understand what is being said and to perceive the underlying message. Helpers must ask themselves, "Does the client's behavior fit his words?" and "What is the client really trying to communicate?"

Another aspect of listening is the concept of selective perception. Selective perception means that individuals sometimes hear only the aspects of another's message that they wish to hear, and disregard the rest. For instance, a helper might ignore the message conveyed by a client's tone of voice and respond only to the usual meaning of the words spoken. Johnson (1981) adds the following:

> There is considerable evidence that you will be more sensitive to perceiving messages that are consistent with your opinions and attitudes. You will tend to misperceive or fail to perceive messages that are opposite to your opinions, beliefs, and attitudes. If you expect a person to act unfriendly, you will be sensitive to anything that can be perceived as rejection and unfriendliness [p.93].

The helper's beliefs and attitudes can distort the message being conveyed. When listening to others, it is essential to be aware of the possibility of selectivity in what you hear and perceive. Effective helpers are always listening for the full message.

Communicating

Communication is the process of transmitting feelings or thoughts so that they are understood. This process involves conveying information verbally or nonverbally through a variety of means such as body movements, facial expressions, and gestures. To communicate, there must be both a sender of a message and a receiver of a message. Generally speaking, all behavior transmits certain information and may, therefore, be involved in communication.

Many aspects of human services work require the ability to communicate. Communication is an integral part of human services, and may take the form of transmitting particular knowledge, information, or skills. For example, when a helper is counseling individuals facing retirement, the content of the communication may focus upon financial planning, housing needs, or social or emotional concerns. At the other end of the life cycle, helpers working in children's human services programs may focus the content of their communication upon the development of basic life skills. Communicating effectively and responding appropriately is often the key factor in determining the success of any attempt to help.

You can easily understand the complexity of communication by considering the example of the game of passing a single message through a series of individuals. In this game, one person thinks of a message and in turn whispers it to another. The next person attempts to whisper the same message to another person, who does the same, passing it to as many people as possible. When the last person tells the entire group what his or her version of the message is, it is usually very different from the original message. How does a relatively simple message become distorted when conveyed to another person? To understand this, we must look at the various factors involved in communication and understand the obstacles and barriers that can distort even the simplest of messages.

Accurate communication occurs between people when the receiver interprets the sender's message the way the sender intended it. Difficulties in communication arise when the receiver imparts to the message a meaning that was not intended. When the sender attempts to convey a message, the receiver interprets the message before he or she can respond to it. All forms of communication require some degree of interpretation, meaning that an individual must construe, understand, and attach individual meaning to a message. It is through this act of interpretation that communication can become distorted. The process of interpretation is always filtered through our individual biases, expectations, and prejudices. As mentioned previously, when information is transmitted, the listener tends to accept what seems to fit into his or her belief system and sometimes rejects or distorts information that is inconsistent with these beliefs. Also, people are sometimes so positive they know what the other person is going to say that they distort the incoming message to match their expectations. For example, if a man who has very low self-esteem asks his boss for a raise, he may take the boss's statement "I'll have to give it some thought" as a sign of refusal.

A common problem in communication occurs when the receiver understands the words of the message but fails to recognize the sender's underlying meaning. For example, a person might say "Sure is a rainy day" in an attempt to change the subject, while the receiver might assume the person is really concerned about the weather. Another example is the client who sits in the office looking down, arms crossed, slouched deeply in his or her chair, who responds to the question "How do you feel?" by saying "Fine." The client's nonverbal behavior, consisting of posture, eye contact, and facial expression seems to indicate the opposite. Which message does one respond to? The answer is both. The helper must hear the words but also be aware of additional information conveyed in the communication.

Helpers must have an awareness of their own styles of communication. Becoming aware of style means that you know when you as a helper might be creating difficulty in communication by sending out conflicting verbal and nonverbal messages to the client. To this degree, you can see how the quality of self-awareness enhances the skill of communicating effectively. Inappropriate use of language can also lead to mishaps in communication. The helper should avoid using words the client may not understand or may find objectionable. The helper's vocabulary must be understandable to the client. Since words do not mean the same thing to all people, the helper must sometimes provide clear definitions and examples of meaning. If the client's message is unclear, the worker has the responsibility of helping the client to clarify its meaning.

Giving Feedback

Giving feedback is the process of conveying to clients perceptions, feelings, observations, or other information concerning their behavior. Feedback basically represents an individual opinion or evaluation of the client by the worker. It helps clients become aware of how they are perceived by others. Clients can then decide to correct errors in judgment, change undesirable behaviors, and to establish goals.

People do not operate in a social vacuum. We often seek out other individuals to give us their evaluation of how well we accomplish a particular task or perform a certain job. For example, the actor or actress often anxiously awaits the theatrical reviewer's evaluation of his or her latest performance. In the same manner, a child proudly displays his or her latest work of art to the parents and awaits the parents' comments. Feedback is a basic requirement of human beings in many aspects of life.

For the human services worker, learning how to provide feedback effectively is an essential task. Danish and Haner (1976) stated that "to be helpful, the feedback must be given in such a way that the receiver (a) understands clearly what is being communicated; and (b) is able to accept the information" (p. 14). Timing is an important factor in the appropriate use of feedback. Is the client receptive to another point of view at this time? Sometimes a client is not receptive because he or she is in a highly emotional state.

The relationship between worker and client is another critical issue in the use of feedback. If one respects and values the opinion of the other, one is more likely to accept what is offered.

The worker has to exercise judgment in regard to clients' abilities to accept feedback concerning their behavior or problems. Consider the example of the client who thinks she has a wonderful sense of humor, and yet people tend to shy away from her when she jokes around. Several individuals may already have informed her that her jokes are not funny, but she may ignore these people, claiming they have no sense of humor. If in the worker's judgment the client would be more receptive to feedback from a helper, the worker can point out to the client that her sense of humor tends to be sarcastic and hurtful, and this may be a reason why peoply shy away from her.

Feedback serves many purposes. It can reaffirm what the client already believes and feels. It can inform clients of aspects of their behavior of which they were not previously aware. It can provide motivation for change, and can also be a source of support during difficult times.

Observing

For the purpose of this discussion we define observing as the process of noting or recognizing an event. An event could be almost anything from the weather to the facial expression of a particular individual. Observing occurs in two stages: receiving sensory input and giving meaning to the information.

The human services worker always looks for any signs or clues to understand more of what is going on with the client. Areas in which clues can be found include:

- facial expressions
- vocal quality
- body posture
- gestures
- clothing
- general appearance
- eye contact
- distance between worker and client

Workers usually rely on the sense of sight to provide them with basic information. The sense of hearing is equally important, however. In fact, all the senses receive messages that can supplement, confirm, or negate the initial impression derived from sight.

For example, the worker notes that the client is slouched, apparently at ease. However, as the interview progresses, the worker hears the client's rapid speech and intermittent stuttering, indicating tension. In effect, the worker's initial impression of the client as being relaxed has now been negated by other sensory information.

This example also illustrates that an important aspect of observation is interpretation, or attaching individual meaning to an occurrence. Another helper might come up with a different interpretation of the behavioral clues.

Confronting

Confrontation is a word that conjures up fear in some individuals. People often associate the word with some form of attack, anger, or hostile behavior. In the context of the helping profession, the term requires a different understanding. Confrontation can be defined as calling to the attention of the client discrepancies between or among the client's thoughts, attitudes, or behaviors (Ivey & Simek-Downing, 1980). A confrontation is actually an invitation to the client to become more aware of and to examine more fully certain aspects of behavior that seem to the counselor to be harmful or self-defeating for the client. It is through the process of confrontation that clients are made aware of specific obstacles that have impeded or could interfere with reaching their desired goals. Through this process, clients optimally learn to accept responsibility for their behavior.

Confrontation need not focus exclusively upon negative aspects of clients' behavior. It can be used to show clients strengths and resources they have overlooked. The acknowledgment of strengths can sometimes produce anxiety, however, since then people can demand more of one. Thus, confrontation involves challenge even when a positive aspect of behavior is pointed out. Before individuals can change, they must perceive a need for change. Confrontation provides one stimulus for change.

Constructively challenging the client can take various forms. Counselors can call attention to the client's self-defeating attitudes, point out discrepancies between what the client says and actually does, focus upon various manipulations or forms of game playing, or, as mentioned previously, address unrecognized areas of strength. Following are some examples of the use of confrontation in counseling.

EXAMPLE A

Client: I am not really interested in a better-paying job. It will probably demand more of my time and I will have to learn new skills and even wear a tie and jacket to work.

Counselor: You say you are not interested in a better job, yet you spend several sessions talking exclusively about it. Is it possible you really want to go after the better job and are afraid of failing, so you have convinced yourself that you really do not want the job? Are you possibly afraid of new demands that could be placed on you?

This confrontation addresses the client's incongruent behavior.

EXAMPLE B

Client: I am really concerned about the shape of the world today. People do nothing to change the situation. People are starving. Trash is scattered all over the streets, crime is everywhere, and people do not get out and talk to one another anymore.

Counselor: You say you are a concerned person, but the bulk of your time is spent sitting in front of the television and drinking beer.

This confrontation focuses the client upon the discrepancy between what he claims concerns him and what he actually does about it.

The misuse of confrontation can have negative effects on clients. If the client is not ready to accept the challenge of the offered information, the confrontation is not helpful. The counselor must time the confrontation so that it is most helpful.

Clarifying

The basic purpose of clarifying is to make clear what information is being conveyed by the client and how it is being received by the counselor. Sometimes difficult situations and painful emotions can create problems with communication. When the counselor clarifies aspects of the client's message, the client knows how the message has been received. The process of clarifying often involves the use of the skills of paraphrasing, highlighting, and summarizing.

Paraphrasing. When the counselor paraphrases a client's message, he or she rewords it. In doing so, the counselor attempts to focus the client's attention on the main element of an immediate message. Through the use of paraphrasing, the counselor conveys to the client that the meaning and the feelings of the message have been received and understood. Consider the following example:

Client: Even though I feel I have a lot of friends, I feel as if no one understands me or really wants to. My mother and father don't listen to me. My teachers ignore me and my girlfriend says I'm no fun to be with anymore.

Counselor: It sounds as if you feel that you have no one you can really talk to.

Client: Yeah, I guess that is how I feel.

In this example, the counselor rewords and restates the client's message and pinpoints the basic feelings. This serves to focus the client upon his main areas of concern, in addition to conveying to the client that the counselor understands what is being expressed.

Highlighting. Highlighting is very similar to paraphrasing, but has a slightly different purpose. Paraphrasing is often done as a response to the client's immediate message. Highlighting, however, is not an immediate response and does not necessarily follow the sequence in which the client is expressing the message. Highlighting is an attempt to capture the recurring theme of messages during a counseling session. In this way, the counselor emphasizes the main aspects of what the client is expressing over a short time. This serves to focus the client's train of thought and draws the client's attention to the main areas of concern being expressed.

Following the previous example, the counselor has just spent twenty minutes listening to the client's appraisal of himself and his many friendships. The counselor is now attempting to highlight the major theme and feelings expressed by the client.

Counselor: Even though you say you have many friends, you still feel that no one really understands you.

The counselor has now identified the major theme of the client's message and is again drawing the client's attention to what he has already expressed as his main concern.

Summarizing. Like paraphrasing and highlighting, summarizing is a means of giving back to the client the essence of what he or she has been trying to convey. The distinction concerns the amount of material covered. Paraphrasing and highlighting concentrate on the immediate aspects of client messages during parts of a single counseling session, whereas summarizing involves restating the chief elements of the client's message over one or a series of counseling sessions (Shulman, 1982). When the worker summarizes the major points of information and recurring themes brought forth by the client over several sessions, the client can develop a broader perspective on and deeper understanding of the depth and significance of specific problem areas. This process brings to the attention of the client changes in feeling and attitudes that may have gone unnoticed. It enables clients to develop a frame of reference in which to see where they were, where they are now, and where they would like to be.

Report Writing

Report writing is a means of recording the interactions between clients and events. Most reports concern client behavior and progress. Report writing is not generally perceived as one of the more exciting skills to acquire within the human services field, but nevertheless, it is one of the most practical and valuable. Report writing in one form or another is necessary in many aspects of the human services field. All professionals and institutions require a consistent method of keeping track of what happens to whom, when, and why, although specific methods and styles of report writing vary. Many human services agencies use a standardized form for the various types of reports. Obviously, writing clearly and using the language accurately are important. More specifically, reports are usually compiled with two basic objectives in mind: to establish a documented record for future reference, and to convey current information regarding a specific case or event (Wicks, 1979).

A counselor working with many clients must keep an accurate report of each one's progress. Clients may be taking medication, which necessitates that a consistent and accurate report be kept on the type of medication, dosage, and consequent reactions. If a client changes counselors, the report of the previous counselor may be requested by the new counselor as a means of gaining background information on the client. In many clinics it is mandatory to keep reports of patient contacts, diagnosis, and treatments. Very often these reports are monitored by state and federal agencies in order to ensure a continuous level of compliance with state and federal regulations.

Reports are crucial when professionals evaluate or consult with public or private agencies, institutions, or schools. For instance, a human services specialist might be brought in to evaluate the effectiveness of a specific program or service. The evaluator would rely heavily upon the records and reports submitted.

FACTORS THAT INFLUENCE THE USE OF SKILLS

This chapter has so far described a variety of skills and characteristics needed for effective helping. There are a number of factors that can influence the way in which the worker applies these skills and characteristics. These factors are discussed in the following sections.

Values

A person's sense of right and wrong, likes and dislikes, and standards of appropriate behavior are all a part of values. One's personal, professional, and societal values develop through one's experiences with famiy, peers, and culture. Of immediate relevance is the fact that the individual's values guide behavior in professional or working relationships. How a worker reacts to a particular client, situation, or problem is partly determined by the worker's values. Most workers of the humanistic orientation accept the principle that the helper should not try to impose values on the client but should help the client clarify his or her own values. To be effective, workers must fully understand their own values and respect the client's right to have different values.

Consider the example of a human services worker who has strong personal values against abortion. The worker is asked to counsel a pregnant teenage client who is unsure about having the child. Obviously, the worker's personal values could have a strong influence on the way he or she goes about the helping process. If the worker pressures the client to make a decision in line with the worker's values, the client may later feel that she betrayed her own sense of what was right in this situation.

How can you as a beginning worker avoid placing values on others? It may help to think about the influences that shaped your values and beliefs. This will help you to appreciate the fact that persons who come from different backgrounds may have different values from your own. Other people feel that their values are "right" just as your values feel "right" to you.

To begin the process of clarifying your values, you might answer these questions:

- What values underlie your desire to help others?
- What social issues do you feel strongly about?
- Which client behaviors would you have trouble accepting?
- Which of your values would you like to change?
- What would you like to accomplish in human services?
- How do you go about solving personal problems?
- Do you readily seek help from others when you need it?

Professional Codes of Ethics

At present there is no single code of ethics that applies to all careers or disciplines in the broad field of human services. Rather, the professional organizations representing individual careers have established separate codes of ethics to provide guidance and direction for their own members. Professional organizations that have established such codes include the American Psychological Association (APA), the National Association of Social Workers (NASW), the

American Medical Association (AMA), and the Council for Standards in Human Service Education (CSHSE).

The general guidelines offered by professional codes of ethics could not possibly instruct the practitioner on what to do or how to behave in all professional situations. Ethical codes do, however, serve various important functions. For example, codes define minimal standards of professional conduct and attempt to ensure that workers meet various standards, requirements, or levels of competency (Corey, Corey, & Callanan, 1984). Ethical codes also define the scope or range of responsibilities for individuals, and help to clarify various common issues of major concern within a particular field. Van Hoose and Kottler (1977) cited additional reasons why such codes exist: (1) they are self-imposed as an alternative to having regulations imposed by legislative bodies; (2) they are designed to prevent internal bickering and disagreement within the profession; and (3) they are designed to help protect the practitioner in areas of malpractice.

There are many areas of overlap among the various codes of ethics. The issue of client confidentiality and the right to privacy is one such area. Various professional codes offer guidelines articulating what is considered to be appropriate or responsible action for the practitioner in matters pertaining to this issue. For example, should a human services worker always share information concerning his or her client with the court if asked to do so? Is the worker ethically obligated to get the client's consent? The issue of client termination is another example. When is it considered to be ethically appropriate to disengage or terminate your work with a particular client? What responsibilities does the worker have to the community at large when working with dangerous or high-risk clients?

For additional information concerning the various professional codes of ethics, refer to the listing of professional organizations at the conclusion of Chapter Six. You can write directly to a professional organization and request a copy of their code of ethics.

Physical and Emotional Well-Being

Even such relatively mild physical maladies as a cold, a toothache, or an upset stomach can alter or diminish one's ability and efficiency in attending to others. While experiencing physical discomfort, we tend to be more focused on ourselves than on other people. In addition to distracting us, physical discomfort can distort the accuracy of sensory information we receive. A worker who feels depressed, run-down, or in a state of mental fatigue is also less likely to be as efficient as he or she ordinarily could be. When the worker is aware of these difficulties, he or she might do well to keep in mind how the difficulties can affect interaction with the client.

Environmental Factors

Physical space influences both the worker and the client. For example, arrangement of furniture influences behavior. Barriers placed between individuals, such as a desk separating a worker from a client, create a more formal, businesslike, less personal style of interaction. This physical separation of several feet is analagous to keeping someone "at arm's length." Many large organizations serving the public often utilize barriers such as desks or counters with large plastic windows to create this type of environment. Acting in an intimate, personal, or less formal manner in this type of setting is often considered inappropriate. Removing the barriers and consequently becoming more physically assessible and closer to others creates a different set of behavioral expectations. The worker should consider these factors.

Background and Life Experience

A person's background consists of elements such as socioeconomic class, cultural heritage, race, and religion. All of these combine to shape one's perception of reality. The person raised in an exclusively upper-class environment probably has a different understanding of economic problems facing the nation than the person raised in more impoverished circumstances. The views of reality of each of these individuals are quite valid and both may be accurate, but they are nevertheless different. This difference, created by exposure to different life circumstances, influences and colors all aspects of observation. Skilled workers must become consciously aware of how their backgrounds influence the application of their skills.

Understanding and use of language is directly influenced by one's background. Words and phrases can convey very different ideas and feelings to people from different backgrounds. For example, the word *fuzz* is a slang expression for the police, used among some groups of people but not others to connote hostility. If you are not used to how the word *fuzz* is used within various groups of individuals, then you may incorrectly interpret this word as an expression of hostility toward authority figures. This can slant your entire understanding of what someone is trying to communicate.

All people develop certain likes and dislikes, shaped by our prior experiences. These likes and dislikes become molded into attitudes and beliefs that bias us either toward or against a particular person, group, object, or situation. A bias can distort a worker's interpretation of the client's situation by setting up preconceived expectations of what a person or group of people are like.

As mentioned earlier, people have a tendency to notice those aspects of behavior that confirm already existing beliefs. For example, if one believes all people over 70 years of age are suffering from senility and loss of intelligence, one tends to look for behavioral signs to confirm this existing belief. Biased individuals tend to hear what they expect to hear and see what they expect to see. The problem with a prejudice or bias is that it can distort the accurate assessment of someone or something (Wicks, 1979), and thus interfere with the effectiveness of one's skills. One way to counteract a bias is to become aware of biases that may develop in people of your background.

Prior Training

As Chapter Four indicated, various *theoretical* approaches to helping are prevalent in the field. The approach a worker follows can influence how he or she perceives the client and therefore can affect which aspects of behavior he or she notes with particular emphasis. For example, the worker who employs a behavioral approach to helping might be more apt to notice and emphasize the client's overt physical manifestation of symptoms such as insomnia, weight loss, or nervous habits. The behaviorally oriented worker might not pay attention to certain aspects of the client's life history that could indicate an early childhood trauma. The psychoanalytically oriented worker, on the other hand, would be much quicker to notice and emphasize the earlier life experiences of the client. Limitations imposed by strict adherence to a specific theoretical approach can limit the scope of one's skills.

THE WORKER IN GROUP SETTINGS

The responsibilities of a human services worker sometimes involve working with groups. This requires using the skills previously discussed in a somewhat different manner, as well as using additional skills. This section will focus on the basics of group dynamics and the skills necessary to facilitate group work. It is intended as an introduction for the beginning human services student; many additional concepts, skills, and techniques can be acquired through advanced training in group work.

Definition of a Group

There are a variety of ways to define a group, and many types of groups exist. For the purpose of our discussion, we can define a group as a collection of people who share a common purpose and who come together to achieve their goals by working together in some form. The primary characteristics of groups include the following:

- Group members perceive themselves to be a part of a group.
- Members are interdependent in some manner.
- Members strive to achieve goals.
- Members influence each other in some way.

Types of Groups

Since human services workers function in a variety of settings, the variety of groups they may be involved with is large. The following categories illustrate the broad range of types of groups:

- families with problems
- goal-oriented groups: task forces, teams, commissions, and so on
- personal growth groups: assertiveness, sensitivity, encounter, T-groups
- treatment groups: group therapy, group counseling around a wide variety of problems and using a wide variety of approaches such as Gestalt, rational-emotive, and transactional-analysis therapies

It should be noted that categories can overlap to some extent. Often groups can have a multiple focus. For example, they may be both therapeutic and educational for members.

Group Leadership Skills

Group leaders share many traits with orchestra conductors (Benjamin, 1978). Both set the pace and the tone for the rest of the group. A worker who leads a group must be aware of the needs and goals of all members. What follows is an examination of basic group leadership skills found to be most useful in and applicable to group settings in the human services field.

Selecting Group Members. In many groups, especially in therapy or counseling groups, the selection of group members is an important consideration. Establishing a balanced group composition is often desirable. The worker might want to provide a varied mix of young and old, male and female, or talkative and quiet. Previous knowledge and information about an individual can help the worker make appropriate decisions concerning a person's suitability to a particular group.

Establishing Goals.   Once the group is established, the leader, together with the group members, must determine the group's objectives and goals. Goals are based on the members' level of functioning. In a group with a low level of functioning, the goals are usually set by the leader. Whether the goals are specific or general, they must be clearly defined and agreed upon by the group members. The leader should normally discuss group goals, suggest procedures, and provide an opportunity for group members to express their views.

Establishing Norms.   Establishing a clear set of group rules at the beginning helps the group to proceed more effectively toward its goals and enables the leader to determine whether or not the group is on the right track. Group rules or guidelines might address the issue of confidentiality by having participants agree to discuss group matters only within the confines of the group itself. Another rule might involve allowing each member to finish talking before another member can interrupt.

Intervening.   The helper intervenes by stepping in and attempting to change, modify, or point out something that is occurring in the group. Intervening is not focused exclusively on blocking negative aspects of a client's behavior. It can also be used to point out the positive aspects. For example, a helper may intervene between two clients who are arguing over a particular issue to point out to one of the clients that she is finally standing up for what she believes in. The leader may also intervene when one member violates the established rules of the group.

Sometimes groups get stuck. The leader may intervene in a group discussion when the discussion has reached an impasse. The leader may then suggest additional or alternative ways of viewing the situation or problem. The leader may also intervene by introducing a specific therapeutic technique, such as role playing, to help clarify and bring additional insights to a particular problem a client or group of clients may be experiencing. Knowing how and when to move in is as important in group work as it is in interviewing.

Promoting Interaction. By skillfully facilitating, the group leader helps to promote and bring about interaction among the group members. Promoting interaction can lead to the establishing of clear channels of communication among clients. When group members are linked to one another, they begin to work together and relate personally to one another. To be effective as a facilitator, the leader needs to be insightful and sensitive. The leader has to find ways of relating the concerns of one individual to the concerns or struggles of another. This provides further opportunities for mutual support and helps to develop a feeling of interconnectedness and cohesiveness.

The result of this process can be the creation of a climate of safety and acceptance in which members trust one another and are therefore likely to engage in productive interchanges (Corey & Corey, 1977). As a facilitator, the group leader helps the participants to express their problems, provides support as members explore aspects of themselves, and essentially helps group members reach their individual goals through this mutually influencing process.

Appraising/Evaluating. The group leader must appraise the ongoing process and goals of the group. It is particularly helpful to do this after each group meeting. The leader must reflect on what is happening in the group, the direction it seems to be taking, how it helps certain participants and not others, and the types of interventions that may be helpful in the next group session. Often a leader will suggest that the members become part of this process by sharing their evaluations of what is happening in the group with group members. In this process, group members can become more aware of how they are influenced by others and how others may be influenced by them. As a result of the process, constructive changes or new goals can be implemented to enable the group to fulfill more of each member's stated needs.

Termination in the Group. The issue of termination emerges in every group in various ways. Workers must know how to end each group session. Sessions can be terminated in a number of ways. The leader can suggest to members how to transfer what they have learned in the group to other life situations or environments. The leader can summarize what happened during a session or can ask the members to think about some point that had emerged. The leader can also end a session by suggesting minigoals for clients to work on.

Workers must know when it is most appropriate for a certain member to leave the group. In this decision, the worker must consider and evaluate all available information pertaining to the client,

An example of a community program that offers a variety of services to the handicapped population.

such as the client's stated goals, his or her past and present abilities to achieve stated goals, and whether the group is still useful for the client's present situation.

A worker must also know when an entire group has completed its work so that it is time to dissolve the group. Has the group achieved its stated purposes or goals? If the leader has previously highlighted a clear set of group goals, developed constructive group guidelines, and consistently monitored the group's progress, the group is now in a good position to decide about termination.

THE WORKER IN THE COMMUNITY

As human services systems have developed in order to identify and meet human needs, new and diverse activities and functional roles have been created for workers. Workers are spending increasing time in community settings because of the need to locate services for clients, to enlist the aid of various organizations in developing new services, and to provide information that might help to prevent problems. As any system gets larger, workers need additional skills and knowledge to understand and use effectively the resources available within the system. The individual and group skills previously examined in this chapter are, of course, components of all human services activities. As the contemporary worker has become more involved in various aspects and activities of the community, the need for additional knowledge and skills has emerged. Additional skills useful for the community worker are:

- advocating
- negotiating
- organizing
- coordinating
- educating
- planning

- consulting
- gathering information
- acting as liaison
- lobbying
- reaching out

By examining some of the functional roles and activities most often performed by workers in the community, you can begin to understand why these skills are needed and how they might be utilized.

Client Advocacy

When functioning as a client advocate, the human services worker represents clients by helping them obtain whatever services they need. The worker attempts to bring community resources to the individual or group. In this context, the worker identifies and assesses the needs of the client or group, and matches the available community resources to the client's or group's needs. For example, a client may be entitled to social security or welfare benefits but may be denied these services for improper reasons or because of lack of information. The helper's work then involves educating the client about all available services. The worker may literally act for clients, confronting and negotiating bureaucratic mazes to ensure that they receive all the governmental services to which they are entitled. Often this work involves coordinating and gathering a substantial amount of information concerning the various programs of service available and the procedures necessary to qualify for such programs.

As the client's representative, the worker actually pleads the client's case to other individuals who represent different services or agencies within the larger system. This can often be extremely frustrating, and it is all too easy to lose one's patience and temper. Negotiating skills here are very useful. Knowing when to be forceful and when to compromise often makes the difference between getting needed services and not getting them.

Community Organizing

As an organizer, the human services worker acts to bring various sections of the community together to create, improve, or maintain programs. Some examples of this organizing function might include the development of a job-training program within a community or setting up an after-school program using already existing playground facilities. An organizer brings together various agencies and programs and uses all available resources to resolve a particular problem.

To accomplish these tasks, the worker must know the community political structure and the various financial realities. Functioning in this capacity often brings the worker into the political arena. Knowing who has the power to accomplish a particular task is very important. It helps if the worker is a skilled and articulate speaker, since it is often necessary to plead one's case before groups and committees. Being able to work independently and under pressure is another important attribute of the community organizer.

Community Outreach

Human services workers who perform outreach activities can generally be found working directly in the client's environment. In many instances a client may be unable or unwilling due to physical or emotional illness to come to a specific human services center. In this case, the outreach worker actually visits the client's residence and helps with a variety of concerns related to all aspects of daily living. A typical service involving these types of activities is a homebound elderly program. Elderly individuals can become, through illness or other factors, unable to accomplish certain tasks for themselves. The worker's activities here might involve helping the client to shop for groceries, teaching the client how to budget money more effectively, informing and educating the client about health and nutrition concerns, and actually helping the client to learn or relearn many daily activities that other people take for granted.

Other outreach activities and services focus upon the recently discharged psychiatric patient, who may require some form of help to make the transition back into community living. Here the worker might be involved in teaching a client how to utilize forms of public transportation, linking clients to other services available in the community, and helping clients to develop a range of personal interests that could enhance their quality of life. It is often the outreach worker who is the prime liaison between clients in the community and available community services.

Coordinating Services

Service coordination is becoming more common and visible in today's human services systems. The service coordinator is responsible for overseeing a certain caseload of clients. The primary task is to make sure the identified clients receive access to a system of coordinated services designed to meet their individual needs. Through personal interviews and gathering previous reports and evaluations from other workers, the service coordinator determines which available services it is appropriate to channel the client to. For example, a client seeing an outpatient counselor once a week for specific problems may also be unemployed and in need of vocational training. Unemployment and lack of money may have also caused the client to be in need of adequate housing. The service coordinator must evaluate all of this client's needs and try to develop a coordinated treatment plan designed to meet the stated needs.

Often the service coordinator meets regularly with staff representatives from the various services or programs the client is involved with to discuss and monitor the client's progress and make necessary adjustments. The service coordinator becomes primarily responsible for the client within the context of the services system. The ability to gather information, to plan and coordinate services, and to work effectively with a variety of professionals from different parts of the system are required for this work activity.

Providing Information

One of the major tasks confronting human services is to educate and inform the public. Often, people can prevent smaller problems from becoming larger ones if they only know who to turn to for help, what legal rights they possess, and what alternatives are available to them. Access to information can actually prevent some prevalent social problems.

To provide information to the community, human services workers are involved with many aspects of our daily lives. For example, workers can be found visiting local high schools to provide current information on such topics as drug abuse, birth control, or alcoholism. In other segments of the community, workers are likely to be involved with civic or church-related groups, providing information concerning social security benefits, welfare procedure, or family planning. Many community mental health centers have a specific consultation and education department whose designated task is to provide these types of information to a particular community. A more in-depth examination of the role of prevention in the human services field is provided in Chapter Eight.

ADDITIONAL READING

Corsini, R. (Ed.). (1973). *Current psychotherapies.* Itasca, IL: F. E. Peacock.
Johnson, D. W., & Johnson, F. P. (1982). *Joining together: Group theory and group skills* (2nd ed.). Englewood Cliffs, NJ: Prentice-Hall.

Knapp, M. L. (1972). *Nonverbal communication in human interaction.* New York: Holt, Rinehart & Winston.

Kottler, J. A. (1983). *Pragmatic group leadership.* Monterey, CA: Brooks/Cole.

Krupar, K. (1973). *Communication games.* New York: The Free Press.

REFERENCES

Avila, D. L., Combs, A. W., & Purkey, W. W. (1978). *The helping relationship sourcebook.* Boston: Allyn & Bacon.

Benjamin, A. (1978). *Behavior in small groups.* Boston: Houghton Mifflin.

Brammer, L. M. (1973). *The helping relationship—Process and skills.* Englewood Cliffs, NJ: Prentice-Hall.

Brill, N. (1973). *Working with people.* Philadelphia: J. B. Lippincott.

Carkhuff, R. R., & Berenson, B. G. (1967). *Beyond counseling and therapy.* New York: Holt, Rinehart & Winston.

Combs, A. W., Avila, D. L., & Purkey, W. W. (1978). *Helping relationships.* Boston: Allyn & Bacon.

Corey, G., & Corey, M. S. (1977). *Groups: Process and practice.* Monterey, CA: Brooks/Cole.

Corey, G., Corey, M., & Callanan, P. (1984). *Issues and ethics in the helping professions.* Monterey, CA: Brooks/Cole.

Cowen, E. L., Leibowitz, E., & Leibowitz, G. (1968). Utilization of retired people as mental health aides with children. *American Journal of Orthopsychiatry, 38,* 900–909.

Danish, S. J., & Haner, A. L. (1976). *Helping skills: A basic training program.* New York: Human Services Press.

Ivey, A., & Simek-Downing, L. (1980). *Counseling and psychotherapy: Skills, techniques, and practice.* Englewood Cliffs, NJ: Prentice-Hall.

Johnson, D. W. (1981). *Reaching out—Interpersonal effectiveness and self-actualization* (2nd ed.). Englewood Cliffs, NJ: Prentice-Hall.

Rogers, C. R. (1961). *On becoming a person.* Boston: Houghton Mifflin.

Shulman, E. D. (1982). *Intervention in the human services (3rd ed.).* St. Louis: C. V. Mosby.

Truax, C. B., & Carkhuff, R. R. (1967). *Toward effective counseling and psychotherapy.* Chicago: Aldine.

Van Hoose, W., & Kottler, J. (1977). *Ethical and legal issues in counseling and psychotherapy.* San Francisco: Jossey-Bass.

Wicks, R. J. (1979). *Helping others: Ways of listening, sharing, and counseling.* New York: Chilton.

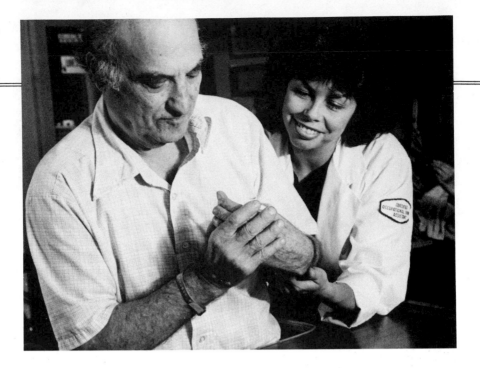

CAREERS IN HUMAN SERVICES

INTRODUCTION

Human services share the goal of helping people to live healthier and more productive lives. The range of career fields within human services that share this goal is broad, and includes mental health, education, health, social services, vocational rehabilitation, child care, and housing. There are a variety of specific job titles within each of these fields. Considering the wide range of career options, it is not surprising that the beginning worker often feels uncertain about which path to follow. This chapter is intended to provide basic career information to help you make an informed choice.

We have selected for coverage here a representative cross section of human services careers, as it is not possible to describe in the space of a chapter all the career options. The emphasis is on career fields that together are attracting the large majority of individuals entering human services today. These are paraprofessional work, therapeutic recreation, creative arts therapy, psychiatric nursing, occupational therapy, clinical psychology, social work, and psychiatry. Since psychiatry demands lengthy, difficult, and costly training, this career may not attract the same numbers of students as other career options in the human services field. It is examined in this chapter because the majority of human services workers are likely to come into contact with psychiatrists in their professional work. Some knowledge of the psychiatrists' background and training may therefore be helpful.

You will notice that a great deal of overlap exists among careers in terms of work setting, duties, and levels of responsibility. To help you obtain additional information about each career field described, names and addresses of professional organizations associated with each field are provided at the conclusion of this chapter.

PARAPROFESSIONAL WORK

Paraprofessionals are those workers who do not have formal education beyond the baccalaureate level. As the National Organization of Human Services (1982) points out, such workers are not traditionally affiliated with any established profession, but are salaried staff members who perform a variety of functions for people within human services organizations. For example, in the field of mental health, a staff member who has attained a master's degree in psychology is classified as a professional; a staff member holding a baccalaureate or associate degree or less is considered a paraprofessional.

Functions

The term _paraprofessional_ is derived from the Greek root meaning "alongside of." In this sense it implies a working relationship alongside of a professional. Paraprofessionals are also called generalist workers, new professionals, beginning professionals, community workers, lay therapists, and indigenous workers. As the assortment of titles suggests, the work roles and functions of paraprofessionals vary greatly. Paraprofessionals represent the largest number of workers and usually have the most contact with those in need. In some instances, the duties of paraprofessionals are similar to those of professionals.

The paraprofessional may perform some of the same duties as the professional, but the extent of decision making, the level of responsibility, and the range and depth of activity is not as great (Schmolling, Burger, & Youkeles, 1981). For example, as a staff member working within a social service agency, a paraprofessional might perform preliminary interviews and client screening, make home visits, gather information, perform administrative functions including the preparation of reports or setting of fee schedules, and act as a member of a treatment team. The professional worker might also perform these functions but, in addition, might make diagnoses, provide short- and long-term psychotherapy, and plan specific courses of treatment or action. Although an overlap of duties may exist, the professional most often acts in a supervisory capacity and is, therefore, given greater responsibility for all work performed.

During the 1960s the manpower shortage in human services greatly spurred the training and utilization of paraprofessionals. The new workers not only helped alleviate the shortage but provided services in many ways (Sobey, 1969). However, the influx of paraprofessional workers into the field caused tension and controversy to develop between the paraprofessionals and professionals in many agencies. The tension was caused, in part, by the belief of paraprofessionals (and certain professionals as well) that advanced graduate or professional training was not always necessary in order to satisfactorily perform many functions in human services. Others believed that advanced education and/or professional training was essential for many tasks. This controversy, which is discussed further in Chapter Nine, continues to the present day.

There are many specific job titles within the broad category of paraprofessional work. Different institutions, agencies, and programs use various titles to refer to paraprofessionals. For example, a state psychiatric hospital may use the job titles of psychiatric aide, mental health aide, mental health technician, or mental health trainee. A social service system might utilize the job titles of social work aide, social work associate, or community worker. Not only are there a variety of titles, but other designations are used to refer to a specific level of work and responsibility within a given job title. For example, as a mental health aide, one might be at level I, II, III, IV, or V. Each higher level usually denotes a greater degree of responsibility and/or supervisory function and also carries with it a higher rate of salary and greater prestige. These various levels indicate a career ladder approach in human services similar to that of the civil service system.

The following examples illustrate more clearly some of the functions of paraprofessionals. It must be emphasized that these examples represent only a limited portrayal of paraprofessional work drawn from a broad range of activities.

EXAMPLE A: SOCIAL WORK ASSISTANT III

Ms. G. has a baccalaureate in psychology and is a paraprofessional under the job title of Social Work Assistant III in a nursing home. She is a member of a treatment team, along with an M.S.W., certified social worker, a master's degree-level psychologist, and a psychiatrist. The team meets twice weekly, during which time Ms. G. shares information of social and emotional significance observed during daily interactions with specific clients. The goal of these meetings is to develop and monitor treatment plans that may be required for individual clients. Other aspects of her weekly work activities include a great deal of patient contact such as leading a weekly discussion group with clients, transporting nonambulatory clients to meals and appointments, and assisting an art therapist who conducts classes for the clients once a week.

EXAMPLE B: MENTAL HEALTH ASSISTANT II

Mr. F. is a paraprofessional who has an associate of science degree in community mental health and works in a large psychiatric hospital under the job title of Mental Health Assistant II. He already has basic academic and fieldwork experience in the mental health field, but is required to participate in a year-long training program conducted by the hospital for all its paraprofessional staff. These workshop training programs are designed to familiarize the paraprofessional with hospital procedure and to teach specific treatment approaches, methods, and problem-solving techniques. Mr. F'.s primary duties involve working with a professional social worker to conduct daily therapeutic group discussions with the clients, implementing individual treatment programs with clients, attending treatment team meetings with other paraprofessional and professional staff, and performing a variety of clerical duties such as ordering various supplies for the ward to which he is assigned. In addition, Mr. F.

regularly conducts tours through his ward and provides information for visiting students who are currently enrolled in college mental health programs.

EXAMPLE C: PSYCHIATRIC AIDE III

Ms. C. is a paraprofessional who has a high school diploma and 1 year college course work. She works in the day treatment program of a community mental health center under the job title of Psychiatric Aide III. Ms. C. works with former long-term institutionalized patients who attend this program as part of their discharge treatment plan from the hospital. She leads various groups with clients on a daily basis. The group topics often include nutrition and health, current events, money management, basic adult reading and writing, and events and activities available within the community. She often organizes and arranges trips with clients to various activities available in the community. As a member of a treatment team, she works with social workers, psychologists, and psychiatrists to help develop treatment plans for the clients in her program. A great deal of her work involves helping clients with activities of daily living, which include shopping for groceries, getting help with housing problems or welfare problems, buying clothing, and using the public transportation system.

Training and Education

Training for a paraprofessional career is usually accomplished by one of two routes. The first route involves formal completion of a two- or four-year college or university academic human services program. These degree-granting programs prepare the individual for an entry-level position within the human services field. Completion of a two-year program gives the individual the basic course work and fieldwork experiences. A typical program in a two-year community mental health program leading to an associate degree might include such courses as basic psychology, developmental psychology, behavior pathology, interviewing, and fieldwork. Field-based courses have students work directly in community field sites under the supervision of a college faculty member. This two-year program is the primary route to a paraprofessional career. Completion of a four-year college program is usually viewed as preparation for a more advanced professional career.

A four-year program might have class and fieldwork requirements similar to the two-year program, but usually requires more extensive course work in other areas as well. Four-year programs place greater emphasis upon liberal arts studies and offer more advanced coursework in specific types of therapy and additional skills training.

The second route to becoming a paraprofessional is through training offered by specific institutions such as mental hospitals, social service agencies, or community mental health centers. These institutions usually have on-the-job or in-service training programs for individuals who lack a formal college degree but desire a para-professional career. Such programs usually provide basic courses focusing on administrative procedures, patient and staff issues, counseling or treatment methods, medical issues, and other selected topics pertaining to that specific institution. It should be mentioned that there are agencies that hire paraprofessionals but provide little or no training. This lack of paraprofessional training has raised serious questions and concerns.

THERAPEUTIC RECREATION

Therapeutic recreation is the selected use of recreational activities as an aid in the treatment, correction, or rehabilitation of physical or mental disorders. The primary focus of this form of treatment is corrective or rehabilitative. Recreation alone cannot cure a disabil-ity or disease. It can help an individual with a temporary disability regain his or her former level of functioning, or it can help an individual with a permanent disability learn to function maximally within the limits set by the specific disability.

Functions

Recreation therapists work in a variety of treatment and nontreat-ment settings, which include nursing homes, hospitals, mental health centers, rehabilitation institutions, recreation centers, parks, senior citizen centers, and Ys. The recreation therapist is most often part of a treatment team in treatment and/or institutional settings. Such a team may consist of a physician, a psychologist, a social worker, a nurse, or representatives from other fields as necessitated by the individual needs of a patient. Nontreatment settings usually find the recreation therapist working independently. In either setting, this specialist can function with individuals or groups. Recreation can have an educative function in addition to having therapeutic value and providing pleasure. The educative functions are present in many aspects of a recreation therapist's work, but these functions are most clearly evident in nontreatment settings such as YMCAs, park pro-grams, and senior citizen centers.

In nontreatment settings the recreation therapist designs and implements programs for special populations such as children with disabilities, individuals with weight problems, or senior citizens who desire a constructive and consistent fitness program. In addition to developing such programs, the specialist spends time instructing individuals in the rudiments of such a program. The specialist often conducts brief classes to explain the benefits of the program, teaches individuals how to use any equipment involved in the program, and monitors individuals' progress toward desired goals.

As previously mentioned, in treatment settings such as mental hospitals, mental health centers, or rehabilitation centers, the recreation therapist's work activities are usually coordinated with recommendations from the treatment team. Consider the example of a patient in a mental hospital who has a history of aggressive and antisocial behavior. One of the recommendations of the treatment team is that the patient slowly be introduced to recreation activities that might serve as an outlet for pent-up anger and frustration and facilitate the development of a sense of social cooperation. The recreation therapist develops a suitable treatment approach to achieve these goals. The patient is initially introduced to activities that can be performed alone, such as playing basketball, jogging, and swimming. Over a period of weeks and months the specialist may give the patient some instructions as to the finer points of the activity, and possibly do the activity with the patient. After another length of time, the patient may wish to test his or her skill with another patient or staff member. The hope is that the patient will gradually begin to function more constructively with others, using recreation as the vehicle to attain this goal.

The recreation therapist may also perform various other functions in addition to providing direct services to clients. Administrative duties often involve directing recreation training programs in colleges and universities. Many recreation therapists consult to private and public agencies and institutions. Other specialists may work for city, county, or state government agencies designing or planning recreation programs for specific communities.

Training and Education

To become a professional recreation therapist one must complete a baccalaureate degree, with major emphasis in therapeutic recreation, from an accredited college or university. Such college or university programs usually include course work in recreational leadership, therapeutic recreation, biology, psychology, physical education, and other relevant areas. Many programs require practical fieldwork experience in addition to course work. In this context the aspiring recreation therapist learns to put theory into practice. It is advisable, although not usually mandatory, for the student to gain proficiency in selected sports or activity areas.

Master's degree programs are also available and are another way to enter the field. Individuals with baccalaureate degrees in areas other than therapeutic recreation can pursue a master's degree in the field and enter the field on that level. Of course, pursuing a master's is ordinarily an advantageous way of increasing one's expertise and training in the field, even if one already possesses the baccalaureate in therapeutic recreation. Coursework in master's programs may include therapeutic recreation for special populations, administration of therapeutic recreation services, and consultation in therapeutic recreation.

CREATIVE ARTS THERAPY

Dance, music, and art therapy comprise what are broadly referred to as creative arts therapies or expressive therapies. Creative arts therapists utilize dance, music, or art in a therapeutic manner to facilitate an individual's insight, self-expression, and social awareness. Creative arts utilized in a therapeutic manner can provide a means of nonverbal communication in which an individual can express psychological needs. The fields of dance, music, and art therapy share many common characteristics, which will be discussed, but the fields differ regarding specific training and required skills.

Functions

Creative arts therapists are employed in many settings, which can include public and private hospitals, nursing homes, mental health clinics, rehabilitation centers, senior citizen centers, public and private schools, and halfway houses. Many interesting and innovative programs utilizing the creative arts have been established in prisons and facilities for the terminally ill. The creative arts have been shown to be a useful form of therapy with a wide range of populations, including the learning disabled, emotionally disturbed, retarded, blind, deaf, and physically handicapped.

Many creative arts therapists function as members of therapeutic treatment teams, particularly in agency or institutional set-

An art therapist exploring the client's world.

tings. The creative arts therapist, as a member of this team, makes recommendations regarding a client's plan of treatment, evaluates a client's progress, and works directly with an individual client, group, or family. Consider the following example.

A creative arts specialist with expertise in art therapy is working with an emotionally troubled child in a residential treatment facility. The child is relatively nonverbal and somewhat threatened, unable to talk about her feelings and problems. Psychotherapy, which relies heavily on a person's verbal ability, has thus far been unable to uncover any specifically useful material with which to help the child understand and learn how to cope with her problems. The treatment team recommends art therapy as an appropriate means to facilitate more fruitful insights into this child. The creative arts therapist begins by having the child draw pictures of herself and her family and surroundings. This visual representation of the child's feelings and perceptions reveals a lot about the child's current problems. How the child works with the various art materials, such as oil paints, charcoals, and clay, also indicates and helps release high levels of tension and frustration. The creative arts therapist and the treatment team are now in a more advantageous position from which to evaluate the needs of the child and develop a more complete plan of treatment.

The creative arts therapist with expertise in dance or music can function in a similar manner to the art therapist. Dance therapy focuses on the nonverbal aspects of personality and behavior as represented by an individual's body movement. Music therapy can increase an individual's self-confidence, help develop a sense of accomplishment and personal satisfaction, improve eye-hand coordination, and increase an individual's attention span.

While many creative arts therapists work in institutional settings, others work as consultants and/or maintain private practices in which they work with clients. Some therapists teach in training programs or college or university programs. The creative arts therapist may serve as an administrator in creative arts or expressive therapy departments in virtually all the settings previously described.

Training and Education

As mentioned earlier, training and educational requirements vary somewhat for the different types of creative arts therapists. The professional organization associated with each field develops criteria for professional recognition within the field.

Art. At present, to be recognized as a creative arts therapist with expertise in art and to be professionally qualified to use the title art therapist, one must obtain a master's degree in art therapy or complete a graduate-level training program in an institute or clinic that is accredited by the American Art Therapy Association.

Dance. In the field of dance therapy, the American Dance Therapy Association also considers a master's degree or equivalent graduate-level training to be the minimum for an entry-level position in the field. Successful completion of graduate training qualifies the creative arts therapist with specialization in the field of dance to use the title of dance therapist.

Music. In the field of music, the National Association for Music Therapy considers the completion of a four-year undergraduate degree with major emphasis in music therapy to be sufficient for professional recognition as a music therapist.

PSYCHIATRIC NURSING

Psychiatric nursing is the specialization within the broad field of nursing that places emphasis on treatment of the physical and mental well-being of a patient. Psychiatric nursing is directed toward assisting the patient to maintain and restore optimum levels of physical and mental health.

Functions

Psychiatric nurses are employed in a variety of settings, which may include inpatient and outpatient units of public and private hospitals, community mental health clinics, rehabilitation centers, and residential mental health treatment facilities. Psychiatric nurses can also maintain private practices in which they provide consultation, counseling, or psychotherapy services to individuals, families, or groups. Psychiatric nurse specialists can also teach in a variety of training programs in hospital, clinic, and college or university settings. Psychiatric nurses can function as administrators of such programs and pursue specific research interests in any of the many professional settings available.

The specific work activities and functions of the psychiatric nurse vary considerably depending on the setting. Still, there are common work activities and functions that can be discussed. The psychiatric nurse in the psychiatric hospital setting is often a member of a therapeutic treatment team. He or she meets regularly with other team members, which may include a psychiatrist, a psychologist, a social worker, and other professional and paraprofessional staff. The psychiatric nurse, as a member of this team, is integrally involved in developing individualized treatment plans for patients, implementing treatment, and evaluating progress.

A major portion of a psychiatric nurse's professional time is spent working directly with patients who have physical as well as mental disorders. He or she is a key figure in establishing and maintaining a therapeutic relationship with the client. The psychiatric nurse often explains specific aspects of patients' illnesses to them. If the patient is taking prescribed medication for an illness, the psychiatric nurse can administer the medication and explain what the medication is and does and what to expect. He or she is trained to observe and understand patient behavior. The psychiatric nurse may work as a counselor to patients, helping them to understand and cope with their illness and helping them to regain a higher level of control over their lives. An emotional illness can often interfere with the patient's ability to understand and meet physical health needs. In this case, the psychiatric nurse might teach patients how to take better care of themselves both physically and emotionally.

Training and Education

According to the American Nurses Association and the National League for Nursing, professional recognition as a clinical specialist in psychiatric nursing requires successful completion of an accredited master's degree program in a clinical psychiatric nursing specialty area. Many colleges and universities provide graduate study in child, adolescent, and family psychiatric nursing, which presently comprise the clinical psychiatric nursing specialty areas.

Before attending a master's degree program in psychiatric nursing, one must complete the training required to become a registered nurse. This usually can be accomplished by completing an accredited program of study offered by various hospital nursing programs, two-year community college programs, or four-year baccalaureate degree programs. A typical baccalaureate degree program includes course work and supervised clinical internships. Undergraduate programs usually emphasize courses in anatomy and physiology but also offer other courses such as nursing the emotionally ill, family-centered maternity nursing, nursing of children, emergency helath care, and drug calculations in nursing. The clinical internship offers students practical nursing experience in different settings under the supervision of a faculty member from the student's college or university nursing program.

The American Nurses Association considers a nurse without advanced clinical training (from an accredited master's degree program) to be a general nurse, even if he or she works exclusively in a psychiatric setting. In-service training programs, continuing education programs, and workshops are available for registered nurses who desire more proficiency in psychiatric nursing but are not enrolled in a master's degree program. Nurses at this level can be certified as generalists through the American Nurses Association rather than as clinical psychiatric nurses.

One can apply to the American Nurses Association for professional recognition and certification as a clinical psychiatric nurse upon completion of the master's degree program of study. There are no current universal state certification requirements for psychiatric nursing. Some states require certification for psychiatric nurses while other states, such as New York, presently have no such requirement. Various doctoral programs are available for psychiatric nurses wishing further training and professional recognition beyond the master's level.

OCCUPATIONAL THERAPY

Occupational therapy is the selective and purposeful therapeutic use of activities to aid in the treatment of physical or mental disorders. Occupational therapy can serve as one part of an individual's overall treatment plan (along with other therapeutic approaches such as psychotherapy or physical therapy) or can be the sole therapeutic approach used to aid an individual. The range of uses of occupational therapy is enormous. It has proved a useful treatment for problems such as physical disabilities, emotional or developmental disorders, and injuries due to accidents. It is particularly useful in the teaching of daily living skills. All programs of treatment are designed for a client's specific needs, and may consist of a single activity or a combination of activities. Activities can be educational, recreational, or social in nature and can include prevocational testing and training, personal care activities, and the use of creative arts.

Functions

Occupational therapists are employed in a variety of settings, which include, but are not limited to, hospitals, mental health clinics, nursing homes, rehabilitation centers, day care centers, sheltered workshops, home health care agencies, and public and private schools. The majority of occupational therapists have positions in hospitals and the majority of clients served fall into the physically handicapped and emotionally handicapped target populations. Of course, the everyday activities of an occupational therapist vary according to the setting and target population.

The occupational therapist very often functions as a member of a therapeutic treatment team. Other members of this team might include a psychologist, a psychiatrist, a social worker, or a nurse. As a member of this team, the occupational therapist is the specialist most often called upon to design and implement a program of activities to reduce specific disabilities and develop an atmosphere in which to promote restoration of ability. The treatment approach utilized most often to accomplish this involves three phases: assessment, treatment, and evaluation. Initially, assessment is needed to determine the individual's ability level. Based upon the assessment, a treatment program is developed. At the final stages of treatment an evaluation is done to judge the effectiveness of the program.

Consider the example of an individual who is a stroke victim and has spent considerable time in the hospital. As a result of this illness, the individual must relearn basic skills such as feeding, dressing, walking, and speaking. The illness has also made his former employment difficult, if not impossible, and he must develop new interests and possibly a new career. Once the individual's level of abilities is assessed, a treatment program might include the following:

• teaching the patient to use equipment such as a wheelchair, prosthetic device, crutches, or braces; to aid with eating, walking, speaking, and general mobility

- working with creative materials such as paints or clay to improve coordination, build confidence, and provide a source of exercise
- working with progressively more difficult materials such as leatherwork, ceramics, or printmaking to refine motor coordination, build strength, and increase work tolerance
- prevocational testing to assess the individual's abilities and skills and to explore other talents
- prevocational training to give an individual practical experience in specific jobs

The individual's progress is consistently monitored throughout treatment and overall evaluation is done at the conclusion of the program. This determines whether additional treatment is needed or the individual is ready to resume activities of daily living. A patient may return to visit the occupational therapist periodically to discuss any problems that may arise. Treatment may be simple or complicated, depending on the client's needs. Highly experienced and talented occupational therapists actually design innovative therapeutic devices to meet the needs of a given situation.

While most occupational therapists are involved in direct patient care, many perform a variety of other duties. A certain percentage of occupational therapists teach in college or university programs. Many perform administrative functions as directors of occupational therapy programs in hospitals or clinics. Still others maintain private practices and act as consultants to various programs and agencies.

Training and Education

The field of occupational therapy contains two forms of classification. One can either be a certified occupational therapy assistant (COTA) or a registered occupational therapist (OTR). Each requires a different form of preparation.

A certified occupational therapy assistant is one who completes an approved two-year associate degree program in occupational therapy from an accredited junior or community college. There are also various educational institutions that have one-year certificate-granting programs. Most programs require a combination of coursework and fieldwork training. A certified occupational therapy assistant most often works under the supervision of a registered occupational therapist.

The registered occupational therapist is required to complete a four-year course of study in an approved college or university program. The individual is then awarded a bachelor of arts or sciences in occupational therapy. A passing grade on a national certification exam administered by the American Occupational Therapy Association is required to be considered professionally competent for employment. Graduates of approved four-year programs are immediately eligible to take this certification examination. In certain situations, certified occupational therapy assistants can become eligible to take this exam (through an accumulation of a minimum of four years of job-related experience). Upon successful completion of the exam the assistant can become a registered occupational therapist. A variety of master's degree programs in occupational therapy exist for those individuals who seek more advanced training in specific areas of the field.

CLINICAL PSYCHOLOGY

Clinical psychology is the specialization within the broad field of general psychology that focuses on the diagnosis and treatment of mental and emotional disorders. Of specific interest to clinical psychologists are the causes of abnormal behavior. Clinical psychologists utilize all applicable scientific methods in their investigation of behavior. These methods may include psychological testing, controlled experiments, and direct observation.

Functions

Clinical psychologists engage in a wide variety of work activities including research, testing, counseling, psychotherapy, teaching, supervising, and consulting. This range of work activities may be performed in psychiatric hospitals, mental health clinics, hospitals, training institutes, public and private schools, research centers, colleges and universities, and federal, state, and local government programs. The type of setting often defines the clinical psychologist's primary work activities and the range of his or her responsibilities. To illustrate this diversity of settings and work activities consider the following examples.

SETTING A: PSYCHIATRIC HOSPITAL

The clinical psychologist conducts individual and group psychotherapy sessions with patients. As a member of the ward treatment team he or she helps to develop and monitor individual treatment plans for patients. A clinical psychologist often administers a battery of psychological tests to a patient in an effort to better determine the nature and scope of the client's problems. This specialist may conduct a group ward meeting with all the patients twice weekly to discuss problems or grievances, disseminate new information that may affect patients, and help the patients to adjust to the ward environment.

The clinical psychologist may be called upon to conduct a staff workshop in his or her particular area of expertise, as part of the hospital's ongoing staff development program. As a member of the senior clinical staff, he or she can also supervise the work of various other paraprofessional and professional staff members. As a representative of the hospital, the clinical psychologist often consults with other hospitals, agencies, programs, or the court system in reference to specific patients, program development, or treatment issues. The clinical psychologist may also maintain a private practice with individuals or groups, in addition to these primary work responsibilities.

SETTING B: PUBLIC OR PRIVATE SCHOOL

In a school setting, the clinical psychologist is most often involved with the counseling of children to help promote their social and intellectual development. Students who are most often in need of the services of a clinical psychologist might include those with learnig disabilities, maladaptive behavior problems, or those experiencing temporary crisis situations. The clinical psychologist often administers standardized psychological tests to help determine the nature of a student's present problems.

The clinical psychologist frequently consults with teachers concerning the specific needs of students. He or she may, in cooperation with teachers, develop special programs of instruction for those students whose disabilities require such individualized programs.

SETTING C: COMMUNITY MENTAL HEALTH CENTER

The majority of clinical psychologists functioning in these settings serve as clinical members of outpatient treatment programs. Other primary work activities vary according to the nature and scope of the clinic. For example, while some clinics may be organized solely for outpatient services, others may provide additional services such as day treatment programs, social programs, medical services, prevocational training, and residential services. The clincical psychologist may be involved in any or all such available services, depending on interest and expertise. In the outpatient setting, the clinical psychologist usually maintains a caseload of clients. The number of patients in a given caseload varies depending upon the size of the clinic, number of other staff members, and number of clients being served. An average number of clients being treated by a single clinical psychologist per week might be 25. The methods of treatment utilized by clinical psychologists vary greatly. The treatment method often depends upon which psychological theory or theories the particular clinical psychologist believes to be most effective. The treatment approaches most often practiced are derived from the psychoanalytic, humanistic, or behavioristic models, described in Chapter Four. The outpatient clinician conducts individual and/or group or family sessions with his or her clients to treat specific problems. The clinical psychologist works in a treatment team, with the help of other staff members, to design and monitor individual client treatment plans. As a supervisor, the clinical psychologist oversees the training and quality of work of other paraprofessional and professional staff.

The growth of a community psychology approach to mental illness means community mental health clinics maintain close ties with other people and agencies in the community. The clinical psychologist may become involved with helping to plan and establish community service and prevention programs such as after-school programs for troubled youth, services and workshops on drug prevention or teenage sexuality, or social programs for the elderly.

Training and Education

Training for a career in the field of clinical psychology begins with the attainment of the baccalaureate degree with a major emphasis in psychology. This degree alone does not qualify an individual to become a psychologist; further graduate-level preparation is required. Many individuals pursue a master's degree in psychology as their final degree, while others consider the master's-level training an intermediate step before entering a doctoral program in clinical psychology. Individuals can enter a Ph.D. program in clinical psychology directly after attaining the B.A. degree.

One can become a master's-level psychologist and function in the field. Job opportunities and salaries are, however, generally less than those available to the Ph.D.-level psychologist. The doctoral-level training most widely accepted is a Ph.D. program approved by the American Psychological Association. Most Ph.D. programs require five years of graduate study, during which time the student completes a range of course work and a clinical internship of approximately one year's duration. The student is placed in a setting such as a psychiatric hospital to fulfill his or her internship requirement. The student intern is supervised in performing a variety of tasks in which he or she could be involved after the completion of graduate study. Internships usually provide a good experience for the student to learn firsthand what it is actually like to perform the duties of a psychologist. The last phase of graduate study, after all course work and internship requirements have been met, involves writing a formal dissertation. The dissertation is an original piece of research conducted by the student under the supervision of a committee of selected faculty members. The student is awarded the Ph.D. upon successful completion of his or her dissertation.

A new type of doctoral program, granting a Psy.D. degree, recently has been approved by the American Psychological Association. A number of graduate schools are offering this new degree. A doctoral dissertation is not required, as the major focus of the training is the development of clinical skills. This type of program is designed to appeal to those individuals more interested in clinical psychology as opposed to research or academics.

Most states have some form of licensing and/or certification requirements, including a written examination, that must be fulfilled. In certain states, licensing law restricts the use of the title psychologist to those individuals who have met the requirements of that state. These laws are designed to stop unqualified individuals from practicing therapy.

SOCIAL WORK

The field of social work focuses on helping individuals to realize their potential in order to live as fully and successfully as possible. The practice of social work addresses itself to the full range of human problems that confront individuals in almost all areas of life. Social workers help individuals, families, and groups to cope with personal problems, and also try to help shape society to be more sensitive and responsive to human needs. Since human problems frequently overlap professional boundaries, social workers often function within the many allied human services fields such as health, criminal justice, community service, or education.

Functions

As previously described, social workers function in a variety of settings with a variety of duties and responsibilities. Some examples of social work settings are mental health clinics, public and private

Social worker interviewing a family.

hospitals, nursing homes, rehabilitation centers, health care agencies, public and private schools, social service agencies, correctional institutions, senior citizen centers, or colleges and universities. When one refers to different kinds of social workers, one is usually referring to the setting in which the social worker is employed rather than to basic differences in training or social work practice (Schmolling, Burger, & Youkeles, 1981).

Although individual functions and activities vary among social workers, there are common work activities. One such activity involves face-to-face contact with clients or those receiving services. This personal contact is referred to as direct practice. Direct practice can be performed in most settings. For example, the social worker employed by a psychiatric facility (psychiatric social worker) might work with individuals or groups to help them solve their specific emotional problems. The social worker employed by a school system (school social worker) might counsel individual students concerning specific school or social problems. The social worker might work directly with families in social service or family agencies. A series of therapeutic sessions might be utilized to help the family to improve communication and solve specific family problems. The social worker employed by a community agency might function as a community organizer and have direct contact with many elements of the community. The social worker in this role usually helps individuals to improve conditions and services within their specific neighborhood. Many social workers also maintain private practices in which they offer a range of psychotherapy services to individuals, families, or groups.

Many social workers provide supervision to other professional and nonprofessional staff. A more experienced social worker might supervise the work of others by providing advice about developing individual client treatment programs and alternative treatment approaches, or offering suggestions concerning how workers can improve their professional competence.

Another common work activity in the social work field is administration. The amount and extent of administrative responsibility vary according to the experience and training of the individual as well as with the type of employment setting. For example, the duties of a senior administrator of an agency or facility might include designing specific programs of service, developing and monitoring budgets, supervising personnel, and evaluating the effectiveness of programs. In general, a senior administrator is responsible for making sure the various programs fulfill their stated missions or purposes.

The social worker may work closely with various agencies, facilities, or branches of government as a consultant. For example, he or she may be requested by the court system to give a professional opinion or provide specific information regarding a client who is accused or convicted of a crime. Consultants may also help an agency develop or reorganize a particular department or program.

Many social workers engage in research or education activities. Experienced social workers can function as teachers or professors in social work training programs at colleges and universities. Social workers involved in research may investigate programs, develop theories, or gather data concerning who needs help, where and what type of help is needed, or how a service may be improved.

Training and Education

The National Association of Social Work, the governing body in the field, determines the criteria for the professional social worker. Currently, the minimum requirement set forth for acceptance as a professional social worker is satisfactory completion of a baccalaureate program in social work and acceptance for membership status in the National Association of Social Work. The college program must be accredited by the Council on Social Work Education.

Bachelor's degree programs in social work (B.S.W.) prepare individuals for entry-level positions in the field. Course work stresses different aspects of the field, which might include the history of social work and the practice of social work in different settings. In addition to course work emphasizing social work, the student is exposed to a broad liberal arts background. All accredited programs require the student to complete 300 hours of supervised fieldwork. The student is placed in a selected social work field site and, under the supervision of a professional social worker, gains experience working directly with clients.

Traditionally, the only route available to becoming a professional social worker has been to attain a master's degree in social work (M.S.W.). This requires completion of a graduate program (usually two years of full-time study). The recent development of B.S.W. progiams means the M.S.W. is not the only route to social work; however, the master's degree is often necessary for advancement in the field. In fact, many professional social work agencies, institutions, and facilities set the M.S.W. as a requirement for supervisory positions.

One does not necessarily have to possess a B.S.W. degree to gain acceptance into an M.S.W. degree program. Individuals possessing undergraduate degrees in other fields, such as psychology or sociology, may be accepted for graduate study, provided they meet other criteria established by individual schools.

M.S.W. training requires two years of supervised fieldwork. The course work, for the most part, pertains exclusively to the profession of social work, with many schools emphasizing the common elements of direct practice and increasing the student's knowledge of the field. M.S.W. degree-granting programs, like all B.S.W. programs, must be accredited by the Council on Social Work Education.

In recent years, doctor of social work (D.S.W.) programs have been established in various colleges and universities. This doctoral-level program seems to attract social workers whose primary interests are in pursuing advanced-level training in the areas of teaching, administration, and social policy. A doctor of social work program, like many other doctoral programs, usually takes an average of four years to complete and includes a program of required course work and the successful completion of a doctoral dissertation.

PSYCHIATRY

Psychiatry is the medical specialty that investigates, diagnoses, and treats mental, emotional, or behavioral disorders. Psychiatrists are initially trained as medical doctors. As such they are the only category of human services professionals legally authorized to prescribe medicine.

Functions

Psychiatrists, because of their extensive training and preparation, generally occupy positions of elevated status within the human services field. This is reflected by their high salaries and the scope and depth of their responsibilities. For example, within a therapeutic team comprised of other human services workers, the psychiatrist often functions in a leadership or supervisory capacity. The majority of psychiatrists maintain some type of private practice, but few contribute all their professional time to treating patients in a private setting. The psychiatrist may also work in a clinic or hospital setting, perform consultations, conduct research, teach, or occupy an administrative position. A psychiatrist's specific function varies according to the setting in which he or she is working, but all licensed psychiatrists can prescribe medication.

The psychiatrist who works in a psychiatric hospital is involved in many activities. For example, he or she normally carries a specified caseload of patients. As mentioned earlier, the psychiatrist is most likely also a member of a hospital team in which patient treatment plans are developed and monitored and the possible discharge of improved patients is discussed. The psychiatrist is often called upon to consult with other workers in the hospital concerning specific cases in which a psychiatric opinion is requested. Psychiatrists also act as expert consultants to courts, prisons, and other public and private institutions.

Many psychiatrists engage in work that is primarily administrative, such as directing a psychiatric hospital staff or program, directing a mental health clinic, or overseeing a governmental program such as the National Institute of Mental Health. The psychiatrist serving in this capacity is largely involved in the development of programs, budget preparation and monitoring, and staff management. As an administrator, the psychiatrist establishes the framework within which other professionals work.

Research and teaching are other possible career areas for the psychiatrist. Research opportunities and interests are varied, and the range of possible research subjects is enormous. For example, the psychiatrist might study the effect of a drug upon a specific disorder, the impact that maternal stress has on the newborn child, or the effects of a new treatment approach. As a teacher, the psychiatrist may be found in medical schools, institutes, and colleges and universities.

An additional area of specialization now emerging for the psychiatrist is that of community psychiatry. Community psychiatry is based on the belief that the community should play a more vital role in preventing and treating mental illness. Prevention and treatment are accomplished by means of a variety of community programs. The psychiatrist involved in this field is most likely employed by a community mental health center. In this context he or she might be involved with designing such community programs as residential centers for ex-institutionalized patients, working with schools to establish programs for troubled youth, or designing social programs for senior citizens.

Training and Education

The training of a psychiatrist is lengthy and demanding. Many individuals do not realize that preparation for such a career actually begins as early as high school with the attainment of excellent grades. A solid aptitude for science and mathematics is necessary because a great deal of required course work is in these areas. The aspiring psychiatrist usually majors in a premedical course of study in undergraduate school. A premed program frequently includes courses in inorganic and organic chemistry, physics, biology, and advanced mathematics.

Application to medical school is made after the student has been granted a baccalaureate degree. Medical school is a highly demanding four-year course of study. During these four years the student learns the practice of medicine. The student is considered a full-fledged physician upon graduation from medical school.

Following medical school, the new physician must enroll in another course of study called the residency. It is during this four-year program that the physician specializes in the field of psychiatry. The training may take place in one of several settings, which include university medical centers, accredited psychiatric hospitals, or psychiatric divisions of general hospitals. The course work and practice is devoted exclusively to psychiatry and it is within this framework that the physician sharpens his or her clinical skills.

The psychiatrist is able to take an examination certifying competency in the field upon satisfactory completion of his or her residency training. He or she is not awarded a certificate in the specialty of psychiatry until passing the national exam administered by the American Board of Psychiatry and Neurology. This certification is not a legal requirement for a physician to practice psychiatry, but the board-certified psychiatrist normally has more career opportunities and enjoys greater acceptance in the medical community.

PROFESSIONAL ORGANIZATIONS

For more detailed information about the career areas discussed in this chapter, you can write to any of the organizations listed on pp. 200–201.

Paraprofessional Work

National Organization of Human Services
Box 999, Loretto Station
Denver, CO 80236

Council for Standards in Human Services Education,
Southern Regional Education Board
130 Sixth Street, N.W.
Atlanta, GA 30313

Therapeutic Recreation

The National Therapeutic Recreation Society
1601 North Kent Street
Arlington, VA 22209

Creative Arts Therapy (Art, Dance, and Music)

American Art Therapy Association
427 E. Preston Street
Baltimore, MD 21202

American Dance Therapy Association
Suite 230, 2000 Century Plaza
Columbia, MD 21044

National Association for Music Therapy Inc.
P.O. Box 610
Lawrence, KA 66044

Psychiatric Nursing

National League for Nursing
10 Columbus Circle
New York, NY 10019

Occupational Therapy

American Occupational Therapy Association
6000 Executive Boulevard
Rockville, MD 20852

Clinical Psychology

American Psychological Association
1200 Seventeenth Street N.W.
Washington, DC 20036

Social Work

Council on Social Work Education
111 Eighth Avenue
New York, NY 10011

National Association of Social Workers
1425 H Street N.W., Suite 600
Washington, DC 20005

Psychiatry

American Medical Association
535 North Dearborn Street
Chicago, IL 60610

American Psychiatric Association
1700 Eighteenth Street N.W.
Washington, DC 20009

ADDITIONAL READING

Barton, W. E., & Sanborn, C. J. (Eds.). (1978). *Law and the mental health professions: Friction at the interface.* New York: International Universities Press.

Monohan, J. (Ed.). (1976). *Community mental health and the criminal justice system.* Elmsford, NY: Pergamon Press.

Morse, S. J., & Watson, R. I., Jr. (1977). *Psychotherapies: A comparative casebook.* New York: Holt, Rinehart & Winston.

Porter, R. A., Peters, J. A., & Headry, H. R. (1982). Using community development for prevention in Appalachia. *Social Work, 27,* 302–307.

Walsh, J. A. (1982). Prevention in mental health: Organizational and ideological perspectives. *Social Work, 27,* 298–301.

Whittington, H. G. (1972). *Clinical practice in community mental health centers.* New York: International Universities Press.

REFERENCES

National Organization of Human Services Newsletter. (Fall, 1982).

Schmolling, P., Burger, W., & Youkeles, M. (1981). *Helping people: A guide to careers in mental health.* Englewood Cliffs, NJ: Prentice-Hall.

Sobey, F. (1969, November). *Nonprofessional personnel in mental health programs: A summary report based on a study of projected support by the National Institute under contract #PL4366-967* (No. 5028). Washington, DC: National Clearinghouse for Mental Health Information..

SOCIAL POLICY

INTRODUCTION

Social policy, a topic usually discussed in advanced courses, is considered by many to be too complex to be included in introductory courses. We, however, believe that social policy is a most appropriate topic for introductory courses in human services. Without an understanding of social policy, the human services worker cannot appreciate the significant impact it has upon the design and delivery of services. We will try to show some ways, direct and indirect, in which social policies affect the human services worker and the consumer of human services.

The first section of this chapter provides a general description of social policies with regard to what they do and who they affect. The remaining sections focus on making and implementing social policies.

Throughout the chapter, we try to show the relevance of social policy to the individual human services worker. In one section, there is a discussion of the role of the human services worker in introducing or initiating policy proposals. This is followed by a discussion of when and how the worker might influence the formulation or the final form of social policy. Finally, examples are given of how the human services worker affects existing policy and how policy affects the worker. The general focus is on the connections between social policy, the human services worker, and the delivery of human services. For you to understand these connections, a discussion of definitions, development, and implementation of social policies is required. Definitions of social policy are discussed first.

WHAT IS SOCIAL POLICY?

A policy, according to the *Random House Dictionary* (1978), is "a guiding principle or course of action adopted toward an objective or objectives." The word *social*, according to the same dictionary, refers to "the life, welfare, and relations of human beings in a community." Gil (1981) summed it up very well when he wrote that "social policies are a special type of policies, namely, policies which deliberately pertain to the quality of life and to the circumstances of living in society, and to intra-societal relationships among individuals, groups, and society as a whole" (p. 13).

Titmus (1974) made it clear that the study of social policy includes an understanding of the political, social, and economic forces in society. While such an understanding is beyond the scope of this text, it is certainly worth mentioning. He claimed that "social policy can be seen as a positive instrument for change; as . . . part of the whole political process" (p. 26). Another definition of social policy is that of Huttman (1981), who saw social policies as "plans of action and strategies for providing services" (p. 2). She added that social policies have the goal of sound human relations. Another definition dealing with a particular kind of social policy, and one of more than passing interest to human services workers, namely social welfare policy, is the one given by Prigmore & Atherton (1979): "Social welfare policy is a generic term for the guidelines used for decision making on social welfare programs and issues" (p. 8).

Although there are many definitions of social policy, they all seem to agree that social policy is characterized by the following aspects:

- Social policy is problem-oriented—that is, it seeks to improve an existing or anticipated condition.
- Social policy is action-oriented—that is, it outlines or describes programs that seek to effect change.
- Social policy is focused on individuals or groups, such as the target populations described in Chapter Two.
- Making social policy involves making choices regarding the kind and/or extent of changes to be made.

While there are many other aspects of social policy, for the purpose of this discussion the four indicated above will be highlighted.

What impels a society, or a group, or individuals for that matter, to expend hard-earned and limited resources to help those in need? Is such behavior a demonstration of democratic values, religious beliefs, or a matter of survival for society? There appears to be no single answer. In the past, all of these factors have played a significant part in the efforts to help those in need. We now take a brief look at past social policies.

Social Policy in the Past

Social policies in preliterate societies were not perceived as such. They were plans for survival—to assure food, shelter, and protection against predators, hostile groups, and hostile environments. Physical survival was the goal. The success of the plans depended upon the mutual efforts of the family or tribe. Without these efforts, individual survival was jeopardized.

As families or tribes settled in one place and developed villages of relative permanence, and as populations increased, more of the support necessary for survival was provided by the extended family. In these different circumstances, those without a family were still able to survive, if only marginally. When communities grew even larger and more complex, organized religion began to provide aid to those who had no family or whose family did not have the resources or ability to provide the needed support. Caring for the mentally ill, homeless children, the physically disabled, and the hungry became a major concern of organized religion. These humanitarian efforts seemed to prevent the turmoil and conflict that often result from threats to survival. Keep in mind the important fact that efforts and plans designed to improve the life of those in need also eliminated a threat to the existing power structure. Large numbers of hungry, desperate people were frequently candidates for riot and rebellion.

Social Policy in Modern Times

The rapid and significant changes that typify modern industrial society caused organized religion, private organizations, and individuals to increase their efforts to help those in need. The loosening of family bonds, the increase in crime, and the increase in the numbers of mentally ill, elderly poor and disabled, and persons living in poverty made it impossible for existing institutions to provide the necessary support for those in need. Their values, plans, and policies did not undergo basic changes; they just did not have the resources in the form of funds, manpower, or material to provide the needed help.

As problems grew in size, number, and complexity, governments had to step in to develop and implement programs to prevent starvation and to provide opportunities for gaining resources for an adequate life. An underlying purpose was to reduce dissatisfaction with the existing political or power structure. When one looks at the bottom line, it is obvious that social policies do not stem from humanitarian values alone but also derive from the desire of those in power to remain in control of society's wealth and resources. This is why governments focus on social policies that deal with basic needs such as food, shelter, clothing, and medical care.

Private human services agencies also deal with these kinds of problems, but on a very much smaller scale. In addition, they focus on providing help in meeting the higher-level needs, such as belonging and self-actualization, described in Chapter One.

For the most part, they try to help people adjust to the existing social and economic structure. Agencies, in effect, seek to maintain the status quo.

There are human services workers, however, who believe that the way to help is by changing society through social policies that distribute resources and power more equitably among all people— namely to the poor. Regardless of the basic motives behind social policy, it seems clear that unless and until more successful or satisfying programs are devised to provide for the basic needs of people who are unable to provide them for themselves, much suffering, turmoil, and conflict will result.

PURPOSE AND TYPES OF SOCIAL POLICY

The purpose of social policy today, put simply, is to improve the lives of people. Most often policy is designed to meet the needs of selected populations such as those mentioned in Chapter Two. Accordingly, there are many different types of social policies. The most familiar type of policy is social welfare policy, mentioned earlier. Other types include housing policy, mental health policy, child welfare policy, and unemployment policy. Within each of these general categories there are more specific plans or policies. For example, in the case of housing policy, the focus might be on housing for the elderly or perhaps housing for the poor or for migrants. Mental health policy could include policies dealing with aftercare services, outpatient clinics, or prevention programs. So while the common purpose of social policy is to meet needs, it is important to recognize that there are many kinds of policies that affect almost all human needs. We recommend that you read Huttman (1981) for a more detailed understanding of this subject.

THE SCOPE OF SOCIAL POLICY

Social policy affects most, if not all, people in society, from the cradle to the grave. For example, there are social policies that deal with abortion, birth control, child care, child abuse, teenage drinking, young adult drug abuse, marriage, divorce, as well as policies relating to older adults, and yes—even death. The number and kinds of policies and programs implemented and/or proposed by federal, state, local, and private agencies are indeed impressive. It should be noted that because of the sheer number of programs implemented, one can find inconsistencies in purposes and goals.

Not only do social policies affect us throughout our life span, they also affect us in almost every aspect of our lives. Most certainly they affect us in regard to Maslow's hierarchy of needs described in Chapter One. For example, policies dealing with basic physiological or survival needs such as hunger and thirst try to prevent malnutrition and eliminate starvation in our society. The food stamp program is one example of such a policy. Safety needs are met through housing and law enforcement policies, to name just a few. An example is a recently initiated program to provide shelter for the homeless population in New York City. Other kinds of safety needs are met by programs focusing on automobile safety, food and drug monitoring, and public transportation. Programs dealing with these and other needs are often influenced by other kinds of government policies.

Other kinds of government policies include foreign policies, economic policies, educational policies, transportation policies, and defense policies. It is important to recognize that social policies are not the only policies focused on improving society in one way or another. One might claim that transportation policies could be considered a form of social policy because good transportation improves society. The same could be said for economic, educational, and other policies.

When one considers all the different types of policies, at least two things become quite clear. First, there are a tremendous number of policies and programs dealing with issues in every aspect of our lives. Second, there is a need to decide the relative importance of different policies. For example, the need to distribute surplus food to the poor is seen by some in power as less important than increasing the number of submarines. The "guns or butter" issue is at present clearly being decided in favor of defense over social policies. There is also a hierarchy of importance in the various social policies. Some people claim that providing funds for the AFDC program is more important than providing outpatient services in the community for released mental health patients. Regardless of how one determines which policy is more important than the others, it is inevitable that policies are in competition with each other.

This competition is resolved through compromise and the exercise of power. It is rare for everyone to agree on which social policies to promote, or on which policies are more important. Gilbert and Specht (1974) stated clearly that "different choice preferences will be registered by different policy planners, depending upon the values, theories, and assumptions given the most worth and credence" (p. 49). The concept that compromise and power provide the means for resolving the competition between social policies is discussed in the following sections.

THE MAKING OF SOCIAL POLICY

As indicated earlier, one of the aspects of social policy is that it is problem-oriented. Another way of putting it is that social policy attempts to improve the lives of people who need help in meeting certain needs. If people were able to meet their needs through their own efforts, society would not need to develop programs to help them. It is when the needs cannot be met by the individual that social policies and programs are brought to bear.

As noted earlier, there are often very serious differences and controversies regarding the kind and extent of help required, how the help should be provided, and who deserves or needs the help. How, then, is social policy made? Since it is problem-oriented, it begins by focusing on unmet needs.

Identifying Unmet Needs

The first step in social policy formulation is to identify unmet needs. On the surface this seems like a very simple task. However, there are some problems even here. In this tremendously complex society of ours, there are so many unmet needs that it is difficult to select those that demand a social policy and program. Could there be, should there be, policies and programs that meet *all* the unmet needs of *all* the people *all* the time? If not, the question arises, whose needs and which needs should we attempt to meet? Shall we be concerned about the unmet needs of the wealthy, or concentrate on the needs of the poor? If, as most people might agree, we should focus primarily on survival or life-sustaining needs such as adequate food, what direction shall we go from there? What about other unmet needs? Should we be concerned only about the unmet needs that are beyond the control of the individual, or should we also help people who contribute to their own difficulties because of ignorance, poor judgment, or foolishness? Another question needs to be asked. Should social policies be based on the number of people affected? If so, how many people constitute the required number to merit the introduction of a policy and program?

Another major problem in regard to policy formulation is that society is in a constant state of change. And not only is society changing, but individuals, workers, planners, and organizers are changing with society. Alinsky (1971) made the point about an organizer that "truth to him is relative and changing; everything to him is relative and changing" (p. 11). The same holds true for the social planner. Change is not an easy or comfortable process to undergo. It is a process that often, if not always, brings on conflict with oneself or with others, for people change at different rates and in different directions. Other questions come to mind. Don't social problems change without intervention in a changing society? For example, not long ago unmarried couples living together were not only frowned upon but actively discouraged and prohibited. Today, in an ever-increasing number of states and jurisdictions, unmarried couples living together are permitted and recognized legally in many ways. A changing society in effect has eliminated a problem and affected social policies. Aren't some problems temporary, and how can one know if they are or not, or how temporary they are?

A final question: Who answers all the questions posed above, and how?

Who Identifies Social Problems?

Who has the power to determine which issue should be identified as a social problem that requires the formulation of a social policy for its resolution? Power in this context refers to the ability to influence, sway, and somehow persuade a significant number of individuals to also recognize and declare an unmet need as a social problem. According to Alinsky (1971), it is this kind of power that begets even greater power. In other words, the more people one influences, the more influence one can exert. Such power, however, is not easily come by. In fact, many professionals in the human services field, such as Meyer (1983), feel that "politicians control the power to define. Who is to be defined as poor, sick, unemployed, homeless, or uncared for . . . ?" (p. 99). She went on to state unequivocally that "the criteria used to define these conditions are political and economic." Does this mean that a poor person cannot determine or identify social problems? Not at all! Brager and Specht (1965) pointed out that the large number of low-income persons and their ability to affect public opinion provide a degree of power that cannot be ignored. Alinsky (1971) also recognized that when people are made aware of a specific cause, they can, when organized, wield tremendous power.

It is clear that private citizens, regardless of their economic status, can be instrumental in identifying social problems. A lay person may not identify the problem as Maslow or other professionals might, but that does not mean that the identification is any less accurate. In fact, problems are often more clearly and accurately identified by such individuals. Recently, for example, a California mother of a developmentally disabled young man suggested an idea that was quickly developed into a full-fledged program. The idea was to pair such young men with older adults, each providing needed services for the other, thus enabling them to live together but independently of their families. The young adult would provide shopping, cooking, and cleaning services, while the older adult would teach academic and vocational skills that could enable the young person to become truly independent. This is an excellent example of how a social problem was identified by a private citizen. Usually, however, an individual's problem does not become identified as a social problem just because it is known by the individual. As indicated above, numbers are essential when trying to identify a problem as a social problem. In most instances the private individual needs the help of human services experts and others to have a problem recognized and established as a social problem.

The human services worker when working with a population to meet certain needs often becomes aware of other needs that are not being met. For example, in the mid-1940s in New York City, workers helping older adults with public assistance recognized that these people were also very lonely. The workers then influenced others to provide the older persons with a place to meet other older adults. The facility became a recreation center for the older adults in the community. Additional services were added as other problems such as those with nutrition and health were recognized. From this modest beginning and others like it, the senior center movement was born.

The objective of the worker is to try to obtain the appropriate services for those in need. Human services workers can be, and often are, instrumental in determining unmet needs and in influencing policy. In order to accomplish this task, the worker must assess the number of individuals involved and the kind and degree of disadvantage involved. Furthermore, the reasons for the lack of services must also be established, for they will have a direct bearing on decisions the worker must make in an attempt to rectify the problem.

Among the many reasons for a lack of needed services in a community, four seem to be prevalent. First, there might not be any resources in the community (or anywhere else, for that matter) to provide the needed service. Second, the resources might be available in the community but the individuals in need might not be aware of their existence. Third, even if the resources are known, those in need might not know how to use such resources. Fourth, those in need might not be eligible for such services—that is, they might not meet age, sex, racial, income-level, neighborhood, or other criteria determined by the providers of service. In the instances where lack of knowledge of existing resources or how to use such resources is the major stumbling block, the worker's major role might be to supply the needed information to those seeking such services. Where there are no resources or where eligibility requirements are not met, the worker may be required to enter the realm of social policy in order to meet the needs of clients.

Austin, Skelding, and Smith (1977) pointed out that risks are involved when fighting for the rights of those in need and attempting to affect policy. Advocating, they rightly claimed, often means speaking out, confronting agencies, and risking one's job. Not long ago in Illinois, a worker discovered that residents of a center where he was working were to be transferred to an unlicensed nursing home. Upon learning of this situation, the worker notified the families of these residents of the plans and their right to oppose the move. The worker went further and represented the residents and their families at a hearing, and was instrumental in preventing the proposed transfer. His action resulted in a threat to his job and a written reprimand in his file. The worker filed a grievance through his union and won. He then went on with the help of his union and lobbied successfully for new state regulations preventing such transfers and assuring competent service for older persons.

This example raises the question that all human services workers ask themselves at one time or another: Should you try to defend the consumer's right to service, or should you keep quiet and accept things as they are? Increasingly, human services workers and agencies are standing up and being counted when the need arises. Unfortunately, this does not occur as often as one might wish. Azarnoff and Seliger (1982) indicated clearly that "advocacy has risks which impede action for many staff people. Dismissal or loss of advancement must be considered as a realistic threat" (p. 209). Whether or not one is successful in obtaining the needed services is often a function of how one goes about the attempt. The worker must exercise tact, skill, and a judicial use of power to win support for new programs.

Initiating Social Policy

Once a problem has been identified as a social problem, the next step might be to inform others about the situation. Informing and educating other workers and clients is one of the necessary steps in the process. The human services worker, usually a member of an agency staff, might inform his coworkers and/or supervisor of an unmet need. The worker might then try to enlist their aid in an attempt to meet the need. By informing other clients, the worker makes others aware of the problem and thus may arouse additional interest and support. The hope and intent is to mobilize as much strength as possible in the effort to obtain the needed service.

This kind of an approach often leads to contacts with individuals and groups who have the influence and resources to help resolve the problem. These influential persons include politicians, professionals and their organizations, and government officials who might initiate an investigation in order to determine the breadth and depth of a particular problem. The results of the investigation are then examined and presented to those who make the decisions regarding programs and policies. These decision makers include executive board members of voluntary agencies, and local, state, or federal legislators or civil servants.

Sometimes it is the client population together with human services workers who initiate the move toward the introduction of new programs and policies. Many years ago on the Lower East Side of New York City, the director of a summer sleep-away camp of a sectarian agency was approached by community residents of various faiths and races to discuss providing camping services for their children. The community members pointed out the desperate need for these services that could not be met by other agencies in the community. They also pointed out that many children attending the director's camp did not live in the community. The director agreed to accept some of the children in question. Within a relatively short period of time the agency served all those who desired service, with the understanding that the agency would maintain its sectarian nature and goals. Community members in this example used their power to influence policy of a community agency. Until recently it was the agencies who determined their policies, and the recipients of service did not have the power to change or affect them significantly.

Baker and Northman (1981) suggested that citizen involvement in policy determination is really a form of redistribution of power that previously did not allow for such sharing. Dobelstein (1980), on the other hand, asserted that "even in the present consumer-oriented society, those who are the principal recipients of welfare policies are rarely involved in making welfare decisions" (p. 30). While one might agree with the latter point of view, we believe that it may be a mistake to underestimate the power of the consumer and/or the human services worker to affect policy. It is sometimes impossible to tell in advance if one will be able to affect programs and policies, and to what extent. Actually, one may be able to affect such decisions more than one might imagine. As far as the individual worker is concerned, opportunities for initiating programs occur more frequently on the local than on the state or federal levels. As an ancient Chinese philosopher was reported to have said, "A journey of a thousand miles starts with a single step."

FACTORS IN ESTABLISHING POLICY

Azarnoff and Seliger (1982) affirmed that the president and Congress pass the laws and formulate policies based upon their perceptions of what the public wants and needs. What is the basis of their perceptions? Often it is the results of research or the pressure of groups and individuals lobbying for or against a certain policy. We look at these factors in this section.

Research

The basic sources of information used in deciding policy are studies, surveys, experiments, reports, and records. Data gathered from these sources are examined, interpreted, discussed, and presented to the president and Congress for their consideration. This process also takes place on the state and the local level, and involves the legislatures and executives of each jurisdiction. Voluntary agencies formulate their policies and programs in essentially the same manner. Data are gathered, examined, interpreted, discussed, and presented to the executive and board of directors for their decisions. It is rare indeed that agencies, governmental or voluntary, devise policies or programs without going through this process. Sound research and its application, while not a guarantee of perfect policies or programs, is an extremely useful tool in developing sound social policies and programs.

The Community Mental Health Centers Act of 1963 is an excellent example of how research can be used to develop policies and programs to help the mentally ill. In this instance, it was a presidential commission that gathered data on the increasing numbers of people in need of mental health services. The lack of trained personnel, facilities, and resources was highlighted in the report of the commission. Congress adopted legislation that provided funds to set up community mental health centers throughout the country. In addition, funds for training more personnel were made available. The intent was to reduce the number of people needing long-term hospitalization. Much was accomplished but, as with almost any complex problem, solutions were only partially achieved and other problems were created. Unfortunately, the research in this instance did not provide enough data to avoid some of the problems that developed. Some problems are not the fault of the research. In too many instances, the information asked for is limited to specific and existing problems rather than predicting and preventing future problems.

It has sometimes happened that research, surveys, and studies have been devised to prove a point, rather than to gather data and let the chips fall where they may. Other situations have occurred in which the individuals conducting the research (often human services workers themselves) had little knowledge of acceptable methods of gathering and interpreting valid and reliable data. Anecdotal records and similarly limited types of studies have all too frequently been the basis for program policy changes. These approaches are at best questionable. There have also been instances when agencies have ignored or discarded data that did not enhance the image or viability of the agency. Capoccia and Googins (1982) suggested that in an environment of limited choice of policy decisions or limited funding, mobilization of interested groups and the exercise of power becomes more important than research in assessing needs. They added that the more limited the choices, the less the chances are for determining need through an objective or rational process.

The results of biased or inadequate research have sometimes led to poorly planned policies and programs. Such policies might be considered politically practical but they also might be useless and destructive to those they are intended to serve. Witness the deinstitutionalization policy and program of the last decade for the mentally disabled. The title of a report to the Congress in 1977 by the Comptroller of the United States gives an idea of the results of this policy: *Returning the Mentally Disabled to the Community: Government Needs to Do More.* The report refers both to the positive aspects of the various programs and to the many problems resulting from a lack of facilities and services, as well as to the inadequacy of follow-up for those returned to the community. Mechanic (1980) was more specific in this regard. He stated that "large numbers of mental patients were released from hospitals into the community without adequate preparation, . . . appropriate services, or consideration of the social costs" (p. 83). He added, significantly, that while the thrust for such programs came from many sources, a major one was the economic pressures on state governments. He pointed out that the programs were generally supported by mental health professionals due to overly optimistic views of anticipated results. What did result in many instances was patient "dumping," leading to community fears and resistance, and victimization of patients by the unscrupulous due to the lack of support services. More adequate research regarding the needed criteria for facilities for patients, the number of patients involved, and the level of support services might have led to more successful programs.

Pressure and Lobbying

When one studies the development of social policies on the federal level, one becomes awed by the pressure brought to bear on Congress and the president to influence the development and purposes of social policies and programs before a final decision is made. Azarnoff and Seliger (1982) described the legislative process as a vehicle to obtain different points of view and, possibly, to change

One of the many nonprofessional groups that affect social policy through their representatives and by testifying before legislative bodies.

programs and policies. They emphasized that "the legislative process is not neutral or value free" (p. 75). White (1982) confirmed this view in his description of the rapid growth in the number of lobbyists who try to affect legislation. He wrote that in the first half of 1981, over 1000 new lobbyists registered in Washington. His report on a recent survey told about the existence of more than 50 lobbies for minorities, over 30 for social agencies, more than 30 for women's groups, and many others. This does not include the offices of almost 30 states and 70 cities that are in Washington trying to obtain their share of the pie, as well as to influence programs and policies that could help their constituents. When one adds the countless individuals and groups, including many human services worker organizations, that march, testify, send letters, make calls, and otherwise attempt to influence the lawmakers, it becomes clear that the pressures on Congress and the president are awesome.

The question then is how does all this constant pressure affect their perception and decisions regarding policies and programs. It becomes quite apparent that regardless of what decisions are made, not everyone will be happy. The same pressures exist on state and local levels of government and within voluntary or private agencies, although on a smaller scale. The general outcome is that the decision makers try to give important groups, those with clout, at least some of what they want.

Opposition

Opposition refers to efforts to defeat proposed policies or changes in existing policies or programs. These efforts play an important role in determining the final form of accepted policies and programs. Sometimes there is little change in the original proposal as a result of opposition, but in some instances one might have some trouble in recognizing the original idea. The degree of transformation is related to the strength of the opposition and the nature of the compromise reached by the opposing groups. Compromises might be in philosophy, funding, resources, politics, or a combination of these factors.

For example, federal legislation regarding abortion, while certainly recognizable from the original proposal, had to undergo change in order to be passed. Opponents to the legislation sought to make all abortions illegal except in specific medical emergencies. Proponents felt that the decision to have an abortion should rest with the pregnant woman. The struggle between the opposing forces led to an important compromise concerning the age of the fetus at which abortion was considered to be illegal. This compromise helped to secure passage of the bill. Political considerations were the major basis for proposal and acceptance of the compromise. The moral issues are still alive and may never be resolved. However, if there had been little or no opposition to the original policy, the final legislation and the entire abortion issue might have been significantly different.

Opposition is frequently based not upon moral, political, or philosophical issues, but rather on self-serving economic factors. The survival of an agency or program has been known to be a major obstacle to new policies or policy changes. Jobs of human services workers are often at stake, and this factor, as difficult as it might be to acknowledge, has been known to be a major obstacle to eliminating or changing an obsolete or ineffective agency or program.

THE IMPLEMENTATION OF SOCIAL POLICY

Once a policy has been decided upon, regardless of its purpose or limits, a program must be devised and carried out if the policy is to have any impact. Remember, a policy is a plan or guide. It tells us what to do, not how to do it. For example, there is a policy stating that child abuse should be eliminated and prevented. This policy has been established by many organizations, public and private, concerned with child welfare. These agencies often make funds available to help in the effort. There are many ways one could approach the problem. Some agencies might focus on working with young parents who were victims of child abuse themselves. Others might provide information and education through the media. Yet another approach would be to attempt to discover the cause of child abuse through research and then develop a program to deal with those causes. In an actual program, any one or a combination of these approaches is considered an effort to implement the policy of preventing child abuse.

The discussion that follows provides some idea of what is involved in developing programs to implement social policy. It includes additional insights regarding opportunities for human services workers to affect programs and policies. The purpose is merely to introduce you to some of the factors at work in the implementation of social policy.

Funding

Money! Money makes the world go 'round! Money talks! Money isn't everything! There seems to be some truth in all those comments. With regard to social policies, it is almost certain that the availability of funds determines whether or not a policy is implemented. Money also determines the degree to which a policy is implemented. For example, the policy of most states is to provide adequate treatment and living facilities for patients in mental hospitals. In practice, however, there are too many institutions that provide little or no treatment along with minimal custodial care. Unfortunately, the same holds true with regard to many institutions serving the aged, the retarded, and juvenile offenders. In most cases, the excuse given for these conditions is lack of funds. This is very frequently the case. What is also true, however, is that how one uses available funds is a significant factor in determining the degree to which a policy is implemented and the degree of effectiveness of a program. In other words, efficient use of funds may make up, in part, for the limited amount of funds. On the other hand, it should be understood that ample funds do not guarantee the effective implementation of policies.

Another problem of funding social policies occurs when a policy is decided upon and no funds are appropriated to carry out the policy. In some cases monies are appropriated but are not permitted to be spent (Fill, 1974). An example of this type of problem came about when the policy of busing children from one area to another to integrate schools was proclaimed by the courts. Funding to provide the buses was sometimes not forthcoming from other branches of government to carry out the mandated policy. Federal, state, and local governments have often mandated programs without providing sufficient funds to implement them effectively. Obviously, funds are vital to the process of implementing policy.

Another important aspect of funding is the pressure of current trends in the field of human services. In the view of Brager and Holloway (1978), "Human service agencies are vulnerable to program fads and fashions . . . . New programs and ideas sometimes attract more than a fair share of limited funds" (p. 49). They intimated that this might be due to competition for available limited funds, and the fact that funding sources sometimes demonstrate more interest in particular aspects of service. In New York City, for example, the drive to provide shelter and food for the homeless became the issue of the winter of 1982–83. Shelters were established, staff were assigned to get the homeless to the shelters, and even the mayor hit the street trying to convince the homeless to take advantage of the shelters and services provided. It was obvious to all that a class action suit against the city, and the accompanying publicity, triggered the sudden concern for the homeless. After all, weren't they there before the winter of 1982–83? The recent movement toward deinstitutionalization is yet another example of a current trend in the field of human services.

It is clear that funding affects policies and policies affect funding. It is also clear that human services workers are seriously affected in their efforts to carry out policies depending upon the level of funding available to them.

Interpretation of Policy

A second factor that has significant impact upon policy implementation is the way policy is interpreted. Interpreting policy means more than just explaining policy. According to the *Random House Dictionary* (1978), interpretation is "construing or understanding in a particular way." It involves an understanding or conception of another's words or deeds. The question here, of course, is how social policies are interpreted. It is useful, at this point, to make a distinction between general policy and operational policy. For example, the elimination of poverty is a general policy. How one goes about eliminating poverty—for example, through welfare programs or government work programs—involves operational policy (Huttman, 1981). In other words, a general policy states a broad objective, while operational policy is concerned with the methods and procedures used to meet the objective.

There is usually little controversy regarding the interpretation of general policies. Few would argue with the policy of trying to eliminate poverty. Problems arise, however, on the operational level when it becomes necessary to determine the income at which a person or family is considered to be living in poverty. Further questions then arise. To what extent should people be helped, under what conditions, and for how long? Different states, jurisdictions, and agencies have different criteria for resolving such questions.

For example, Congress recently tightened eligibility rules for the social security disability program. It was felt that the government was providing funds to disabled people who were able to work. It was subsequently reported ("U.S. Agency Calls," 1983) that decisions to stop disability payments were being based on an extremely hardline interpretation. It was reported that an examiner said unless a claimant was "flat on his back in an institution," "comatose," or "in a catatonic state" he or she would not meet the criteria for continued payment. The policy was thus being interpreted to mean that if one could walk, one could work and would therefore no longer be eligible for disability payments. This interpretation of a general policy eliminated claimants whose disabilities were serious enough to prevent them from working in a competitive society. Furthermore, the decisions were based on written records. There were no face-to-face interviews that would have helped to provide a more accurate basis on which to make a decision. This would have prevented some of the obviously destructive decisions that were made. The stopping of payments on the basis of written records alone is an example of interpretation of an operational policy.

It is apparent that policies can be significantly affected when interpreted differently by those who determine policy and those who implement policy. To complicate matters, both the target population and the general public also become involved in interpreting policy. For example, in discussions in 1982 and 1983 on proposed modification of the social security program, many of those receiving benefits interpreted the planned change as an attempt to reduce their benefits. Many others of the general public shared this view. Some younger people, for instance, interpreted the suggested change as an attempt to reduce future benefits through changing the retirement age from 65 to 68 over the years.

When conflicting interpretations of policy cannot be resolved, the courts are called upon to give their interpretation of policy. New York City recently sought to be relieved of certain requirements and responsibilities regarding services and facilities for sheltering the homeless. These requirements dictated the number of lavatories and showers in the shelters. The city did not want to be held responsible for providing food, bathing facilities, and sleeping quarters under the same roof. Those seeking adequate shelter and care for the homeless resisted the changes the city sought. The issue went to the courts to determine how the policy of caring for the homeless would be implemented.

Who Implements Policy?

A third significant factor in implementing policies is the question of who implements them. Human services workers are usually the ones who actually deliver or provide the services to those in need. These workers include those described in Chapter Six and others such as vocational counselors, community developers, and the police. Human services workers are instrumental in the successful implementation of policies and programs. The degree of success of these policies and programs is determined by the amount and kind of training the worker has received. Recently we attended a conference of human services workers and researchers concerned with providing psychotherapeutic services to minority groups. It became very clear, in the papers presented and the discussions that followed, that the training of those providing services to minority populations was not adequate to assure success of such programs. A lack of sensitivity and a lack of knowledge regarding the needs of minority group members was a major obstacle to successful interventions.

It is clear that training of human services workers, regardless of the type or level of service, is critical to the successful implementation of programs and policies. The increasing trend toward registration, licensing, and testing of human services workers attests to the importance of training and competence in the view of consumers of human services and employers of human services workers. Improved competency and training not only increase the chances of successful implementation of programs, but also increase the abilities and credibility of workers in their efforts to identify the needs of people and to develop new social policies or improve old ones.

ADDITIONAL READING

Biklen, D. P. (1983). *Community organizing: Theory and practice.* Englewood Cliffs, NJ: Prentice-Hall.
Etzioni, A. (1976). *Social problems.* Englewood Cliffs, NJ: Prentice-Hall.
Feagin, S. R. (1975). *Subordinating the poor: Welfare and American beliefs.* Englewood Cliffs, NJ: Prentice-Hall.

Galper, J. H. (1975). *The politics of social services.* Englewood Cliffs, NJ: Prentice-Hall.

Johnson, W. H. (1980). *Rural human services: A book of readings.* Itasca, IL: F. E. Peacock.

Julian, J. (1980). *Social problems* (3rd ed.). Englewood Cliffs, NJ: Prentice-Hall.

Mills, C. W. (1959). *The power elite.* New York: Oxford University Press.

Parenti, M. (1978). *Power and the powerless.* New York: St. Martin's Press.

Piven, F. F., & Cloward, R. A. (1971). *Regulating the poor: The functions of public welfare.* New York: Vintage.

Schenk, Q. F., & Schenk, E. L. (1981). *Welfare, society, and the helping professions: An introduction.* New York: Macmillan.

Scull, A. T. (1977). *Decarceration: Community treatment and the deviant—A radical view.* Englewood Cliffs, NJ: Prentice-Hall.

Tallman, I. (1976). *Passion, action, and politics: A perspective on social problems and social problem solving.* San Francisco: W.H. Freeman.

Weinberger, P. E. (1974). *Perspectives on social welfare: An introductory anthology* (2nd ed.). New York: Macmillan.

REFERENCES

Alinsky, S. D. (1971). *Rules for radicals.* New York: Vintage Books.

Austin, M. J., Skelding, A. H., & Smith, P. L. (1977). *Delivering human services: An introductory programmed text.* New York: Harper & Row.

Azarnoff, R. S., & Seliger, J. S. (1982). *Delivering human services.* Englewood Cliffs, NJ: Prentice-Hall.

Baker, F., & Northman, J. E. (1981). *Helping: Human services for the 80s.* St. Louis: C.V. Mosby.

Brager, G., & Holloway, S. (1978). *Changing human service organizations: Politics and practice.* New York: The Free Press.

Brager, G., & Specht, H. (1965). Mobilizing the poor for social action. In *The Social Welfare Forum, 1965* (pp. 197–210). New York: Columbia University Press.

Capoccia, V. A., & Googins, B. (1982). Social planning in an environment of limited choice. *New England Journal of Human Services, 2,* 31–36.

Dobelstein, A. W. (1980). *Politics, economics, and public welfare.* Englewood Cliffs, NJ: Prentice-Hall.

Fill, H. J. (1974). *The mental breakdown of a nation.* New York: New Viewpoints.

Gil, D. G. (1981). *Unravelling social policy: Theory, analysis, and political action towards social equality* (3rd ed.). Cambridge, MA: Schenkman.

Gilbert, N., & Specht, H. (1974). *Dimensions of social welfare policy.* Englewood Cliffs, NJ: Prentice-Hall.

Huttman, E. D. (1981). *Introduction to social policy.* New York: McGraw-Hill.

Mechanic, D. (1980). *Mental health and social policy* (2nd ed.). Englewood Cliffs, NJ: Prentice-Hall.

Meyer, C. H. (1983). The power to define problems. *Social Work, 28,* 99.

Prigmore, C. S., & Atherton, C. R. (1979). *Social welfare policy: Analysis and formulation.* Lexington, MA: D.C. Heath.

Titmus, R. M. (1974). *Social policy: An introduction.* New York: Pantheon Books.

U.S. agency calls cuts in disability pay improper. (1983, April 7). *The New York Times,* p. B14.

White, T. H. (1982). *America in search of itself: The making of the president 1956–1980.* New York: Harper & Row.

PREVENTION
IN HUMAN SERVICES

INTRODUCTION

"No major disorder in a population has ever been eliminated by providing one-to-one treatment," stated the report of the Task Panel on Prevention of the President's Commission on Mental Health (1978, p. 214). Does this mean that treatment of major disorders is of no use? Not at all! Treatment and rehabilitation are essential methods of working with patients. They are, however, not the only effective tools of human services. What the statement does mean is that other approaches are needed if society hopes to successfully cope with the increasing number of individuals who are dysfunctional. One such approach is preventing disorders from developing in the first place.

Although prevention in the human services is not a new idea, it is rarely addressed in introductory human services texts. When it *is* discussed in such texts, it is most often covered only briefly. We applaud the recent growth of prevention programs in the human services, and are convinced of the great potential of these programs. For this reason we feel that it is essential to introduce the subject of prevention to those planning to enter the field of human services. It should be clear to you that human services are not limited to the repairing or patching up of dysfunctional persons through treatment and rehabilitation. Furthermore, by introducing the concept of prevention in an introductory text, we hope that human services training programs will be encouraged to begin covering prevention with the same thoroughness now given to treatment and rehabilitation. Adequate information on prevention programs also offers the human services student another option regarding career choice.

The first part of the chapter focuses on what prevention is and what it is one seeks to prevent. A brief history of prevention efforts follow. The remainder of the chapter includes a discussion of the different levels of prevention and the rationale for importance of prevention efforts. The chapter ends with an examination of current prevention programs and obstacles or barriers to the development of prevention programs.

DEFINING PREVENTION AND ITS TARGETS

To *prevent* means to keep something from happening. In the field of medicine, it is quite clear what one attempts to prevent. Illness, injury, and premature or unnecessary death are the three major targets of prevention programs in medicine. In the human services, not including medicine, the major targets are not so clearly defined or identified. The Task Panel on Prevention of the President's Commission on Mental Health (1978) felt strongly that efforts should focus on the prevention of "persistent, destructive, maladaptive behaviors" (p. 219). Such behaviors include child abuse, drug abuse, criminal activities, and desertion of family, among many others.

The panel also stated that disorders should be the target of prevention programs. It is clear that there are many stressful situations, such as puberty, illness, and death, that cannot be kept from occurring, particularly by those faced with the problems. The goal, then, would be to prevent the situation from causing the kind of psychological and social disorders mentioned above. For example, during the deep recession of the early 1980s, millions of people were put out of work. Unemployment led to the loss of homes for some, the loss of medical benefits for others, the need for some to apply for welfare, and general fear and uncertainty for all. These misfortunes led to increased family disorganization, alcoholism, depression, and similar disorders for millions of individuals and families. These individuals had neither the resources nor the skills to cope with the loss of their jobs and incomes. How to keep disorders caused by loss of income from occurring or how to prevent them from becoming severe enough so that "normal" functioning is impaired is the focus of prevention efforts in the human services. One might consider the unemployment insurance program, for example, an effort to prevent the breakdown of the jobless. It does at least temporarily reduce the stresses associated with unemployment.

PREVENTION IN THE PAST

In this section we focus on the history of prevention efforts in the human services. Because it is impossible to separate the history of prevention programs from the history of human services, some of the material discussed here will necessarily overlap material in Chapter Three.

Preliterate and Ancient Civilizations

People have always tried to find ways to prevent hunger, injury, illness, and death. In preliterate civilizations, rituals, prayer, and sacrifices were used in the hope of preventing such catastrophes. These preventive rituals focused not only on hostile animals, environments, and people, but also on the weather and other natural phenomena that influenced the supply of food.

Ancient civilizations also used many of the "preventive" methods of preliterate groups such as prayer and ritual. However, a movement away from the priest, shaman, or religious healer slowly developed. There was an increasing awareness that in many cases illness and death were due to natural rather than supernatural phenomena. In fact, some early efforts at prevention were successful even though the actual causes of the diseases were not known. In ancient Greece, for example, Hippocrates noted that a particular disease, now thought to be malaria, developed and spread near swamps. When people avoided these areas, or when the swamps were filled in, the disease abated (M. Bloom, 1981). Ancient Rome also contributed to the prevention of disease, even though the Romans might not have been aware of doing so. Their sewers and aqueducts were built to overcome unpleasant living conditions brought on by waste products and poor-tasting water. In effect, they prevented illness caused by poor sanitation and contaminated water.

The Dark Ages and the Renaissance

With the coming of the Dark Ages, medical practices reverted to an emphasis on prayer and rituals. According to Catalano (1979), medicine in Europe at that time became more of a combination of pagan myth and Christian prayer, then considered the best protection against illnesses of any kind. This change is described in more detail in Chapter Three. Prevention efforts related to illness, hunger, and poverty made little headway during the Middle Ages. The Church did, however, provide care and food to many in need, which prevented hunger and the accompanying stress-related problems.

The Renaissance and the Age of Reason saw a return to acceptance of more scientific medical practices. Quarantines were used to prevent the spread of disease. Inoculation against smallpox was developed. This was a powerful preventive measure, for it kept a specific disease from occurring. New drugs were found to be useful in treating and preventing diseases. During the 17th and 18th centuries, other practices and discoveries prevented some diseases. Sanitation projects were improved, general cleanliness was promoted, and a beginning understanding of contagion all helped in prevention of diseases. The lack of knowledge of causes of specific illnesses was not always an obstacle. Scurvy, for example, was practically eliminated without an understanding of vitamin deficiency or of how a diet that included fresh fruit and vegetables prevented it from occurring. Most prevention efforts were made in relation to physical illness. Mental illness was perceived in a different way by both most medical doctors and the public at large. The treatment of the mentally ill was influenced by religious beliefs. During this time the prevention of mental illness was, therefore, based upon a belief in prayer, ritual, and living a life free of sin.

The 19th and 20th Centuries

The 19th and 20th centuries saw even greater advances in medicine. Pasteur introduced the germ theory of disease. Ehrlich introduced the idea of a chemical "magic bullet" against specific diseases, the idea that a single medication could cure or prevent a particular disease. Clinical laboratory diagnosis and specialization became the trend. In the field of mental illness, advances were also being made but at a slower rate. Haindorf, in the early 19th century, introduced the concept that emotional conflicts that disturb the normal functioning of the body result in mental illness. Groos, before Freud, believed that man is affected by physical forces he is not aware of and that these forces determine his behavior (Alexander & Selesnick, 1966).

Some significant though rudimentary efforts to prevent mental illness were made in the latter part of the 19th century and the early 20th century. For example, the settlement house movement represented a major attempt to help people deal with the perils and pressures of poverty, hunger, crime, poor education, sweatshops, and filthy living conditions. The primary focus was not on the prevention of mental illness, but rather on helping the millions of immigrants coming to America to establish themselves in their new homeland. Exploitation of these people, many of whom did not even know the language, was the rule. Human services workers of that era were convinced that this exploitation and its attendant hardships contributed to high rates of juvenile delinquency, crime, alcoholism, and poor health. Efforts to prevent these conditions from occurring were a major focus of the settlement house movement. Settlement house workers attempted to help the exploited overcome their poverty through education. Some progressive politicians also tried to alleviate the plight of the poor. Such attempts continued over many years. However, the settlement house movement and cooperating politicians did not have the political power to make significant changes in the distribution of resources to reduce or eliminate the stress brought on by poverty. They did, however, help sensitize the general public to the plight of poor immigrants.

The movement that probably attained the greatest success in preventing the exploitation of the poor was the union movement. Unions were formed and supported by exploited workers. Their efforts were supported by the settlement houses, other institutions, and liberal political leaders. The unions not only prevented exploitation of their members, through the collective bargaining process, but also initiated and actively promoted legislation that increased opportunities for the poor to break the cycle of poverty and its accompanyin disorders. The minimum wage laws and unemployment insurance are examples of such legislation. The unions, in effect, brought about a significant increase of resources for their members and millions of others entering or already in the work force. While the working person did not suddenly become rich, he or she was much better off financially than before the advent of unions. Economic pressures, one of the avowed causes of emotional stress, was, for many, significantly reduced.

The latter part of the 19th century and early part of the 20th century also saw movement in determining the relationship between some physical and behavioral problems. There was a recognition that syphilis in its later stages caused many behavioral problems such as impulsive and bizarre actions. During the first 20 years of the 20th century, the mental hygiene movement, one of the most significant reform movements, was initiated by Clifford Beers and his associates. The main impetus for this movement was the autobiography of Beers, a former institutionalized mental patient. His book, *A Mind That Found Itself*, helped establish the National Committee for Mental Hygiene. One of the stated aims of the committee was the prevention of mental disorders. An article in the first issue of the committee's journal, *Mental Hygiene*, stated that "a healthy life-style could save people from insanity, hence the importance of educating the public as a means of preventing mental illness" (Dain, 1980, p. 103).

Most prevention programs in this country prior to the 1960s were aimed at physical diseases and were carried out largely by the Public Health Service. It was not until the 1960s that prevention efforts related to disabling behaviors were again seriously considered. Federal laws were passed that had an impact on prevention effort in mental health and behavioral disorders. Some of the more familiar pieces of legislation were the following:

- the Community Mental Health Centers Act of 1963
- the Economic Opportunities Act of 1964—the War on Poverty
- the Comprehensive Alcohol Abuse and Alcoholism Prevention, Treatment, and Rehabilitation Act of 1970
- the Child Abuse Prevention and Treatment Act of 1974
- the Juvenile Justice and Delinquency Prevention Act of 1974

- the establishment of an Office of Prevention within the National Institute of Mental Health in 1982

It should be noted that four of the acts listed specifically include prevention in their titles. The other two, although not specifying prevention in their titles, most certainly had prevention efforts as an integral part of their programs. In addition, Congress began to earmark funds for research in prevention activities. On the state level since 1974, approximately 12 states have established or are organizing statewide prevention units focused on the prevention of behavioral disorders. Initially, eight of them were financed by state funds alone. Some of the programs are more advanced than others; a few are still in the final planning stages (Johnston, 1980). In other states, efforts are being made to establish similar programs. In New York State, for example, the New York City Coalition for Prevention in Mental Health, a group made up of consumers, human services workers, and educators representing themselves and different agencies, is advocating that the state establish an office of prevention. Heller et al. (1984) noted that with the reduction of funds for human services programs as of 1980, federal and state policies once again emphasized treatment efforts over prevention programs "even though the help offered might only be palliative" (pp. 177–178).

LEVELS OF PREVENTION

The various state and federal prevention programs mentioned above focus their efforts on different levels of prevention. The concept of levels originated with the Public Health Service, and includes primary, secondary, and tertiary levels of prevention. Before discussing these levels it must be made clear that there are controversies within the field of human services regarding the definition of each level. These differences will be described after a definition and example of each of the three levels of prevention.

Primary prevention in the human services is designed to prevent a disorder, disability, or dysfunction from occurring in the first place. An example of primary prevention might be a program to help the unemployed learn new skills and use support networks. Such a program might help prevent depression, alcoholism, and other psychological disorders from taking place. In the medical field, the shots given to prevent polio, the flu, or tetanus are examples of primary prevention at work.

Secondary prevention can be defined as the early detection and treatment of dysfunction. If, for example, parents noticed that their teenage child was beginning to use alcohol and do poorly in school, and sought and obtained help for their child, that would be secondary prevention. In such an instance, the aim would be to help the youngster refrain from using alcohol and to improve in school work. Secondary prevention in medicine is similar. An individual, for example, goes to the doctor with the complaints of headache and slight fever, and is diagnosed as having a touch of the flu. The treatment is then focused on eliminating the symptoms and getting the patient well.

Tertiary prevention is generally defined in terms of efforts to rehabilitate and return to the community those afflicted with severe mental disorders. For example, there are mental patients who suffer from delusions—that is, they believe they are someone else, such as Napoleon, God, or Superman. They even try to behave as such figures and it is this behavior that keeps them from functioning successfully in society. In many such cases these people are placed in institutions. They remain there until they are able to regain enough of a hold on reality to return to the community. A medical example might be an individual who lost a leg, was fitted with an artificial one, and was taught to walk with the new leg.

A more detailed examination of the levels of prevention provides one with a greater understanding of the different concepts of prevention held by different individuals and groups in human services.

Primary Prevention

Primary prevention is seen by Price, Bader, and Ketterer (1980), Cowen (1980), and the Task Panel on Prevention (1978) as being principally concerned with the reduction of new cases of disorders in a community. If, for example, families with severely retarded children were helped to learn new ways of dealing with their children and how to use all the resources provided for such problems, it might well prevent the onset of family strife, or any other disorder that would further keep the retarded individual (or members of the family) from functioning at their potential. Stemming the ever-increasing number of disorders that develop among families facing different problems is one goal of primary prevention. Another example is one involving child abuse. Studies have indicated that people who were abused as children are more likely to become child abusers, delinquents, and prone to various kinds of societal violence. If such individuals are identified, they can be helped to learn other ways of dealing with their children prior to becoming parents. This

School daze.

School is tough enough without
having to learn through a mind
softened with drugs.

So get the education you deserve,
and learn how to say no to drugs.

Send for a free booklet, *Peer Pressure: It's Okay To Say No.* Write: Say No To Drugs, P.O. Box 1635, Rockville, Maryland 20850.

An example of primary prevention efforts.

approach might well prevent that type of destructive and maladaptive behavior from occurring at all.

The Task Panel on Prevention (1978) claims that "primary prevention involves building the strengths, resources, and competence in individuals, families, and communities that can reduce the flow of a variety of unfortunate outcomes—each characterized by enormous human and societal costs" (p. 213). In other words, primary prevention involves providing education and training programs to help the families of severely retarded children and the potential child abusers learn different ways of interacting with their children. When one looks at the "flow of unfortunate outcomes," such as divorce, desertion, delinquency, and depression, brought on by these or other problems, one can clearly imagine "the enormous human and societal costs," and thus the need for primary prevention programs.

An additional but critical aspect of primary prevention efforts, according to Cowen (1982), is that they must be group- or mass-oriented. This does not mean that primary prevention programs may not deal with individuals, but rather that the major focus must be on large and/or specific populations. These populations are referred to as target populations, high-risk groups, or the general population. While these groups may not be demonstrating any disorders, their circumstances, as described above, are such that many of them are probably vulnerable or open to such disorders. These groups function, live in the community, and show no signs of disorder.

Secondary Prevention

Secondary prevention, according to Goodstein and Calhoun (1982), "involves early diagnosis and treatment of a disorder at a stage when problems may be nipped in the bud" (p. 499). Price et al. (1980) see the goal of secondary prevention somewhat differently, as an attempt "to shorten the duration of the disorder by early and prompt treatment" (p. 10). If, for example, a young child of an alcoholic parent began to show signs of withdrawal and the nonalcoholic parent took the youngster for help, this would be considered by many to be secondary prevention. It would include diagnosis and treatment in an attempt to "nip the problem in the bud" or at least to shorten the duration of the problem.

There are those, however, who would claim this help is treatment of an existing disorder. The maladaptive behavior—withdrawal—has already begun; it has not been prevented or kept from occurring. What, then, if anything, has been prevented? Those who claim that early and prompt treatment is secondary prevention assert that if the intervention or treatment is successful, the signs of withdrawal are reduced or eliminated. In effect, intervention has prevented increased or continued withdrawal and therefore should be considered to be a significant prevention effort. One could argue either way as to whether one should call the example described above treatment or prevention.

In our view, the very existence of a disorder takes the effort out of the realm of prevention and places it in the category of treatment. Though it is true that prevention efforts could focus on an individual, the major thrust of prevention is that of reaching groups at risk, target populations, or the general population. While this may be a technical point, it does have significance as an obstacle to the development of primary prevention programs. This point shall be discussed more fully later in the chapter.

Tertiary Prevention

Tertiary prevention, according to Price et al. (1980), is an attempt "to reduce the severity and disability associated with a particular disorder" (p. 10). Goodstein and Calhoun (1982) describe tertiary prevention in more detail. From their point of view, "tertiary prevention includes efforts to reduce the overall damaging effect of a disorder, to shorten its duration, and to rehabilitate those afflicted for reentry into the community" (p. 499). What seems to come through in both these perceptions is that the focus is on working to overcome a disorder that has developed to the point where it keeps the individual from functioning appropriately or effectively in the community.

If those delusional individuals referred to earlier were treated in an institution and were again able to live and function in the community, this would be considered tertiary prevention by many in the human services. Here again one might ask what is being prevented. From one point of view, permanent disability or continued institutionalization is the prevention target. Another point of view—one to which we subscribe— states that the process of tertiary prevention is actually rehabilitation. That is, it restores the individual(s) to better health. It should be noted that most tertiary prevention programs are not focused on a mass of people or on large groups of people but rather on individuals and/or small groups.

WHY AN EMPHASIS
ON PRIMARY PREVENTION IS CRUCIAL

What is so important about the idea of primary prevention in the human services? Four major reasons have been put forward to support primary prevention as a top priority. One reason was provided at the very beginning of this chapter: according to the Task Panel on Prevention (1978) and others in the Public Health Service and in private practice, there has never been a major disease or disorder eliminated through treatment alone. If this is so, it becomes clear that treatment and rehabilitation efforts cannot hope to completely eliminate serious disorders. Furthermore, treatment and rehabilitation have been practiced for years, and it is clear that both processes have not been able to stem the growing tide of disorders in our society.

The second reason is that there are not enough human services personnel to treat or rehabilitate all those in need. Human services educators recognize that the training of personnel cannot keep up with the increasing numbers of people in need of treatment. This is true in spite of the fact that the primary focus of training has been, and still is, on treatment and rehabilitation. To make things more difficult, the economic policies of the early 1980s have caused a reduction not only in the number of individuals being trained, but also in the number of personnel who are already providing the needed services. This decrease in workers has occurred in spite of an increase in the number of people in need of support and help due to problems of unemployment, people living longer and becoming more dependent, more families breaking up, and increasing child abuse, among other trends. Bloom (1981) points out that a few years ago an estimated 10% of the United States population needed help with such problems. The estimate is now that up to 15% of the population are in need of this kind of support.

This situation reminds one of the story of a man fishing off the bank of a wide and fast-flowing stream. While fishing, he sees a person being swept along with the current. He quickly throws the person a line and pulls him to safety. Before he can do anything more he spots another person being swept downstream and he pulls him out also. Just as he does this, he sees a few more people struggling in the current. He calls for help as he pulls someone else out of the surging water. Others come to help as still more people are caught in the current. However, it soon becomes impossible to pull everyone out of danger. There are too many victims and not enough helpers. As more and more people float downstream, more and more are lost. It finally dawns on someone to head upstream and try to keep people from falling into the stream in the first place. Many feel that human services workers had best head upstream before they too become less and less effective.

The third reason why primary prevention should be a priority is that society pays a huge cost for disorders that are not prevented. The Task Panel on Prevention (1978), for example, put its emphasis on the prevention of disorders, each of which is "characterized by enormous human and society costs" (p. 213). In 1977, the Alcohol, Drug Abuse, and Mental Health Administration stated that the cost of treatment and care for alcoholism, drug abuse, and mental illness was a minimum of $106 billion for that year alone. This estimate was considered low by the investigators due to a lack of adequate data on the cost of lost productivity and other related costs such as loss of taxes on salaries and sales due to less buying power, which reduces demand for goods and services and therefore jobs (Cruze et al., 1977). The costs today are certainly much higher than they were in 1977.

Can these astronomical dollar costs be kept from increasing? There are some answers to this question in *A Community Guidebook: Planning for Prevention Programs* (Wisconsin Department of Health and Social Services, 1978). In the case of a nervous mental breakdown, according to the authors of the guidebook, it costs approximately $2500 for 28 days in the hospital and 9 outpatient visits. Supportive services for the rest of the year add another $2500. One person having ten episodes during his adult life would cost about $50,000, not including loss of salaries and production. Five thousand dollars a year in prevention efforts could buy each year almost 400 two-hour supportive group meetings, serving a total of almost 500 people. These meetings would be led by a human services worker. In addition, two human services workers seeing eight to ten children twice a week for one year could be hired. If just one case of recurring mental illness was prevented in those groups, in one year the $5000 would be saved, and $50,000 would be saved over ten years. These figures make it clear that prevention programs that promote positive mental and physical health can save substantial sums of money over extended periods of time.

The fourth reason for the promotion of primary prevention is that emotional and behavioral disorders exact an enormous human cost. Human costs have to do with personal pain and suffering. Perhaps the only way you can truly realize these costs is for us to try to personalize them. Everyone has had to face, at some time or another, a painful or terrible experience. Some remember the fear of being left behind when parents separated. Some remember the shame of having a "drunkard" in the family. Others who have had a mentally ill person living in the same house can still feel the anxiety, fear, and frustration in that situation. The guilt, shame, and apprehension of having a retarded child still affects many others. The anger and fear of living with a drug addict is still with many. The terror after being abused, mugged, or raped does not leave a person or their loved ones.

How many can recall the gut-wrenching pain and sense of helplessness of watching a loved one suffer and die due to illness? How many remember the rage and bitterness they felt when their disabled child, or they themselves, were made fun of or denied an opportunity to go to school? There is also the feeling of desperation, frustration, and rage known by Blacks, Hispanics, or other minority group members when they or their children are abused and denied the opportunity to grow and prosper. The enormous human costs are the tremendous assaults on the emotions and strength of those affected directly and indirectly. Some of the effects radically change the lives of those who, without help, cannot cope successfully with such traumas, and too often become alcoholics, abusers, addicts, mentally ill, or develop some other disorder, thus increasing the number of people needing treatment and rehabilitation.

Primary prevention programs are geared to help people learn how to deal positively and successfully with their problems and stress. If such programs prevent people from developing any of the disorders described above, the human cost will have been reduced. We believe that a greater number of prevention programs make possible a greater reduction in human and societal costs.

The acknowledged inability of treatment and rehabilitation

programs alone to stem the tide of people in need of human services makes increased primary prevention efforts almost mandatory. An examination of the present level of primary prevention programs will be helpful at this point.

A SAMPLE OF PRIMARY PREVENTION PROGRAMS

A brief look at different kinds of primary prevention programs will give you a sense of the scope of such efforts and a clear idea of the goals of primary prevention programs. Primary prevention programs have been growing in number since the mid-1970s. Many of them have been short-term, research, experimental, or demonstration programs limited in terms of time and funding. Much of the data derived from these programs indicate positive results in improving individuals' abilities to cope with stress. These data and results can be and have been used to develop additional theories and programs focused on long-term results. There are programs, although too few from the point of view of proponents of primary prevention, that are ongoing. In any case, it should be noted that the final results of these long-term programs are not yet available, for it is impossible to tell whether or not the targeted disorders have been prevented for the entire life span of those in the various programs.

One dramatic and ongoing primary prevention program is the Scared Straight program. This program, aimed at preventing juvenile delinquency, started in the late 1970s and was reported on national television. Those who saw that program could hardly forget it. Briefly, a group of teenagers not yet involved with the criminal justice system but considered to be a high-risk group in relation to criminal acts, visited a state prison. The visit included, in addition to a tour of the facility, a meeting with a volunteer group of inmates, among them murderers, rapists, and other hardened criminals. The meeting, actually run by the inmates, was aimed at frightening the teenagers enough to make sure that they would "go straight." This was done through graphic descriptions of what goes on in prisons, including homosexual rapes, forms of slavery, boredom, fear, rage, and other forms of verbal and physical abuse. The teenagers were also verbally abused in no uncertain terms and the abuse was intensified if the inmates thought the teenagers were not listening or not taking the program seriously enough. The visiting teenagers were cursed at in violent street language, called stupid, and threatened. The shock and fear was clearly apparent on the faces of the teenagers. In interviews after the visit, it was obvious that this shock and fear was still with many of the visitors. It was felt that because the program was shown on national television it reached a very large number of teenagers and others. This program has continued and been established in states throughout the country.

Tableman et al. (1982) described a pilot program of stress management training involving women on public assistance who were generally isolated and subjected to more than average stress in their lives. None of the women were in crisis, nor did they display maladaptive behaviors that required treatment. The women took part in ten sessions during which they learned skills and methods of reducing stress that helped them change their perceptions of their situations. The program resulted in significant change in the lives of the participants. They were no longer isolated and were able to function more effectively with less stress, thus preventing the kinds of behavioral disorders discussed earlier. The program has been further tested and used with different populations living under stressful conditions.

Another primary prevention program was developed by the Catholic church because of the tremendous increase in the number of divorces. Couples wishing to be married in the church now go through a series of group meetings, led by a clergyman, discussing the responsibilities, joys, and strains of marriage. Childbirth, child rearing, sex, and other aspects of marriage are among the many topics discussed. The goal is to prevent many of the problems occurring in marriages from becoming serious enough to cause behavioral disorders, family disintegration, and divorce.

The Task Panel on Prevention (1978), mentioned earlier, recommended that "top priority for program development, training, and research in primary prevention should be directed toward infants and young children and their environments" (p. 240). The panel felt that "earlier is better" in primary prevention. One such program—the Optimum Growth Project, a community-based research demonstration plan of a Florida community mental health center—was developed to influence the living conditions of disadvantaged children, ages 0 to 5. Specifically, the intent was to change those conditions that often cause mental disabilities. The plan involved two groups of expectant mothers. One group received specific services, which included regular home visits by mental health workers, task and skill training, parent education, group parent meetings, testing of infants, regular checkups, and other services. The second group did not receive these services. The two groups of parents and children will be compared when the target children complete kindergarten.

On the other end of the age scale, Bennett (1982) described a brief demonstration program on the prevention of deterioration in the elderly. Essentially, the program was one of friendly visiting of isolated older adults. Two groups of older adults with no known behavioral disorders but who were considered social isolates were visited in their homes by trained volunteers. One group was visited on a regular schedule over a six-month period, and the second group was visited once at the beginning of the study and once at the end of the study. The specific purpose of the program was to reduce the social isolation of the older adults and improve social adjustment, mental state, and awareness of issues that affected them such as social security and food stamps. There were improvements in personal grooming and apartment upkeep of the visited group. There was also an increase in social contacts. In addition, there was improvement in the mental state of the group that was visited regularly. They were more relaxed and trusting of the visitors at the end of the program. They were also more accepting and at ease with others whom they met in the house or on the street. There was little, if any, improvement in the group that was visited only twice. It is true that these are only short-term results. Whether or not the program will prevent mental deterioration or institutionalization for the rest of the lives of the group members is open to question. The fact that they did improve and not regress during that six-month period and shortly after, during the evaluation period, provides some clues to helping older adults maintain themselves in the community in a positive lifestyle for increased periods of time.

The last primary prevention program to be described here centers on promoting mental health in rural areas through informal helping (D'Augelli & Vallance, 1981). Provision of human services in rural areas is more difficult than in urban areas. For example, because of the smaller populations living in rural areas, isolation is usually greater and transportation is not readily available. Many rural residents have close family and community ties, and asking for help from "outsiders" is not looked upon with much favor. Some rural communities have an informal system of helpers. The project under discussion was designed to not only encourage such a system but also to teach members of the community to train those residents who make up this informal system. The focus is to build on the existing strengths of the community by training the local helpers to become more efficient in helping residents deal with personal problems, job loss, sudden illness or injury, and other problems in living. This approach permits local residents to teach other local residents skills in the helping process, and thus they do not have to share problems with or ask for help from "outsiders." This method also increases the number of helpers and provides increased sources of support to those who are faced with problems in living, before maladaptive behaviors are developed. This particular prevention program is an ongoing one staffed by local volunteers.

OBSTACLES TO THE DEVELOPMENT
OF PRIMARY PREVENTION PROGRAMS

Although there are a growing number of primary prevention programs operating throughout the country, funding for such programs is quite limited in comparison to the funds available for
treatment and/or rehabilitation programs. That no one would
object to the elimination or significant reduction of the disorders
described earlier seems certain. Why, then, the persistent resistance
to funding and development of primary prevention programs in the
human services field? There seem to be three major categories of
obstacles to such funding and development: professional, political,
and economic. An examination of just a sampling of these obstacles
will give you a greater understanding of the problems surrounding
the introduction of primary prevention programs. Note that these
problems are very closely interrelated.

Professional Issues

Professional issues that create problems regarding the growth of
primary prevention programs include the training, practice, philosophy, and ethics of human services workers and the human services professions. Very few two- or four-year training programs for
human services workers discuss, much less focus on, the teaching of
primary prevention theory or skills. Few, if any at all, train workers
for careers in the field of primary prevention. Graduate school
training is equally limited in terms of primary prevention. For the
most part, the training of human services workers is focused on
treatment and/or rehabilitation theories and skills. This training
leads, naturally, to practice concentrated on treatment and rehabilitation. These services are, in addition, the major services of most
agencies in which human services workers are employed.

From a theoretical or philosophical perspective, the fact that
primary prevention is not seen the same way by all human services
workers creates an additional obstacle to the growth of primary
prevention programs. There is no *one* definition of primary prevention acceptable among human services workers. Furthermore, a
group of mental health professionals, in a report to the New York
State Commission of Mental Health (Prevost, 1982) stated that "the
distinctions among primary, secondary, and tertiary prevention do
not provide meaningful guidance for the formulation of programs
and policies" (p. 3). The group added that the concepts have triggered more arguments than action. For example, when a particular

disorder, such as drug abuse, is *treated* successfully, it might be claimed by some that the successful treatment actually *prevented* a potential crime, and thus is really primary prevention. This perception does not include the element of intent, considered to be an essential aspect of primary prevention in mental health (Cowen, 1980). The intent in the example is to stop the drug abuse and not to stop a crime.

Another issue that causes hesitation and confusion centers around whether primary prevention efforts should concentrate on the causes of disorders or the "trigger" or "spark" that sets off a disorder. To add to the dilemma, the question of whether to approach disorders from the viewpoint of a biological, psychological, or a sociological emphasis is raised. In a biological approach, disorders are thought to be caused by physical problems such as brain damage, chemical imbalances, pollution, physical disability, or other similar difficulties. In a psychological approach, disorders are thought to be caused by a lack of knowledge or an inability to cope with emotional stress. In a sociological approach, disorders are thought to be caused by institutions or systems that do little to eliminate racism, unemployment, crime, poverty, hunger, poor housing, and similar societal ills.

These and other professional problems cause many to be hesitant and reluctant to expend their resources and efforts on primary prevention to any degree similar to those given for treatment and rehabilitation programs.

Ethical questions regarding primary prevention programs also arise from the point of view of some human services workers. Some workers claim that if primary prevention programs were aimed at high-risk groups, unforeseen and unfortunate consequences could occur. High-risk groups, for example, could include children from broken homes or children with alcoholic parents. The children would have to be identified as such, and this could lead to additional problems and violation of privacy. The children would have little or no voice in this matter, yet they might be adversely affected. Another ethical issue raised by some is that if primary prevention programs are aimed at entire communities or populations, what responsibility do providers have to those in the community who feel no need or want no part of such programs?

Political Issues

Political issues are also obstacles to the development of primary prevention programs. For example, ours is a crisis-oriented society. That is, our society does not usually act or react to problems unless they become great enough to affect large numbers of people and bad enough to frighten large numbers of people. It is at those times that the storm of protest or concern becomes large enough to move legislators and legislatures to attempt to deal with the problem. This is usually done through the rapid passage of legislation and funding. Witness the recent public outcry, programs, legislation, and publicity that has developed around the problem of drunken driving. The unanimity of support for a crackdown on this problem made it comparatively simple for the various jurisdictions to pass legislation and develop programs to deal with the problem. The lack of a sense of crisis in the view of the public and many human services workers in addition to the lack of unanimity among professionals regarding the efficacy of primary prevention programs provides little impetus for the political system to press for the development and funding of such programs. Furthermore, how can one justify the use of limited resources to prevent disorders that only *might* occur?

Economic Obstacles

Economic obstacles to primary prevention efforts pointed out by the Task Panel on Prevention (1978) include limited resources and present funding practices. Limited funding of human services also limits the development of new and uncertain or unproven programs. To take increasingly scarce resources away from treatment and rehabilitation programs and from people who are in immediate need of assistance, to fund new and, in the eyes of many, questionable primary prevention programs is not acceptable to many in the human services field. Furthermore, the cost of primary prevention programs serving large populations is very high, even though the cost per person is much less than the cost of treatment and rehabilitation of one person. In addition, hospitals and other human services institutions are not prepared or geared for primary prevention programs, but are certainly dependent upon the income derived from their treatment and rehabilitation services. Primary prevention programs might well affect that income adversely. The same threat to income faces those human services workers in private practice. Recipients of third-party payments through their clients' medical insurance could also be affected financially.

CONCLUSION

We believe that these and other obstacles to primary prevention can be overcome. Our strong bias in favor of primary prevention programs has been made obvious purposefully. We just do not believe that the human services profession needs to, or can afford to, stand still regarding the development of primary prevention programs until critics are satisfied and all unanswered questions are answered. We do believe that there has been sufficient research to warrant significant increases in funding of primary prevention programs and continued research in this area. The old cliche "an ounce of prevention is worth a pound of cure" is particularly appropriate here. From an economic, social, professional, and moral perspective it is clear to us that the human services must become more than a "repair shop" for individuals and society. Primary prevention programs are essential in the fight against dysfunctions, disorders, and disabilities.

ADDITIONAL READING

Addams, J. (1969). *A centennial reader.* New York: Macmillan.

Anletta, K. (1982). *The underclass.* New York: Random House.

Barton, W. E., & Sanborn, C. J. (Eds.). (1978). *Law and the mental health professions: Friction at the interface.* New York: International Universities Press.

Marti-Ibannez, F. (Ed.). (1962). *The epic of medicine.* New York: Clarkson N. Potter.

McConville, B. J. (1982, December). Secondary prevention in child psychiatry: An overview with ideas for action. *Canada's Mental Health, 30* (4), 4–7.

Plant, T. F. A. (1980). Prevention policy: The federal perspective. In R. H. Price, F. Ketterer, B. C. Bader, & J. Monahan (Eds.), *Prevention in mental health: Research, policy, and practice* (Vol. 1). Beverly Hills, CA: Sage Publications.

Porter, R. A., Peters, J. A., & Headry, H. R. (1982, July). Using community development for prevention in Appalachia. *Social Work, 27,* 302–307.

Walsh, J. A. (1982, July). Prevention in mental health: Organizational and ideological perspectives. *Social Work, 27,* 298–301.

REFERENCES

Alexander, F. G., & Selesnick, S. T. (1966). *The history of psychiatry: An evaluation of psychiatric practice from prehistoric time to the present.* New York: Harper & Row.

Bennett, R. (1982, June). *Prevention of deterioration in the elderly: A case for friendly visiting.* Paper read at An Ounce of Prevention II, New York City Coalition for Prevention in Mental Health, Hunter College, New York.

Bloom, B. L. (1981, December). The logic and urgency of primary prevention. *Hospital and Community Psychiatry, 23,* 839–843.

Bloom, M. (1981). *Primary prevention: The possible science.* Englewood Cliffs, NJ: Prentice-Hall.

Caplan, G. (1964). *Principles of Preventive Psychiatry.* New York: Basic Books; p. 16.

Catalano, R. (1979). *Health, behavior and the community: An ecological perspective.* New York: Pergamon Press.

Cowen, E. L. (1980). The wooing of primary prevention. *American Journal of Community Psychology, 8,* 258–284.

Cowen, E. L. (1982, Spring). Primary prevention research: Barriers, needs and opportunities. *Journal of Primary Prevention,* 131–137.

Cruze, A. M., et al. (1977). *Final report: Selected measures of economic costs to society of alcohol and drug abuse and mental illness* (Vol. 1). Washington, DC: Alcohol, Drug Abuse, and Mental Health Administration.

Dain, N. (1980). *Clifford W. Beers: Advocate for the insane.* Pittsburgh, PA: University of Pittsburgh Press.

D'Augelli, A. R., & Vallance, T. R. (1981). The helping community: Promoting mental health in rural areas through informal helping. *Journal of Rural Community Psychology.*

Goodstein, L. D., & Calhoun, J. F. (1982). *Understanding abnormal behavior: Description, explanation, management.* Reading, MA: Addison-Wesley.

Heller, K., Price, R. H., Reinharz, S., Riger, S., Wandersman, A., and D'Aunno, T. A. (1984). *Psychology and community change: Challenges of the future* (2nd ed.). Homewood, IL: Dorsey.

Johnston, J. E. (1980, September). *The role of the state mental health authority in prevention* (Mental Health Policy Monograph Series No. 6). Nashville, TN: Vanderbilt University, Vanderbilt Institute for Public Policy Studies, Center for the Study of Families and Children.

Prevost, J. A. (1982, March). *Policy framework for preventive services.* New York: New York State Office of Mental Health.

Price, R. H., Bader, B. C., & Ketterer, R. F. (1980). Prevention in community mental health—The state of the art. In R. H. Price, F. Ketterer, B. C. Bader, & J. Monahan (Eds.), *Prevention in mental health: Research, policy, and practice* (Vol. 1). Beverly Hills, CA: Sage Publications.

Tableman, B., Marceniak, D., Johnson, D., & Rodgers, R. (1982). Stress management training for women on public assistance. *American Journal of Community Psychology, 10,* 357–367.

Task Panel on Prevention. (1978). *Report.* Washington, DC: President's Commission on Mental Health.

Wisconsin Department of Health and Social Services, Division of Community Services. (1978). *A Community Guidebook: Planning for Prevention Programs.* Madison, WI: Author.

CURRENT CONTROVERSIES AND ISSUES

INTRODUCTION

You might gather by now that the human services field is quite complex. Complete agreement regarding philosophies, methods, goals, services, funding, or anything else just does not exist nor, from our point of view, should it. There are times when controversies and differences are stimulating, healthy, valid, and lead to creative solutions. At other times they are repetitious, meaningless, and destructive. Too frequently they use time, energy, and resources that might better be used providing needed services.

The purpose of this chapter is to present a sampling of basic controversies and issues in the field of human services that have not yet been resolved. The questions raised in this chapter influence all human services workers. Some issues affect the human services worker more directly than others, but they all impact upon the worker and the services provided. Prior knowledge of these and other controversies helps workers know what they might expect from colleagues, politicians, consumers of human services, and the general public. This knowledge can be instrumental in helping the worker provide more effective services.

The controversies described in this chapter have been touched upon in previous chapters, and are discussed in more detail here. We do not attempt to resolve these issues here. Our views are often implied by the way we present issues. Furthermore, we do not expect you to come to any specific conclusions or agree with any particular point of view. Issues change, conditions change, people change, and different issues constantly emerge. The idea is to examine them and understand their significance to human services workers and to the provision of human services, for they very frequently raise questions regarding one's personal and professional values and ethics.

GOVERNMENT: HOW MUCH SUPPORT FOR THE NEEDY?

In recent years, the annual struggle over the federal budget has highlighted a major controversy affecting human services workers and programs. The Reagan Administration and Congress have significantly reduced funding for some programs that provide a safety net to help the truly needy. Some human services workers claim that such reductions are unjustified, unfeeling, and unnecessary. The Reagan Administration has disagreed and asserted that there were too many people receiving support who were not truly needy. It has proposed reductions in food stamp funding and cuts in school lunch programs (highlighted at one time by an effort to consider tomato catsup as a vegetable, thus cutting costs). The Administration has also raised premiums for Medicare and delayed cost-of-living benefits for social security recipients. Those opposing the Administration are convinced that these cutbacks serve to create further stress and problems for those who are in most need of support. The proposed budget for the fiscal year beginning October 1984 included additional cuts in funding for social programs. Reductions of over $9 billion were contemplated in the following programs: food, nutrition, food stamps, housing for the poor, legal services for the poor, and Aid to Families with Dependent Children (AFDC), among others (Pear, 1984; "Child Abuse," 1983). The pressures on the needy increase even more.

These proposed additional cuts came at a time when the number of people living in poverty had been rapidly increasing. The Census Bureau, according to the *New York Times* (Pear, 1984), reported that between 1979 and 1982 there was a sharp increase in the number of people living in poverty. The Bureau further reported that even when adding noncash benefits such as food stamps and housing subsidies, there was a significant increase in the *rate* of poverty from 1979 to 1982. There has been no indication that the rate of growth in numbers of people living in poverty has significantly declined since then. Miller (1983), focusing only on children, pointed out that since 1980 over 2 million children have become impoverished. He asserted that more than one child in every five children (over 22 million) live in poverty. In spite of this recent rapid growth in the number of people in need, the proposed budget recommended that social services training and education programs be reduced 12% over the next five years. Galbraith (1984) felt that this problem is primarily a "guns or butter" issue. He pointed out that "military spending has become the principal ... cause of the present and prospective budget deficit. And ... this spending has been presented by the Administration as a basic reason for curtailed or reduced spending on behalf of the poor."

The reduction of federal funding for social programs threatens the very existence of some programs. Fulton (1981) saw the problem early on, and predicted the results. He pointed out the following:

> The reduction in federal domestic programs came at a time when fiscal problems and taxpayer resistance make it unlikely that state and local governments will be able to replace most of the lost federal money. This means that in many cases there will likely be no governmental services or benefits to replace those being reduced [p. 30].

The Reagan Administration, in an effort to help the states serve their constituents in spite of the federal reductions, developed the block grants program. Block grants take the place of federal funding and implementation of individual programs. The federal government gives the states lump sums of money to provide the programs and services for which the federal government is no longer responsible. These programs include maternal and health care, social services, and alcoholism, drug abuse, and mental health services. It has become clear, however, that the block grants mean less money to the states (Cunningham, 1984). Peirce (1982) pointed out that "leaders of the government were in Washington, warning of the havoc the administration's repeated budget cuts were causing on the state and local level" (p. 15). Fulton's prediction has come true—the states and local governments cannot make up the funds lost through federal budget cuts. Meanwhile, the number of poor people increases. A report in the *New York Times* ("Congress Study," 1984) of a recent congressional study pointed out that over one half million people "were made poor as a result of budget restrictions in social programs that Congress approved at the request of the Reagan Administration." The study also stated that over one and a half million people were made poor because of the 1981–82 recession.

What does all this mean to the human services worker? The Community Council of Greater New York (1983), in a definitive study of over 120 programs, reported that between 1981 and 1982 about 10% of the programs had been ended, and specific services had been dropped in another 10% of programs. Close to 30% of the programs studied had to reduce staff, and almost another 10% of the programs were contemplating such a move. About 20% of the programs had reduced the level of services, with others planning to do the same. Fees were increased and services were denied due to changed eligibility criteria in other programs.

Similar steps have been taken in programs throughout the country since these steps were taken in New York in 1981–1982. The human services worker is directly affected by such changes due to the threat of loss of jobs, increased work load, greater frustration, and doubts about governmental willingness to assume its responsibilities toward needy people.

The proposed cuts in budgets of social programs raise key questions regarding the role of government in providing services. Who has the major and/or ultimate responsibilities for the welfare of those in need? Is it the local, state, or federal government? Does government have responsibilities for the welfare of only those who are poor? These and other questions will always be raised as long as there are people in need, funds are limited, and those in power make decisions that reflect their values and philosophies.

TARGET POPULATIONS: THE STRUGGLE FOR SUPPORT

One controversy in the human services centers around the effects of a conservative government on social programs. The basic question is: Whose benefits shall be cut?

Regardless of who has control of the purse strings, be they liberals or conservatives, there will always be a limited amount of funds made available for social programs. The general trend has been that in times of prosperity and/or when liberals are in power, social programs are funded more generously. When conservatives are in power, as is the case at present, support for social programs is usually significantly reduced. The major question then becomes: Which programs shall be reduced or eliminated? Shall it be programs serving the elderly, or school lunch programs, or programs for the physically disabled? What about programs for the homeless, the mentally ill and retarded, or for the poor? Who chooses? What criteria would you use in making these choices? These kinds of questions and their answers create all kinds of tensions in the human services field. Peirce (1982) perhaps answered some of these questions when discussing budget cuts made by the federal government. He pointed out that "the stark fact is that the budget cuts it makes are far deeper in subsidized housing, in job training, in welfare and education programs of primary benefit to poor people than to programs the middle class utilizes most—social security, Medicare, civil service, and military pension levels" (p. 14). The report of the study by the Community Council of Greater New York (1983) referred to earlier confirms Peirce's statement. The study was focused on the impact of government funding reductions on agencies in New York City. The report indicated that in over 10% of the agencies studied, programs in adult and youth employment and training, information, and referral, and in home care were ended.

While it is generally acknowledged that all of the groups receiving support have a legitimate claim to that support, it becomes clear that some programs will lose funding. Several things happen in situations like this. First, the agencies serving the different target populations, and the members of those populations, start competing strenuously with one another for available funds. The most articulate and organized of the various target populations, the one with the most political influence, generally is more successful in gaining support and funds. As an example, the recent outcry by the recipients of social security benefits about the threat of reduced benefits tempered such efforts.

When funds are cut and staff reductions occur, caseloads tend to increase. This then requires a screening process that assures that those in most need get service, while others are turned away. According to a report in the *NASW News* ("Child Abuse," 1983), child welfare agencies are turning away clients that could use prevention programs in child abuse, so that active child abuse cases can be served. Without the prevention program, additional child abuse cases may well occur. The increased caseload puts additional pressure on the workers, and services often suffer. Competition and struggle for existence shift the focus, energies, and resources away from a unified effort by target populations and the human services field to increase overall funding for social programs. This kind of competition seems to demand that the strong shall survive and the weak shall perish.

PARAPROFESSIONAL AND PROFESSIONAL HUMAN SERVICES WORKERS

Two major and muted struggles have developed among human services workers in the last two decades. Both struggles involve money, status, and levels of responsibility. One conflict occurs between paraprofessional and professional human services workers. The other conflict occurs among professional human services workers. Fortunately these quarrels have not had significant ill effects on the direct services provided by the human services workers themselves. It is nonetheless important to know and understand the different points of view of the various contestants, as well as to recognize that all is not sweetness and light in the helping professions. A brief description of the issues follows.

Since the introduction of indigenous community leaders as paraprofessionals in the War on Poverty of the 1960s, the number of paraprofessionals in the human services has grown steadily and rapidly. In addition, the responsibilities, knowledge, training, and competence of paraprofessionals has, from their point of view, increased to a level comparable to that of professional human services workers. Furthermore, large numbers of paraprofessionals, and some professional human services workers, believe strongly that many paraprofessionals outperform professional workers. A trainer of paraprofessionals cited by Sobey (1970) stated that non-professionals are often superior to professionals. These convictions on the part of paraprofessionals are the basis for strong feelings about differences in pay, status, responsibilities, and opportunities for advancement between paraprofessional and professional human services workers. "Aides are expressing growing resentment at what they perceive as a system of double standards—one for them, the other for credentialed professionals," stated Birnbach (1981, p. 553).

As mentioned in Chapter Six, a paraprofessional is one who has not had formal education above a B.A. degree. Professionals are those who have advanced degrees. Paraprofessionals assert that while they do not have graduate degrees, the combination of their life experiences and limited formal education are "credentials" equal to those obtained through advanced formal education. Human services workers with advanced degrees feel that their advanced intensive training provides them with greater knowledge and skill in providing specific services, and enables them to function at a significantly higher level than paraprofessionals. Professionalism, they assert, is based upon the attainment of a specific body of knowledge unique to that field and gained only through professional schools. Much of the knowledge and skills referred to by professionals deal with clinical functions in addition to supervisory and educational responsibilities directly related to their specific profession. These professions might include psychology, occupational therapy, social work, and others described in Chapter Six. You will be faced with this issue in one way or another, to one degree or another, as a human services worker.

Paraprofessional efforts to gain recognition and parity with professionals is duplicated among the professionals themselves. The issue centers around which professionals shall be eligible for third-party payment without the need of being supervised by those with higher standing or credentials. Third-party payment is payment to the professional by an insurance company, such as Blue Cross, or Medicaid, for services provided to the client. Third-party payment permits many more individuals to obtain help that they previously could not afford. Third-party payment also significantly increases the amount of income for agencies and professionals providing services to the needy.

Who, then, among the professionals, is eligible to receive these third-party payments? Most human services professionals, particularly those in private practice, are eager to be included in such programs. Medical doctors and psychiatrists are included in all such programs. In some jurisdictions psychologists are included and in others they are not. Social workers and other human services professionals are also not included everywhere. In some situations some professionals are included in these programs only if they are supervised by a professional of another discipline. For example, a psychiatrist might supervise a psychologist or social worker. It goes without saying that professionals in one discipline object strenuously to being supervised by those in other disciplines. It is obvious that large sums of money are at stake and that status and recognition by the public and government regarding the competence of various professions is involved (Turkington, 1984).

Acceptance into these insurance programs is achieved for the most part through legislative action at local, state, or national levels. Therefore the professional organizations representing the different disciplines lobby to have their members included in these programs. Professional groups already included in the plans often oppose the inclusion of new groups, claiming that they are only trying to protect the public. Some think that there is enough to go around for everyone, and that the constant competition for higher status, recognition, and control does little for the image and dignity of professional human services workers.

DEINSTITUTIONALIZATION: DOES IT WORK?

Is the deinstitutionalization policy for the mentally ill working? "No," replied the witness at a New York State Assembly Committee on Mental Health hearing ("Is Deinstitutionalization Working?" 1983). The witness was a psychiatrist and an expert in the field of mental health. When one reads about "The Plight of Homeless Mentally Ill" (Cordes, 1984), one can clearly understand the basis of the reply given by the witness. On the other hand, O'Shaughnessy (1984) described the "Bronx Chamber of Horrors" in a way that gives urgency to devising a policy that does work. O'Shaughnessy described the fearful conditions in a state psychiatric center where patients have been physically abused and where treatment is minimal, as is staff. It is clear that the institution is overcrowded and there is a sense of desperation permeating it. Does that mean that patients should be "dumped"—that is, released into the community before they are able to function on their own? Should they be sent into the community that ignores them at best and abuses them at worst? There are just not enough adequate resources in the community to serve those who are deinstitutionalized (Cordes, 1984).

Deinstitutionalization, or decarceration, is the practice of releasing individuals who were inmates in institutions such as mental hospitals and prisons. The hope is that they are released into a community with facilities and resources to help them live independently, and/or to family or friends who will help them so that they will not need to be institutionalized again. The claims of those in favor of the deinstitutionalization policy are that (1) treatment and rehabilitation are more successfully achieved in the community, (2) it is more humane to treat people in the community in which they live, (3) due to overcrowding, grossly inadequate facilities, and inadequate numbers of personnel, prisons and mental hospitals in effect constitute cruel and inhuman punishment, and (4) it is less costly to provide the necessary services outside the institutions and in the community. Some believe that it is this last factor—less cost—that provided the main impetus for these programs (Mechanic, 1980). Regardless of motives, who can really argue with the concept of deinstitutionalization? The idea certainly sounded sensible and was hailed as the start of a new revolution in the human services.

What is the state of deinstitutionalization today? It is clear that too few communities in which released mental patients live have adequate facilities or resources for proper treatment or rehabilitation. The recent deaths of former mental patients in a rooming house fire triggered an investigation of the facilities and procedures for discharging mental patients. It was discovered that the residential facility was not the safest but that a shortage of decent housing made moving difficult. The investigation also pointed out that the outpatient center was not given sufficient notice of patient discharges and that important information about the patients was not used. Lack of care leaves the released patient in limbo. Having little or no support in the community, the patient often reverts back to the kind of behavior that caused him or her to be institutionalized in the first place. In many instances those individuals are refused readmission to the hospital and are found on the streets or in facilities not geared to help them.

Regardless of why communities do not have adequate resources or provide the necessary services, be it a lack of funds (the reason given by most human services workers) or "We don't want them in our neighborhood" (the reason given by most of the public), it is clear that the results of releasing patients into the community have not met the expectations of the supporters of the program. Most of the released individuals are not only being denied treatment in one way or another, they are often abused physically and emotionally and shunned by the public, often becoming increasingly desperate and in need of help. Some communities use "Greyhound therapy" (Cordes, 1984)—giving the patient a one-way ticket out of town. If and when the patient is accepted back into the institution, the cycle starts all over again. Stabilize them and get them out as quickly as possible is the order of the day. This is what is referred to as the revolving door policy.

There seem to be three realities. First, deinstitutionalization has not solved the problem of treating or rehabilitating mental patients. Second, treatment of the mentally ill in institutions has not improved significantly, and in many instances it has deteriorated. Third, funding or the lack of funding has created even greater problems, not

Question: Should they be released just because prisons are overcrowded?

only for the mentally ill but for the community at large as well. We can only hope that facing these realities will provide a focus for further efforts.

What about releasing criminals from prisons? New York City recently released over 200 inmates. In this instance there was no discussion about how criminals could be rehabilitated easier, faster, or better. They were let go because the court ordered relief from overcrowding in prisons. The court order was supported by families of inmates, human services workers, and prison officials, among others. The claim was that overcrowding and inadequate facilities and staff size created conditions that constituted cruel and unusual punishment. It was believed that such conditions had resulted in violent outbreaks among inmates and that violence would again erupt if conditions were not improved. One solution to a similar condition occurred in 1972. Massachusetts, riddled with scandals regarding the overcrowding and brutality of its juvenile institutions, without warning closed all of them within a month (Scull, 1977).

Today the public seems to be less concerned about the problem of overcrowding and inadequate facilities than about criminals out on the street. The public also is not as eager to pay for building new or additional prisons. Many a bond issue (the borrowing of money) and tax package for building additional space has been turned down by the voters. The courts, on the other hand, are reluctant to sentence any but the worst offenders to already overcrowded settings. Parole and probation personnel are generally so swamped with parolees and probationers that they are unable to provide required services. The result is a revolving door situation with ever-growing numbers of criminals. While overall crime rates have in fact dropped in certain areas, the number of adjudicated criminals and delinquents in the community has increased in others. The dilemma is clear. The public does not want criminals in the streets but the public is not interested in paying for additional prisons and parole and probation services. What are the alternatives?

Other questions about deinstitutionalization arise when one also considers the plight of the mentally retarded, juvenile offenders, and the elderly. What are the specific conditions that would make deinstitutionalization programs work? Are halfway houses, supervised residences, aftercare clinics, and similar community institutions the answer? Finally, is deinstitutionalization automatically preferred?

THE ROLE OF HUMAN SERVICES WORKERS

Is the role of the human services worker to help individuals solve their interpersonal problems? Is it to help them cope with the stress brought on by financial difficulties, physical disabilities, or other outside pressures? Or is it to try to help change those conditions that create the problems in the first place?

During the War on Poverty in the latter part of the 1960s, agencies were formed to fight poverty, racism, and crime, among other problems. Federal, state, and local governments, as well as some private foundations, funded these agencies. The workers in an agency located in a high poverty and crime area helped local residents to learn their rights in the courts. The workers went to court with their clients to protest against police brutality when it occurred. They taught them how to organize and conduct rent strikes when the tenants were not getting service. They also defended people who were on welfare whenever they needed help (Krozney, 1966). The focus of human services workers during those years was mainly on helping people cope with injustice (Morales & Sheafor, 1980). The main concept was gaining and using power, and people did protest and fight against injustice. However, in one case, the protests and struggles aroused those threatened by these actions, who in turn brought pressure on those in power to curtail the funding for such projects. This, in effect, changed the nature of the role of the workers. No longer able to use government funds to fight "the Establishment"—government agencies and supporters—human services workers shifted their focus to helping clients adjust to their situation.

There are still many human services workers who feel that

helping people adjust to their problems is not a very useful activity. To adjust to poverty, racism, crime, mental illness, and similar problems rather than to bend every effort to combat or prevent such problems is seen by many as a losing battle. Poverty still exists and is growing. Crime rates have increased tremendously during the last two decades, although some recent declines in some categories have been noted. The number of people in need of mental health services has increased, even though mental hospitals have released large numbers of patients. Child abuse, wife abuse, divorces all have increased. Treatment and living conditions of the elderly leave much to be desired. All this has occurred in spite of the efforts of human services programs to date.

What else, then, can a human services worker do? "Become more of an activist," urge the activists. "But activists are seen as radicals by the public, government officials, and other human services workers," is often the reply. It is true that activists in the human services do not often win a lot of friends. The activist role usually stirs controversy and involves some risk. Recall the account given in Chapter Seven of the worker who prevented clients from entering an unlicensed nursing home and was reprimanded by his agency. The worker, with the help of his union, not only had the reprimand withdrawn, but initiated action on a state level to change the rules regarding placing people in unlicensed nursing homes. The worker was successful in that instance. Activists, unfortunately, are not always successful, but if there is to be any chance for success in eliminating injustice, there must be activists.

WHOM DO HUMAN SERVICES WORKERS SERVE?

Whom do human services workers serve? The answer to this question seems obvious and simple. In theory, it might be. However, in practice significant issues arise. For example, suppose you are a human services worker in a mental hospital. The policy is to discharge patients as quickly as possible. One of your patients has been selected for discharge and you are asked to follow through, but you are convinced that the patient is not able to function outside the institution. He is generally stabilized in the institution, however, and has been there for over six months without creating trouble, so "get him out" is the word. What do you do? You are working for the hospital and they are under pressure to discharge as many patients as possible in the shortest time possible. You are also responsible for the well-being of the patient. What happens if you do not discharge the patient? What happens if you do discharge the patient? This situation has actually occurred not once but many times in state institutions.

There are several possible answers to the question "Whom do human services workers serve?" They include the client, the agency for which one works, the government, society in general, or themselves. Some workers would claim that it is possible to serve all of the above but not at the same time or to the same degree. In any case, human services workers might soon be required to make difficult choices regarding whom they serve.

An even more complicated situation arises if and when workers who are paid by third parties such as insurance companies or Medicaid must give detailed reports of service to the companies. These reports not only identify the individuals but the nature of the problem and the course of treatment. In effect, this is a break of confidentiality and a way of influencing the treatment provided. The insurance company may attempt to limit or control the course of treatment. Do you as a human services worker go along with this kind of program, thus serving yourself with regard to payment and future patients? Do you refuse such a program and patients enrolled in those programs? Do you work with the patient anyway, even though payment might be reduced? Whom do you really serve—yourself, the insurance company, the client, or all three?

What about the situation in which you might be serving the taxpayer? Such a situation came up when eligibility criteria for disability payments were revised and thousands of disabled persons were denied payments. The object here was to save the taxpayers money, and cut costs to help reduce the federal deficit. What do you do when asked to administer such a program? Where do your human services responsibilities lie? Do they override your fiscal or administrative responsibilities?

The last example involves a much broader issue. It raises the question of not only whom do we serve but when do we serve them and at what cost. As stated previously, all the present efforts of human services have not been able to provide services for all those in need. Choices must be made. How do you, the human services worker, make them? Furthermore, if one chooses to become an activist or to work in prevention programs, those in need of specific help are denied your services. These kinds of choices affect those in need, other human services workers, professional organizations, legislators, and the public in general.

There are many other controversial issues in human services, but those described above should provide you with more than enough material to ponder at this point. It may be confusing but it also can be stimulating and exciting to struggle with these questions and discover your own way as a competent human services worker.

REFERENCES

Birnbach, D. (1981, August). Backward society: Implications for residential treatment and staff training. *Hospital and Community Psychiatry, 32,* 550–555.

Child abuse, neglect on the rise—Study finds links to unemployment. (1983, September). *NASW News,* p. 12.

Community Council of Greater New York. (1983, January 25). Coping with cutbacks: A study of differential impact and response by voluntary reductions. *Human Services,* pp. 1, 2.

Congress study finds Reagan budget curbs put 557,000 people in poverty. (1984, July 26). *The New York Times,* p. A19.

Cordes, C. (1984, February 15). The plight of homeless mentally ill. *APA Monitor,* 1, 3.

Cunningham, S. (1984, March). Social programs asked to tighten belts again: Block grants mean less money. *APA Monitor,* p. 2.

Fulton, R. (1981, Fall). Federal budget making in 1981: A watershed in federal domestic policy. *New England Journal of Human Services, 1,* 21–31.

Galbraith, J. K. (1984, February 5). Reagan vs. the military. *The New York Times,* op. ed. page.

Is deinstitutionalization working? (1983, January 25). *Human Services,* p. 3.

Krozney, H. (1966). *Beyond welfare: Poverty in the super city.* New York: Holt, Rinehart & Winston.

Mechanic, D. (1980). *Mental health and social policy* (2nd ed.). Englewood Cliffs, NJ: Prentice-Hall.

Miller, D. (1983, August 14). Hello poverty; goodbye economic gains. *The New York Times,* op. ed. page.

Morales, A., & Sheafor, B. W. (1980). *Social work: A profession of many faces* (2nd ed.). Boston: Allyn & Bacon.

O'Shaughnessy, P. (1984, March 18). Bronx chamber of horrors: Mental health system in serious condition. *New York Daily News,* p. 46.

Pear, R. (1984, February 24). Rise in poverty from '79 to '82 is found in U.S. *The New York Times,* p. 1.

Peirce, N. R. (1982, Summer). New federalism and the social services: Friends or foes? *New England Journal of Human Services, 2,* 13–19.

Scull , A. T., (1977). *Decarceration: Community treatment and the deviant—A radical view.* Englewood Cliffs, NJ: Prentice-Hall.

Sobey, F. (1970). *The nonprofessional revolution in mental health.* New York: Columbia University Press.

Turkington, C. (1984, February). Preferred providers please and puzzle private practitioners. *APA Monitor,* pp. 10–11.

NAME INDEX

SUBJECT INDEX